Great States!

Over 200 First-Rate Reproducible Activity Sheets to Fascinate and Educate

by Cindy Barden

illustrated by Chris Nye

Teaching & Learning Company

1204 Buchanan St., P.O. Box 10
Carthage, IL 62321

This book belongs to

_____

This book was developed for the Teaching & Learning Company by The Good Neighbor Press, Inc., Grand Junction, CO.

Cover illustration by Chris Nye

Copyright © 1995, Teaching & Learning Company

ISBN No. 1-57310-018-8

Printing No. 987654

Teaching & Learning Company
1204 Buchanan St., P.O. Box 10
Carthage, IL 62321

Table of Contents

To the Teacher iv

Alabama 1

Alaska 5

Arizona 9

Arkansas 14

California 18

Colorado 24

Connecticut 29

Delaware 33

Florida 37

Georgia 43

Hawaii 48

Idaho 53

Illinois 58

Indiana 63

Iowa 67

Kansas 73

Kentucky 78

Louisiana 84

Maine 89

Maryland 94

Massachusetts 98

Michigan 104

Minnesota 108

Mississippi 114

Missouri 118

Montana 123

Nebraska 128

Nevada 132

New Hampshire...137

New Jersey 141

New Mexico...146

New York 151

North Carolina 157

North Dakota...162

Ohio 166

Oklahoma..170

Oregon 174

Pennsylvania...178

Rhode Island...183

South Carolina 188

South Dakota...192

Tennessee..197

Texas 203

Utah...208

Vermont 212

Virginia 216

Washington..221

West Virginia 225

Wisconsin 229

Wyoming 234

Washington, D.C. 240

Answer Key 245

Dear Teacher,

What better way to learn about the United States than to visit each of the fifty states and the District of Columbia? Explore the many natural wonders from the Everglades to the Grand Canyon. Visit national parks, lakes, forests, mountains, swamps and glaciers. Search for the thousands of plants and animals that share our land and water. Meet the people who live and work here. Learn about the early inhabitants and how they lived. You and your students are invited to join a hot air balloon trip across this great nation.

These activities are written for students in third to sixth grades. Select the ones appropriate for your class. Use them in conjunction with other geography, history, language arts and social studies materials. The activities are arranged alphabetically by state but can be used in any order you please. Many of the activities would work well with small groups or could be done as a class. When several activities are included on one page, you may prefer to assign only one or two to your students. With younger students, you could read the explanatory text to the class, discuss the material and complete the activities orally.

Students can have fun playing charades as they learn about the U.S. One student can act out the name of a state or capital. The rest of the class can guess the name of the state or capital.

Play 20 Questions. One student chooses a state. The other students take turns guessing which state has been selected by asking questions. It would be helpful to have a large U.S. map available during the game. Only questions than can be answered "yes" or "no" are allowed. Are you west of the Mississippi River? Are you north of Tennessee? Are you larger than Kentucky? Etc.

Encourage students to keep completed activities in a folder or book for review.

As students learn about each state, ask them whether or not they would like to live in that state and to explain why or why not.

Compare and contrast two states the students have covered. They could be two very similar states, like New Mexico and Arizona, or two very different states, like California and New Hampshire. Have them look for similarities as well as differences.

Encourage students to "adopt a state." Each student can select a state he or she is interested in learning more about and make a scrapbook for that state with pictures and articles from newspapers and magazines. Have students write to the states' chambers of commerce asking for maps and information for their scrapbooks. Addresses can be found in most current almanacs.

An answer key is provided at the end of the book. The review activities could be used as quizzes, open-book activities or group activities.

Two excellent series of books covering each state and Washington, D.C., are published by Childrens Press: From Sea to Shining Sea and America the Beautiful. These books introduce the geography, history, government, economy, culture, famous people and historic sites of each state.

Other books published by Childrens Press are the New True Books which use simple text and color photos to describe the history, wildlife and sites in our country's national parks.

New True Books are also available about many Native American groups.

While researching the material for Great States!, I discovered the 1990 population figures quoted varied from source to source. Some sources had updated their numbers, based on corrections made to the 1990 census; others had not. Some did not include people in the Armed Forces and others living overseas. Population figures used are from the 1995 World Almanac and Book of Facts.

Some variations in the number of square miles reported depended on whether land only or all area within the state, including lakes, rivers, etc., were included. As your students refer to different sources, they should be aware that discrepancies will be found.

Sincerely,

Cindy

Cindy Barden

Welcome to Alabama

Let's start our tour of the United States in Alabama, the "Heart of Dixie." Hang on to your hats. Hot air balloon races are held in Decatur during the annual Alabama Jubilee.

Nicknames: Heart of Dixie, Camellia State, Cotton State and Yellowhammer State

State motto: We Dare Defend Our Rights

State flower: Camellia

State tree: Southern pine

State bird: Yellowhammer

State game bird: Wild turkey

State fish: Tarpon (saltwater) and largemouth bass (freshwater)

State mineral: Red iron ore

State rock: Marble

State fossil: *Basilosaurus cetoides* (a prehistoric whale)

State song: "Alabama"

Capital: Montgomery

Statehood: December 14, 1819, the 22nd state

1990 Population: 4,040,587: the 22nd largest in population

Area: 51,705 square miles: the 29th largest in area

Neighbors: Georgia, Tennessee, Mississippi and Florida

Major crops: Peanuts, cotton, soybeans, hay, corn, wheat, potatoes, pecans, cottonseed and catfish

Please Pass the Peanuts

George Washington Carver, an African American scientist, became famous for making more than 300 new products from peanuts including ink, soap and shaving cream. Through his efforts, peanuts became a major crop in Alabama. Each year a contest is held in Dothan, Alabama, for the best peanut recipe.

Think of a recipe you could make using peanuts in some form. It could be a soup, an appetizer, a dessert or a main dish. Name your new recipe and explain how to make it.

1

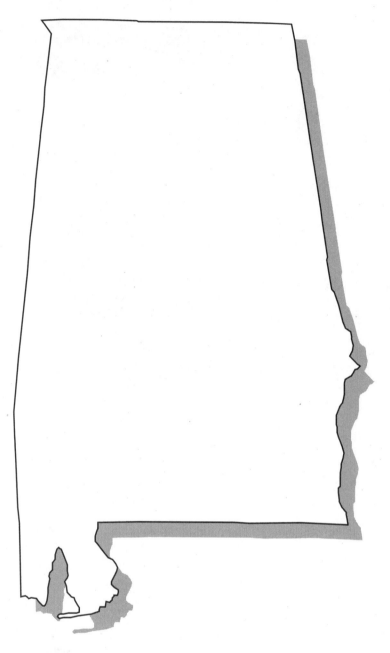

Alabama is bordered by four other states. What are they?

_____, _____,

_____ and _____

Write their approximate locations on the map above.

The Gulf of Mexico is south of Alabama. Color it blue.

Write the names of these major Alabama cities in the correct places on the map: Birmingham, Tuscaloosa, Mobile and Huntsville.

Use the compass to answer these questions. Which direction would you go to get from Alabama . . .

to Tennessee? _____

to Florida? _____

to Georgia? _____

to Mississippi? _____

Did You Know?

- Alabama was named for the Alibamu Indians. The word means "thicket clearers" or "vegetation gatherers."

- In Enterprise, Alabama, a monument was built to honor an insect—the boll weevil. This beetle damaged so much of Alabama's cotton crop that farmers were forced to find other crops to plant.

- People first settled in Alabama about 11,000 years ago. When European explorers arrived, they found the Cherokee, Choctaw and Creeks living in villages. These Native Americans built log homes, grew corn, squash, beans and tobacco. They hunted and fished for food.

- The city of Tuscaloosa was named for Tuskalusa, a Mobilian Indian chief.

- The first Europeans in Alabama were Spanish explorers in the early 1500s. The French established a permanent settlement on Mobile Bay in 1701. Most of Alabama was ceded to England at the end of the French and Indian War in 1763. The Spanish continued to claim the area around Mobile Bay as part of Spanish Florida until 1813.

- Southern leaders met in Montgomery in 1861 where they formed the Confederate States of America. Nicknamed the "Cradle of the Confederacy," Montgomery became the Confederate capital for a short time until it was moved to Richmond, Virginia.

- "Railroad Bill," (Morris Slater) an Alabama train robber in the late 1800s became known as the Black Robin Hood because he gave food and other stolen items to the poor.

- The first electric streetcars in the South ran in Montgomery in 1886. People called it the Lightning Route.

- Joe Louis, born in Lafayette, held the heavyweight boxing title from 1937 to 1949, longer than any other fighter.

- Jesse Owens, born in Oakville, won four gold medals in track at the 1936 Olympics.

- Montgomery became the birthplace of the Civil Rights Movement in 1955 when Rosa Parks was arrested for sitting in the "whites only" section of a city bus. Dr. Martin Luther King, Jr. led protests against her arrest. A year later the Supreme Court decided that segregated buses were not legal.

- The famous University of Alabama football coach "Bear" Bryant got his nickname because he entered a bear-wrestling contest as a youth.

- The city of Birmingham is famous for making steel and iron. A 55-foot statue called "Vulcan, the Iron Man" stands atop Red Mountain. This is the largest cast iron statue in the world. Vulcan was the Roman god of fire, the blacksmith who had his forge under a mountain.

- Famous Alabamians include Hank Aaron, Tallulah Bankhead, "Bear" Bryant, George Washington Carver, Nat King Cole, Bo Jackson, Helen Keller, Harper Lee, Joe Louis, Willie Mays, Jesse Owens, Rosa Parks, Leroy "Satchel" Paige, Lionel Ritchie, Hank Williams, Booker T. Washington and Dinah Washington.

- Find out more about someone from Alabama who was important in the Civil War or the Civil Rights Movement. Write a short report.

Alabama Wildlife

Identify the animals pictured below. You'll find their names in bold in these facts about the wildlife of Alabama.

- The **yellowhammer**, a kind of woodpecker, is Alabama's state bird.

- **Dolphins** swim in the waters of the Gulf of Mexico.

- **Alligators** can be found in Alabama's swamps and bayous.

- The **wild turkey** is the state game bird.

- In Alabama's freshwater lakes, you'll find **largemouth bass**.

- Much of Alabama is covered with forests. Here you'll find **white tail deer**, **raccoons**, **flying squirrels** and **bobcats**.

- **Opossums**, the only marsupials (animals with pouches) found outside of Australia, live in the forests of Alabama.

Welcome to Alaska

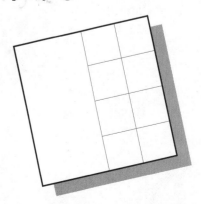

Grab your hats and mittens. It's going to get colder as we head north, far north to Alaska, "the last frontier." If we're lucky, perhaps we'll spot some reindeer, caribou or polar bears as we drift over the largest state.

Nicknames: The Last Frontier and Land of the Midnight Sun
State motto: North to the Future
State flower: Forget-me-not
State tree: Sitka spruce
State bird: Willow ptarmigan
State fish: King salmon
State sea animal: Bowhead whale
State mineral: Gold
State gem: Jade
State fossil: Mastodon
State sport: Dog mushing
State song: "Alaska's Flag"
Capital: Juneau
Statehood: January 3, 1959, the 49th state
1990 Population: 550,043: the 49th largest in population
Area: 591,004 square miles: the largest in area
Neighbors: British Columbia and the Yukon Territory

POPULATION
550,043

How Big Is Alaska?

Alaska is nearly twice as big as Texas, the second largest state, and nearly 500 times larger than Rhode Island.

Although Alaska is the largest state, only Wyoming has fewer people. On the average, less than one person per square mile lives in Alaska.

On the back of this page, draw an 8-inch square. Divide the square in half. Label one half Texas. Divide the other half into eight equal parts. Label the sections to see how many states would fit into an area the size of Alaska.

- Label one section New Jersey, New Hampshire, Massachusetts, Vermont.

- Label one section Connecticut, Hawaii, West Virginia.

- Label one section Indiana.

- Label one section Maine, Rhode Island, Delaware.

- Label four sections Montana.

Alaska's pretty big, isn't it?

Look at the map to the left. On the map above, color the approximate location of the Arctic Ocean blue.

Which two Canadian provinces border Alaska?

_____ and _____

They called themselves *Unangan*, meaning "the people." The Russians called them Aleuts. These people were the earliest known inhabitants of the string of islands southwest of Alaska later called the Aleutian Islands. Label the Aleutian Islands.

What two countries are closest to Alaska?

_____ and _____

Label the Bering Sea and the Pacific Ocean on the state map above.

Using a globe or atlas for a reference, write the names of these major Alaskan cities in the correct places on the map: Anchorage, Fairbanks, Juneau, Barrow, Nome.

Did You Know?

Read the facts about Alaska on this page. Then answer the questions in the next column.

- Does Alaska get a lot of snow? You bet it does. Parts of Alaska average 20 feet of snow in the winter. During one 24-hour period in 1963, 74 inches of snow fell at Mile 47 Camp.

- What do people in Alaska do with all that snow? In 1988 one group built a snowman 63.5 feet tall. They nicknamed it "Super Frosty."

- Alaska and Hawaii are the only two states not bordered by any other states.

- There are more than 3 million lakes and 3,000 rivers in Alaska. The largest lake is Iliamna Lake covering over 1,000 square miles.

- Not only is Mount McKinley the highest point in Alaska, it's also the highest point in North America. The next 15 highest peaks in the U.S. are also in Alaska.

- About 80 of Alaska's mountains are volcanoes.

- The word *Alaska* came from an Aleut word meaning "great land" or "mainland."

- On June 27, 1915, a temperature of 100°F was recorded at Fort Yukon. A record low of -80°F was set at Prospect Creek on January 23, 1971.

- Eskimo ice cream is made with snow, seal oil and berries.

- More than 1,800 islands are part of Alaska.

1. How cold did it get in Alaska?

   _____

2. How many of Alaska's mountains are volcanoes?

   _____

3. What does the word *Alaska* mean?

   _____

4. How many lakes can be found in Alaska?

   _____

5. What is the highest mountain in North America?

   _____

6. Which two states are not bordered by any other states?

   _____

7. What is the largest lake in Alaska?

   _____

8. What is Eskimo ice cream made of?

   _____

9. How many islands are part of Alaska?

   _____

10. Parts of Alaska average 20 feet of snow a year. How many inches is that?

    _____

Learn More About Alaska

To learn more about Alaska, check your encyclopedia, dictionary, atlas or read other books about Alaska. Find one interesting fact about each of the topics listed.

Grizzly bears: _____

_____

_____

Barrow, Alaska: _____

_____

_____

Arctic Circle: _____

_____

_____

Polar bears:_____

_____

_____

Tundra: _____

_____

_____

Kodiak bears: _____

_____

_____

_____

Fjord: _____

_____

_____

_____

Moose: _____

_____

_____

Kayak: _____

_____

_____

Caribou: _____

_____

_____

Umiak:_____

_____

_____

Wooly mammoth: _____

_____

_____

Dall's sheep: _____

_____

_____

Alaska's pipeline: _____

_____

_____

Ptarmigans: _____

_____

_____

*Brrr—
It gets mighty
cold here!*

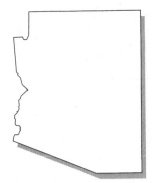

Welcome to Arizona

We'll have a chance to warm up as we head for sunny Arizona. Stow the hats and mittens away. Get out your sunscreen and sunglasses.

Nicknames: Grand Canyon State and Copper State
State motto: God Enriches
State flower: Blossom of the saguaro cactus
State tree: Paloverde
State bird: Cactus wren
State mammal: Ring-tailed cat
State reptile: Ridge-nosed rattlesnake
State amphibian: Arizona tree frog
State gem: Turquoise
State fossil: Petrified wood
State song: "Arizona"
Capital: Phoenix
Statehood: Arizona is sometimes called the Valentine State because it became the 48th state on February 14, 1912.
1990 Population: 3,665,228: the 24th largest in population
Area: 114,000 square miles: the 6th largest in area
Neighbors: New Mexico, Utah, Mexico, Nevada, California and Colorado

The name Arizona may have come from the Papago Indian word *arizonac* meaning "small spring" or from the Aztec word *arizuma* meaning "silver-bearing."

How's the Weather in Arizona?

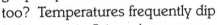

Does it get hot in Arizona? You bet it does. Temperatures in the desert can often be over 100 degrees. On July 7, 1905, the temperature reached 127°F in Parker. But did you know it can get pretty cold in Arizona, too? Temperatures frequently dip below zero in Arizona's snowcapped mountains. A reading of -40°F was recorded at Hawley Lake on January 7, 1971.

State Neckware

Bola ties, which were invented in Arizona, became so popular they were named the state's official neckware. Many bola ties are decorated with silver and turquoise, two of Arizona's natural resources.

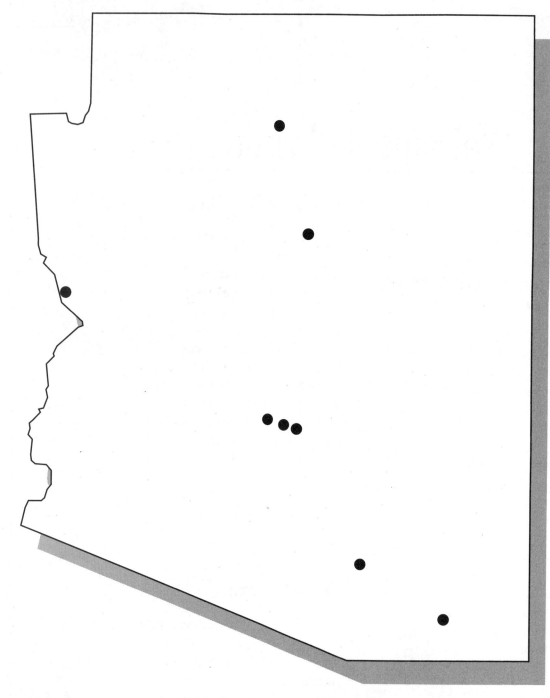

The Sonoran Desert covers most of south-western Arizona. Color it brown.

New Mexico borders Arizona on the east. Label the approximate location of New Mexico on the map to your left.

Mexico borders Arizona on the south. Label the approximate location of Mexico on the map to your left.

Write the names of these major Arizona cities in the correct places on the map: Phoenix, Tucson, Mesa, Tempe and Flagstaff.

Tombstone, Arizona, was the site where Wyatt Earp and Doc Holliday had their famous shoot-out at the OK Corral with the Clanton gang in 1881. Label Tombstone on the map.

The place where Colorado, New Mexico, Utah and Arizona meet is known as Four Corners. Mark this spot with an *X*.

London Bridge was brought to Lake Havasu City from England in 1968. It took three years to reassemble the 952-foot bridge piece by piece. Draw a small bridge to show the location of Lake Havasu City on the map above.

Grand Canyon National Park, the Painted Desert and the Petrified Forest are famous natural landmarks in Arizona. Label them on the map above.

The Early Settlers

- Evidence shows that people settled in Arizona at least 12,000 years ago. The early inhabitants hunted mastodons, wooly mammoths and other prehistoric creatures across the Southwest.

- About 1,000 years ago the Anasazi built their homes in Arizona's cliffs on the northern plateau. Anasazi homes looked much like modern apartment buildings. Instead of stairs or elevators, they used ladders to climb from one level to another.

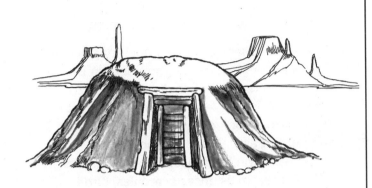

- Other prehistoric Arizonans, the Salados and the Sinaguas were also cliff dwellers. A Sinagua ruin now called Montezuma Castle was five stories high. Nearby is a 100-room Sinagua pueblo.

- The Hopi village of Oraibi was settled over 800 years ago. People still live there making it the oldest settlement in the United States that has been lived in continuously.

- The Apaches were nomadic hunters who lived in the mountains of Arizona. Their cone-shaped homes, covered with reeds and grass were called wickiups. The Navajo hunted and farmed in open country on the Colorado plateau. They lived in log homes covered with earth called hogans.

- The Hohokams were great builders. They dug a complex network of canals from rivers to carry water to their fields. Nearly 700 years ago they built Casa Grande (large house), a 40-foot-high building. People have called it America's First Skyscraper.

Look at the pictures of these early dwelling places. Imagine living here. Write a short story about what you think it would be like to live in a pueblo, wickiup or hogan.

Visit the Deserts of Arizona

Read the information about life in the Arizona desert. Label the animals pictured below.

- The word *desert* suggests a hot, dry place with few plants and animals. The Sonoran Desert which covers most of southwestern Arizona receives little rain—only about two inches a year. It may look empty as you float above it in your hot air balloon, but look closer. The desert is home to thousands of varieties of plants, mammals, insects, reptiles, birds and amphibians.

- Seventy kinds of cactus grow in Arizona's deserts. The largest is the saguaro (seh-gwär-ō) which may be 60 feet tall. Elf owls and gilded flickers are two of the many birds that nest in saguaro cactus. The cactus wren builds its nests in cholla (chô-ya) cactus. Some types of cholla cactus have sprawling arms several yards long. Other types are tree-like and grow up to 15 feet tall. You'll also find yucca plants, organ-pipe cactus and mesquite growing in abundance.

- The large ears of black-tailed jackrabbits help to warn them of predators and aid in removing heat from their bodies. Kangaroo rats live on the tiny amount of water found in the plants they eat. They never need to drink. Coyotes, desert bighorn sheep and wild pigs known as peccaries are other mammals that have adapted to life in the desert.

- A 16- to 20-inch poisonous lizard, the Gila (hē-lah) monster hides in burrows during the day. This colorful lizard hunts for its prey at night when the temperature is cooler.

- Tarantulas and scorpions live in the dry desert. Because they have eight legs, scorpions are related to spiders. They have a poison stinger at the tip of their tails.

- You'll need to be quick to catch a glimpse of a roadrunner. This two-foot long bird would rather run than fly. For short distances, it can run up to 15 miles per hour.

A Pretty Big Hole

• Hundreds of canyons mark the northwest corner of Arizona. Every year millions of visitors from all over the world come to Arizona to see the granddaddy of all canyons—the Grand Canyon. For millions of years, the Colorado River has slowly been forming the largest canyon in the world. Marine fossils found in the limestone walls show that a deep sea once covered the site of the Grand Canyon over 300 million years ago.

• Naturalist John Muir called it the "grandest of God's terrestrial cities." The Grand Canyon is over 200 miles long, about 10 miles across and one mile deep. If you stacked four buildings the height of the Empire State Building on top of one another, they wouldn't reach from the bottom to the top of the Grand Canyon.

• If you want to see the Grand Canyon up close, you can ride down on a mule or hike down on one of the walking trails. It's only one mile down, but the trails are about 20 miles long. It takes most people two or three days to walk down and back up.

• If you decide to make the trip, you'll see plenty of wildlife. Mule deer, porcupines and squirrels live in the forests. Lizards sun themselves on rocks. Harder to spot are the elk, bighorn sheep, bobcats, cougars and coyotes. From the North Rim to the canyon floor, is a

journey from forests to desert. Pines and other large trees grow near the top of the canyon. At the bottom where it's hot and dry, you'll see many different kinds of cactus.

Select one of these topics and write a short story or poem.

1. Imagine riding a mule from the top all the way to the bottom of the Grand Canyon! Describe the sights, sounds and smells around you. How do you feel after several hours riding a mule? What is the greatest sight you see on your trip?

2. Pretend you don't know that the Grand Canyon was formed by the Colorado River over millions of years. Imagine waking up one morning and suddenly finding a Grand Canyon in your backyard. Who or what formed it? Explain how it got there.

3. Imagine you are riding above the Grand Canyon in a hot air balloon. Describe what you see as you descend to the canyon floor.

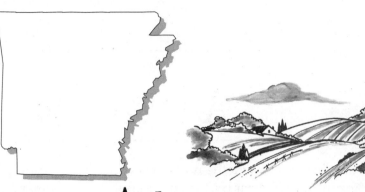

Welcome to Arkansas

From apple blossoms to zither music, you'll find a lot of variety in Arkansas. Let's take time for a soak in the hot springs, then search for diamonds.

Nicknames: Land of Opportunity, Bear State and Wonder State

State motto: The People Rule

State flower: Apple blossom

State tree: Pine tree

State bird: Mockingbird

State insect: Honeybee

State gem: Diamond

State fruit: South Arkansas vine-ripened pink tomato

State beverage: Milk

State musical instrument: Fiddle

State song: "Arkansas"

Capital: Little Rock

Statehood: Arkansas became the 25th state on June 25, 1836.

1990 Population: 2,350,725: the 33rd largest in population

Area: 53,187 square miles: the 27th largest in area

Neighbors: Missouri, Tennessee, Mississippi, Louisiana, Texas and Oklahoma

Did You Know?

- The word *Arkansas* came from the French translation of the word *Ugaxpa*, the name for the Quapaws. The word means "downstream people."

- Toltec Mounds are the remains of a large ceremonial complex built between 700 and 950 A.D. by the people of the Plum Bayou Culture.

- Crater of Diamonds State Park near Murfreesboro is the site of the only active diamond mine in North America. Visitors to the park can keep any diamonds they find.

- Reverend Cephas Washburn started the first school in the Arkansas Territory in 1820 to teach Cherokee children.

- Forests cover about half the land in Arkansas.

- Springs bubble up in the Ozark and Ouachita mountain regions. Mammoth Springs is one of the largest in the country. Hot Springs is known for its 47 hot mineral springs.

What Can You Find in *Little Rock*?

How many words can you make using the letters in the words *Little Rock*? Write your list on another sheet of paper. Try to think of at least 20 words.

14

Label the approximate locations of Arkansas's neighbors: Missouri, Tennessee, Mississippi, Louisiana, Texas and Oklahoma on the Arkansas map.

The Mississippi River forms most of Arkansas's eastern border. Draw a blue line along the Mississippi River.

The capitol building at Little Rock is a one-quarter size replica of the U.S. Capitol in Washington, D.C. Mark the location of Little Rock with a star.

Label the places underlined below on the Arkansas state map.

When it was built in 1986, the Sesquicentennial Sundial in <u>North Little Rock</u> was the largest in the world. Stones from all over the world were donated to create this master timepiece in honor of Arkansas's 150th birthday.

In 1817 <u>Fort Smith</u> was the last outpost of American civilization. During the California gold rush, Fort Smith became a supply base for those traveling west to seek their fortunes.

Both the Union and Confederate armies had headquarters in <u>Fayetteville</u> during the Civil War.

<u>Hot Springs</u> is famous for its hot-water health spas and thoroughbred horse racing.

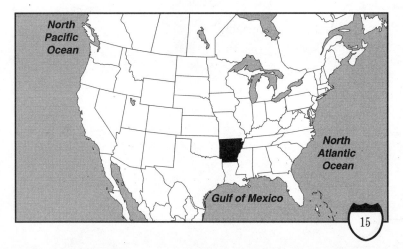

About Arkansas

Read the information about Arkansas. Complete the assigned activities.

- Whether you like folk music, blues, ballads, bluegrass or country music, you're sure to find lots of great old-time fiddling and banjo picking in Arkansas. Traditional Ozark folk music is played on an Autoharp™, mandolin and dulcimer. If you enjoy more classical music, Arkansas has several major symphonies, orchestras and an opera company.

Listen to a recording of Ozark folk music. Describe the shape and sound of an Autoharp™, mandolin or dulcimer.

- If you like your music loud and fun, listen to an Arkansas "kitchen band." The members play tunes on pots and pans, washboards, wash tubs and other kitchen items.

What is a washboard? What is a washtub? Name some other kitchen items you could use to make music.

- Diamonds were discovered near Murfressboro in 1906.

How are diamonds formed?

- The governor of Arkansas closed the high schools in Little Rock in 1958. They reopened the following year.

Why were they closed?

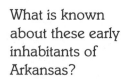

- Bayous can be found in southern Arkansas.

What is a bayou? What types of plants and animals live in Arkansas's bayous?

- Natural gas was discovered near Fort Smith in 1901.

What is natural gas? How was it formed? What is it used for?

- The Plum Bayou culture flourished in central Arkansas from 700 to 950 A.D.

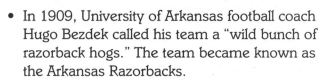

What is known about these early inhabitants of Arkansas?

- In 1909, University of Arkansas football coach Hugo Bezdek called his team a "wild bunch of razorback hogs." The team became known as the Arkansas Razorbacks.

What is a razorback?

The Arkansas Traveler

One rainy day in Arkansas, a traveler stopped to talk to an old man sitting on his porch playing his fiddle.

"Hello there. Can you tell me where this road goes?" asked the traveler.

"Doesn't go anywhere," replied the old man as he played a few notes on his fiddle. "I've lived here all my life, and it's always in the same spot every morning when I get up."

"Could I ask what your name might be?" asked the traveler.

"Well, it might be Dick, and it might be Fred," he replied as he continued his song.

"Shouldn't you fix that leak in your roof?" the traveler asked.

"Can't fix it today. It's raining too hard," the old man explained. He tapped his toe as he played a lively tune.

"You could fix it tomorrow when the sun shines," the traveler suggested.

"Won't have to fix it tomorrow," answered the old man. "When the sun shines, the roof doesn't leak."

As the traveler went on his way, the old man kept playing a jolly tune.

Write a few more lines of silly dialogue between the traveler and the Arkansas fiddler.

Traveler: _____

_____

_____

Fiddler: _____

_____

_____

Traveler: _____

_____

_____

Fiddler: _____

_____

_____

Traveler: _____

_____

_____

Fiddler: _____

_____

Should we stop and chat with the fiddler?

Traveler: _____

_____

_____

_____

Fiddler: _____

_____

_____

17

Welcome to California

Golden poppies, golden trout and gold are all found in the Golden State. Let's travel west to the Pacific Ocean for a visit to California.

Nickname: Golden State
State motto: Eureka (I have found it!)
State flower: Golden poppy
State tree: California redwood
State bird: California valley quail
State animal: Grizzly bear
State fish: Golden trout
State insect: Dog-face butterfly
State marine mammal: Gray whale
State reptile: Desert tortoise
State mineral: Gold
State fossil: Saber-toothed tiger
State song: "I Love You, California"
Capital: Sacramento
Statehood: California became the 31st state on September 9, 1850.
1990 Population: 29,760,021: the largest in population
Area: 158,693 square miles: the 3rd largest in area
Neighbors: Oregon, Nevada, Arizona, Mexico and the Pacific Ocean

Bits and Pieces

- California was named for an imaginary island filled with treasure in a fictional Spanish story of the early 1500s.

- Some people claim that Lombard Street in San Francisco is the steepest and most crooked street in the U.S.

- Only Texas and Alaska are larger than California. Rhode Island could fit inside California nearly 130 times.

- One suburb of Los Angeles was named Tarzana after the character Tarzan created by writer Edgar Rice Burroughs.

- The first crossing of the United States by a helium-filled hot air balloon began in Costa Mesa, California, and ended 2,515 miles away on Blackbeard's Island, Georgia, in 1981.

- One of the most famous Californians isn't a person, it's a mouse. Mickey Mouse was created by Walt Disney in Los Angeles in 1928. What was the name of the first Mickey Mouse cartoon?

- California is home to the world's oldest trees called bristlecone pines. One tree, named Methuselah, is over 4,600 years old. The world's tallest trees, the redwoods, also grow in California. The General Sherman tree is 275 feet tall and measures 103 feet around.

Discussion Question

Why do you think people gave trees names like Methuselah or General Sherman? Pick a tree near your school. As a class, decide on a name for it.

Label the underlined places on the California state map.

Both <u>Los Angeles</u> and <u>San Diego</u> have more people than many entire states.

The three states that border California are <u>Oregon</u>, <u>Nevada</u> and <u>Arizona</u>. Label their approximate locations.

The country of <u>Mexico</u> forms the southern border of California. Label its approximate location.

The <u>Pacific Ocean</u> forms the western border of California.

Some islands off the coast are part of California. Label the islands of <u>Santa Catalina</u>, <u>San Clemente</u>, <u>Santa Barbara</u>, <u>Santa Rosa</u> and <u>Santa Cruz</u>.

<u>San Jose</u> was the first Spanish settlement in California, founded in 1777.

Across the bay is <u>Oakland</u>, San Francisco's sister city.

The state capitol building in <u>Sacramento</u> has a golden dome.

Disneyland opened in <u>Anaheim</u> in 1955.

Label these cities in California:

Long Beach	Fresno	Santa Ana
Carmel	Hollywood	Monterey
Pasadena	Salinas	San Francisco

19

Sunny California

- Most of California has a warm climate, but there are some exceptions. Temperatures in the deserts can often top 100°F Death Valley had a record high temperature of 134°F on July 10, 1913.

- California winters might be warm and sunny in some parts, but not all of California has mild winters. An all-time low temperature of -45°F was recorded in Boca in 1937. In March 1911, more than 37 feet of snow was on the ground at Tamarac. Mother Nature also played a trick on Mount Shasta when she dumped 189 inches of snow during one storm in February 1959.

How many feet high is 189 inches of snow? If that much snow fell on your community at one time, what would happen?

Name the Sport

California has so many professional sports teams, it's difficult to keep them all straight. Name the sport these teams play.

1. San Diego Padres   _____
2. San Diego Chargers   _____
3. Los Angeles Dodgers   _____
4. Los Angeles Rams   _____
5. Los Angeles Raiders   _____
6. Los Angeles Kings   _____
7. Los Angeles Lakers   _____
8. Los Angeles Clippers   _____
9. San Francisco 49ers   _____
10. San Francisco Giants   _____
11. California Angels   _____
12. San Jose Sharks   _____
13. Oakland A's   _____
14. Golden State Warriors   _____
15. Sacramento Kings   _____

Who's Who?

Use reference books to match the names of these people from California with their accomplishments.

1. Wrote *The Grapes of Wrath*
2. Wrote *Call of the Wild*
3. First U.S. woman in space in 1983
4. Most famous child movie star of all time
5. World War II general nicknamed "Old Blood and Guts"
6. The only President who resigned
7. Movie actor who became President in 1981
8. Photographer best known for black and white photos of Yosemite National Park
9. Won seven gold medals in 1972 Summer Olympics
10. Baseball player who made hits in 56 straight games in 1941

_____ Ansel Adams   _____ Joe DiMaggio

_____ Jack London   _____ Richard Nixon

_____ Ronald Reagan   _____ Sally Ride

_____ General Patton   _____ Mark Spitz

_____ John Steinbeck   _____ Shirley Temple

20

Hollywood Squares

To win this game get three correct answers in a row, like tic-tac-toe. Number the squares from 1 to 9. You may put the numbers in any square, in any order.

When your teacher asks the first question, write the answer in the square numbered 1. Write the answer to the second question in the square numbered 2 and so on.

If you have three correct answers in a row, you win.

To the Teacher: Hollywood Squares

When your class finishes studying California, play Hollywood Squares. Ask students to number the squares from one to nine, in any order, before you begin reading the questions. Select nine questions from the list below, appropriate for your class. Make up your own questions if you prefer. Say the number of the question; then read the question. Ask students to write their answers in the boxes with the same number.

Hollywood Squares could be played with questions about other states or with other subjects, such as math or history.

What is the capital of California?   *Sacramento*

Name two cities in California.

True or False: *California* means the color red in Spanish.   *False*

What is the state motto?
    Eureka (I have found it!)

What is the state bird?   *California valley quail*

What is the state animal?   *Grizzly bear*

Name the state reptile.   *Desert tortoise*

What is the state fish?   *Golden trout*

What is the state insect?   *Dog-face butterfly*

What is the state tree?   *California redwood*

Name the state marine mammal.   *Gray whale*

What is the state flower?   *Golden poppy*

What are the oldest type of trees in the world?
    Bristlecone pines

Name the state song.   *"I Love You, California"*

Which state has more people than
    California?   *None*

Which two states are larger than
    California?   *Texas and Alaska*

Name two states that border
    California.   *Arizona, Nevada,
    Oregon*

What is California's nickname?   *Golden State*

Name two people born in California.

What is the state mineral?   *Gold*

In what year did California become a state?
    1850

Name a desert in California.

What is the state fossil?   *Saber-toothed tiger*

What is the name of the tallest type of trees?
    Redwoods

Raisins are made from what fruit?   *Grapes*

What ocean is on the west coast of California?
    Pacific Ocean

What was discovered in California in 1848?
    Gold

What was the first Spanish city in California?
    San Jose

Name someone from California who became
    President.   *Nixon, Reagan*

Name a California football team.

What country borders California on the south?
    Mexico

Name a California baseball team.

Name an island that is part of California.

Name a California hockey team.

Where would you find trolley cars?
    San Francisco

Name a California basketball team.

Name a national park in
California.

Where is Disneyland?
Anaheim

So Much to See in California

Select one of these places in California for a written report. Use drawings or pictures from magazines with your report.

San Diego:

- Juniper Serra Museum
- San Diego Zoo
- Sea World
- Palomar Observatory

Los Angeles:

- La Brea tar pits
- Hollywood

Anaheim:

- Disneyland

Pasadena:

- Tournament of Roses Parade

San Jose:

- The Rosicrucian Egyptian Museum

San Francisco:

- Golden Gate Bridge
- Chinatown
- Fisherman's Wharf

Other Places of Interest:

- Point Reyes National Seashore
- Redwood National Park
- Shasta-Trinity National Forest
- Kings Canyon and Sequoia National Park
- Lava Beds National Monument
- Joshua Tree National Monument
- Cabrillo National Monument
- Lassen Volcanic National Park
- Yosemite National Park
- Inyo National Forest
- Salton Sea National Wildlife Refuge
- Sutter's Fort
- California State Railroad Museum
- State Indian Museum
- San Andreas Fault
- Mohave Desert
- Death Valley
- Colorado Desert
- Big Sur State Park
- Alcatraz Island
- Hearst Castle

Welcome to Colorado

Gold and silver were important during the history of the Centennial State, but red was the color that gave Colorado its name.

Nickname: Centennial State
State motto: Nothing Without Providence
State flower: Rocky Mountain columbine
State tree: Colorado blue spruce
State bird: Lark bunting
State animal: Rocky Mountain bighorn sheep
State gem: Aquamarine
State fossil: Stegosaurus
State song: "Where the Columbines Grow"
Capital: Denver
Statehood: Colorado became the 38th state on August 1, 1876.
1990 Population: 3,294,394: the 26th largest in population
Area: 104,091 square miles: the 8th largest in area
Neighbors: Wyoming, Nebraska, Kansas, Oklahoma, New Mexico, Arizona and Utah

Did You Know?

- More than 1,000 peaks in Colorado are over two miles high. The highest point in Colorado is Mount Elba, 14,433 feet above sea level.
- The word *colorado* is Spanish, meaning the color red.
- Colorado is known as the "Centennial State" because it joined the Union in 1876, 100 years after the founding of our nation.
- Brachiosaurus, tyrannosaurus rex, apatosaurus, stegosaurus and many other types of dinosaurs once lived in Colorado. Colorado has a city named Dinosaur.
- The inventor of the Barbie doll, Ruth Handler, was from Denver. More than one billion of these dolls have been sold all over the world.
- The oldest fossil of a flowering plant found in the U.S. was discovered in Colorado in 1953. It dates back about 65 million years.
- Seven hundred-year-old dried beans left by the Anasazi were preserved by the dry weather. When planted, they grew. In 1983 two men from Colorado started Adobe Milling, a company that sells Anasazi beans.
- The town of Guffey has about 26 people and a most unusual mayor. In 1987 the people elected Paisley, a cat. The town has had a cat for a mayor ever since.

Discussion Questions: What If?

- What if there were no Rocky Mountains in Colorado?
- What if animals were elected to office in other cities?

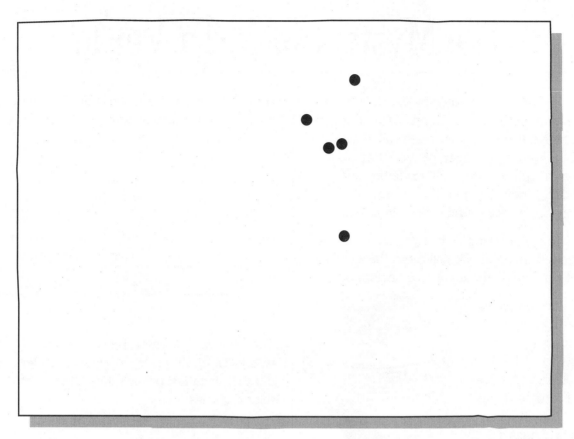

How far is it to Denver? Use a U.S. atlas to find the distances from these major cities to Denver, Colorado.

Milwaukee, WI   _____

New York, NY   _____

Miami, FL   _____

Seattle, WA   _____

Boston, MA   _____

Dallas, TX   _____

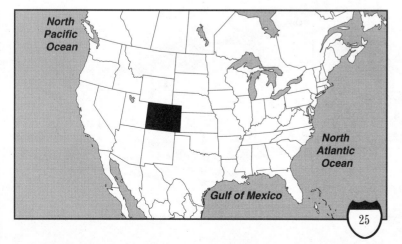

Label the underlined places on the Colorado state map.

Denver is nicknamed the "Mile High City." The 13th step at the state capital is 5,280 feet above sea level—exactly one mile high. About half of all the people in Colorado live in the Denver area.

Colorado Springs was named for the nearby springs and is the second largest city in Colorado.

In the 1950s, only about 2,000 people lived in Aurora. After the discovery of "black gold" (oil), the population shot up to over 220,000.

Boulder was named for the rocks and boulders in the area.

Greeley was named for a New York newspaperman, Horace Greeley, who was credited with giving the advice, "Go West, young man."

Label the approximate locations of the states that border Colorado: Wyoming, Nebraska, Kansas, Oklahoma, New Mexico, Arizona and Utah.

The Mystery of Mesa Verde

While searching for stray cattle in December 1888, Richard Wetherill and Charlie Mason rode across a high flat-topped mountain called Mesa Verde. At the edge of a deep canyon they discovered a magnificent city built under an overhanging cliff. They named it Cliff Palace. After further exploring they found other cliff cities.

Who built these amazing dwellings? The people left no written records. We call them the Anasazi from a Navajo word meaning "the ancient ones."

At Cliff Palace archaeologists have found black on white pottery, woven blankets, stone and bone tools, clothing, bows and arrows. From studying the ruins, they have learned the Anasazi grew corn, beans and squash, hunted deer and rabbits and kept dogs and turkeys. They used no metals.

These cliff dwellings were deserted nearly 700 years ago. By studying burial sites, scientists have discovered the people were short and stocky with black, or sometimes brown hair.

Cliff Palace consists of open plazas and stone houses two to three stories high. In some places, rooms were dug into the ground like basements. To get from one level to another, the people climbed ropes and ladders. To reach their homes, they had to descend the sides of cliffs using ropes, ladders and shallow finger- and toe-hold cuts into the rock.

To protect the treasures found at Mesa Verde, the area was made a national park in 1906.

How were the cliff dwellings at Mesa Verde like a modern apartment building?

_____

_____

_____

_____

The only way to enter the cities under the cliffs was to climb down by ropes and ladders. How did their location protect the cliff dwellers from their enemies?

_____

_____

_____

_____

_____

_____

_____

More to Discover

While visiting Pikes Peak in 1893, Katharine Lee Bates was inspired to write a poem. Her poem became the song "America the Beautiful." Play a recording, sing or read the words to this song to your class.

America the Beautiful

O beautiful for spacious skies,
For amber waves of grain,
For purple mountain majesties
Above the fruited plain!

America! America!
God shed his grace on thee,
And crown thy good with brotherhood
From sea to shining sea.

O beautiful for pilgrim feet,
Whose stern, impassioned stress
A thoroughfare for freedom beat
Across the wilderness!

America! America!
God mend thine every flaw,
Confirm thy soul in self-control,
Thy liberty in law.

O beautiful for heroes proved
In liberating strife,
Who more than self their country loved,
And mercy more than life!

America! America!
May God thy gold refine,
Till all success be nobleness,
And every gain divine.

O beautiful for patriot dream
That sees beyond the years
Thine alabaster cities gleam,
Undimmed by human tears!

America! America!
God shed his grace on thee,
And crown thy good with brotherhood
From sea to shining sea.

Invite students to cut pictures from newspapers and magazines to make a class collage of Colorado.

Encourage students to learn more about one of these places in Colorado. They could work in groups, do individual written or oral reports or form a panel discussion.

Denver:
- Mile High Stadium
- United States Mint
- Molly Brown House

Boulder:
- National Institute of Standards and Technology
- The National Center for Atmospheric Research

Colorado Springs:
- U.S. Olympic Training Complex
- Pro Rodeo Hall of Fame
- World Figure Skating Hall of Fame
- Garden of the Gods
- United States Air Force Academy
- Florissant Fossil Beds National Monument

Pueblo:
- El Pueblo Museum

Grand Junction:
- Dinosaur Valley Museum
- Colorado National Monument
- Rabbit Valley

Other Sites:
- Mesa Verde National Park
- Pikes Peak
- Great Sand Dunes National Monument
- Royal Gorge
- Rocky Mountain National Park
- Blue Mesa Reservoir
- Chimney Rock Archaeological Site
- Gunnison National Monument

National Forests:

Arapaho	Grand Mesa	Gunnison
Pike	Rio Grande	Roosevelt
Routt	San Isabel	San Juan
Uncompahgre	White River	Manti-La Sal

27

Colorado's Riches

The first gold strike in Colorado was made in 1858. As news of the discovery spread, people rushed to Colorado to get rich. Denver, Golden, Boulder and Colorado City began as gold mining towns. Prices were high in the booming gold rush towns. Eggs cost a dollar each and a sack of potatoes went for $15.

By the 1870s people were finding little gold, but in 1878 a "silver rush" began when several silver strikes were made. Leadville and Aspen became important silver mining towns. A silver nugget weighing about 1,840 pounds was discovered in Aspen in 1894.

Many miners searched for gold and silver, but few ever struck it big. Horace Tabor earned $10 million from his Matchless Mine. Known as the "Silver King," Tabor spent his money to build opera houses and mansions. When the price of silver dropped, Tabor and other mine owners went broke. The "Silver King" was lucky to get a job as the postmaster in Denver. His wife moved back to a shack near the Matchless Mine where she died from cold and hunger in 1935.

A second gold rush started in 1890 when Bob Womack found gold in a cow pasture. He sold his claim for $300. Half a billion dollars in gold was mined from that pasture.

Like Horace Tabor, many of the miners who found gold and silver spent it as fast as they earned it. They often went home with less than they had when they started.

Write a short story about how your life would be changed if you found gold in your backyard.

_____
_____
_____
_____
_____
_____
_____
_____
_____
_____
_____
_____
_____
_____
_____
_____
_____
_____
_____
_____

Could that sparkle be gold down there?

28

Welcome to Connecticut

We'll find lots of historic places to visit as we travel east to Connecticut on the Atlantic coast.

Nicknames: Constitution State and Nutmeg State
State motto: He Who Transplanted Still Sustains
State flower: Mountain laurel
State tree: White oak
State bird: Robin
State animal: Sperm whale
State insect: Praying mantis
State mineral: Garnet
State hero: Nathan Hale
State ship: *USS Nautilus*
State song: "Yankee Doodle"
Capital: Hartford
Statehood: Connecticut was the fifth of the original 13 colonies to ratify the constitution on January 9, 1788.
1990 Population: 3,287,116: the 27th largest in population
Population density: 678.5 per square mile
Area: 5,018 square miles: the 3rd smallest in area
Neighbors: New York, Massachusetts, Rhode Island and the Atlantic Ocean

The word *Connecticut* came from a Native American word, *quinnehtukgut* meaning "beside the long tidal river."

Did You Know?

- Sixty percent of the land in Connecticut is covered with forests of oak, beech, birch, hickory, maple, oak, pines and hemlocks.

- During the 1830s and 40s, a movement for the abolition of slavery arose in Connecticut and other states. Through a secret network of "stations" along the Underground Railroad, Connecticut men and women sheltered escaped slaves and helped them to freedom. Harriet Beecher Stowe affected the feelings of thousands with her novel *Uncle Tom's Cabin*, about the evils of slavery.

- The first atomic submarine, the *USS Nautilus*, was built at Groton and launched in 1954.

- In the 1800s, ships from Connecticut traveled all over the world, trading in spices and other goods, giving the state the nickname, "Nutmeg State." What is nutmeg?

- According to the song, Yankee Doodle "stuck a feather in his hat and called it macaroni." At that time, macaroni did not mean a type of noodle. What was a macaroni?

- One type of food is named in the song. Although it sounds like it, "hasty pudding" wasn't made in a microwave. What was hasty pudding?

Label the underlined places on the Connecticut state map.

Three states, <u>New York</u>, <u>Massachusetts</u> and <u>Rhode Island</u> share a border with Connecticut. Label their approximate locations.

<u>Long Island Sound</u> forms the southern border of the state.

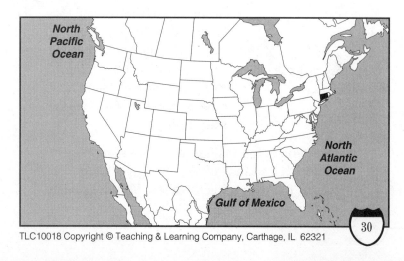

The Dutch established a colony at the site of present day <u>Hartford</u> in 1633.

Visitors can tour the home of Noah Webster in <u>West Hartford</u>.

Nearly 2,000 acres of land in <u>Bridgeport</u> have been set aside for use as city parks.

The First Presbyterian Church in <u>Stamford</u> is shaped like a fish.

Yale University in <u>New Haven</u> has world famous libraries and art museums.

<u>Norwalk</u>'s seafaring days are remembered in the Maritime History Museum on the waterfront.

At one time, <u>Waterbury</u> known as the Brass City, was the center of America's brass industry.

The city of <u>Danbury</u> was once the hat-making capital of America.

Colonial Connecticut

Several groups of Native Americans belonging to the Algonquian-speaking tribes lived in Connecticut in the 1600s when European colonists began settling the area. The Matabesecs, Sequins, Nipmuc, Pequots and Mohegans hunted, fished and farmed. They grew pumpkins, squash, potatoes, tobacco and corn.

Although they had much in common, these groups frequently fought among themselves. Unable to unite against a common enemy, the settlers defeated the individual small groups. Many were killed. Others moved west, away from the white settlers who stole their lands.

The Puritans established the Connecticut Colony as a theocracy—a community ruled by the church. They believed that people should be allowed to elect their leaders. In 1639, a written code of laws called the Fundamental Orders became the first constitution in the New World.

King Charles II granted Connecticut a charter in 1662 that allowed it to elect its own governor and gave the colony other rights. In 1697, the royal governor of New York tried to take over Connecticut Colony and demanded the colonists give him the charter from the king. The colonists refused to return the document and hid it in a hollow oak tree. The tree became known as the Charter Oak.

Until 1765, Connecticut continued to be almost completely independent from England. When their freedom was threatened by the passage of several laws demanding the payment of taxes, two men from Connecticut formed a patriotic group called the Sons of Liberty. Men from several other colonies joined the group in protest of the Stamp Act, the Townshend Acts and other laws passed by England.

Describe the goals and actions of the Sons of Liberty.

_____

_____

_____

_____

_____

_____

_____

_____

Not everyone joined in the rebellion against the Mother Country. Those who remained loyal to England were known as Tories.

Compare the beliefs of the Tories to the Sons of Liberty.

_____

_____

_____

_____

_____

_____

_____

_____

31

Who's Who in Connecticut?

Find one interesting fact about each of the people from Connecticut listed below.

Nathan Hale: _____

_____

_____

Ethan Allen: _____

_____

_____

Harriet Beecher Stowe: _____

_____

_____

Phineas T. Barnum: _____

_____

_____

Noah Webster: _____

_____

_____

Samuel Colt: _____

_____

_____

Benedict Arnold: _____

_____

_____

_____

Charles Goodyear: _____

_____

_____

_____

Clare Booth Luce: _____

_____

_____

Ralph Nader: _____

_____

_____

Eugene O'Neill: _____

_____

_____

Find an interesting fact about these places in Connecticut.

Gilette Castle: _____

_____

_____

P.T. Barnum Museum: _____

_____

_____

Yale University: _____

_____

_____

Dinosaur State Park: _____

_____

_____

_____

Mystic, Connecticut: _____

_____

_____

_____

Do you think we'll see a tyrannosaurus rex at Dinosaur State Park?

32

Welcome to Delaware

Beaches, salt marshes and wetlands mark the eastern coast of the First State where "Liberty and Independence" is the motto.

Nicknames: First State, Diamond State and Blue Hen State
State motto: Liberty and Independence
State flower: Peach blossom
State tree: American holly
State bird: Blue hen chicken
State fish: Weakfish
State insect: Ladybug
State mineral: Sillimanite
State beverage: Milk
State colors: Colonial blue and buff
State song: "Our Delaware"
Capital: Dover
Statehood: Delaware was the first of the 13 original colonies to ratify the Constitution on December 7, 1787, giving it the nickname, "First State."
1990 Population: 666,168: the fifth smallest in population
Area: 2,044 square miles: the second smallest in area. From north to south, the greatest distance in Delaware is only 96 miles. From east to west, the state measures only 39 miles wide.
Neighbors: Pennsylvania, Maryland and the Atlantic Ocean

Did You Know?

- In 1610, Samuel Argall, a Virginia colonist, was swept off course during a storm and took shelter in a bay. He named it De La Warr Bay after Sir Thomas West, Lord De La Warr, the governor of Virginia.

- Delaware's state colors are Colonial blue and buff. The background of the state flag is Colonial blue and the large central diamond is buff-colored.

- Although water forms the eastern border of the state, Delaware has no large lakes. The entire state has only 75 square miles of inland water.

- Delaware was the first to form a convention to write a state constitution which called for election of a president, banned importation of slaves and guaranteed freedom of religion and freedom of the press.

- The movie *Dead Poets' Society* was the first full-length motion picture filmed in Delaware.

- During the Revolutionary War, soldiers from Delaware were nicknamed the Blue Hen's Chickens because they were brave. How did they get that nickname?

TLC10018 Copyright © Teaching & Learning Company, Carthage, IL 62321

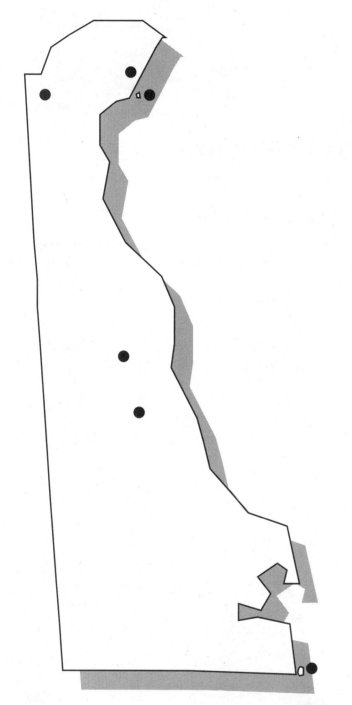

Label the underlined places on the Connecticut state map.

Pennsylvania, Maryland and the Atlantic Ocean form the borders of Delaware. Label their approximate locations. New Jersey lies east of Delaware across Delaware Bay.

Dover has been the capital of Delaware since 1777.

Fort Christina, settled by a group of Dutch and Swedish colonists, became the first permanent white settlement in Delaware. The town was later renamed Wilmington. Old Swedes Church in Wilmington is the oldest church in the U.S. still in use.

Barratt's Chapel was the birthplace of the Methodist Episcopal church in America in 1784. The town of Frederica has been called the "Cradle of Methodism in America"

Cooch's Bridge, near Newark, was the site of Delaware's only Revolutionary War battle. According to tradition, Betsy Ross's flag was first raised in battle here. During Colonial times, Newark was a trade center between Delaware, Pennsylvania and Maryland.

Over 12,000 Confederate soldiers were imprisoned at Fort Delaware on Pea Patch Island during the Civil War. Many prisoners were kept in cold, damp underground cells. Conditions in the prison were so severe that about 2,400 prisoners died there.

The Fenwick Island lighthouse was built in 1852.

North Pacific Ocean

North Atlantic Ocean

Gulf of Mexico

The Swedes in Delaware

- The English navigator Henry Hudson, working for the Netherlands, was probably the first European to reach Delaware during his search for the Northwest Passage. He and his crew explored Delaware Bay in 1609.

What was the Northwest Passage? Did Hudson find it?

- Cornelius Mey and Cornelius Henderson explored the land around Delaware Bay for the Netherlands in 1614 and 1616. A small group of Dutch colonists began a settlement called Zwaanendael (Valley of the Swans) in 1631, but only one member of the group survived.

What happened to the colonists at Zwaanendael?

- Led by Peter Minuit, another group of Dutch and Swedish colonists landed in Delaware at a place known as The Rocks. They built Fort Christina, named for the queen of Sweden. This became the first permanent white settlement in Delaware. After the Dutch left the area to settle in New Amsterdam, Fort Christina became the heart of New Sweden, a string of settlements along the Delaware River from Wilmington nearly to Philadelphia.

Who was Peter Minuit?

- Delaware might be a small state, but there wasn't anything small about Johan Printz, the governor of New Sweden from 1643 to 1653. He reportedly stood seven feet tall and weighed 400 pounds. The Lenape referred to him as "Big Tub." He is still remembered in this nursery rhyme:

> No governor of Delaware, before or since, Has weighed as much as Johan Printz.

- The days of New Sweden were limited. After being defeated by Peter Stuyvesant in 1655, the Swedish colonists were allowed to keep their property, but New Sweden no longer existed.

- Although Sweden did not occupy much of the New World or remain for very long, their influence has remained. Called the Old Swedes Church, services are still conducted at Holy Trinity Church in Wilmington, founded in 1698.

- The Swedish pioneers built log cabins, a type of architecture which kept out the cold better than the lumber houses built by English colonists.

How were log cabins constructed? What kept the logs from falling off each other? What was used to keep cold air from getting between logs? Why would log cabins be warmer than houses made of lumber? Use illustrations to explain your answers.

North or South?

Although it became illegal in 1776 to import slaves, slavery remained legal in Delaware. The issue of slavery made Delaware a divided state. Free Blacks had few rights in Delaware. Patty Cannon headed a gang who seized hundreds of free Blacks over a 40-year period and sold them in southern states. In contrast, members of Delaware's Underground Railroad helped thousands of slaves reach freedom.

After Lincoln was elected President, William Burton, governor of Delaware, tried to persuade the state legislature to join the southern states that seceded from the Union. Delaware remained with the Union, but hundreds from the state joined the Confederate Army.

When Lincoln issued the Emancipation Proclamation on January 1, 1863, he freed all slaves in the Confederate states. Slavery in the Union states was still legal. Slaves in Delaware and Kansas were not freed until the Thirteenth Amendment to the Constitution passed in 1865.

Virginia, North Carolina, South Carolina, Tennessee, Alabama, Georgia, Florida, Mississippi, Arkansas, Louisiana and Texas joined together to form the Confederate States of America.

On the map below, color Delaware blue.

Color the states that seceded red.

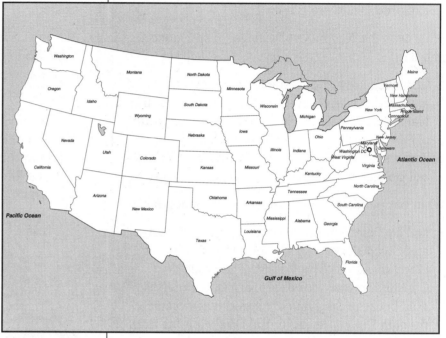

Do you think there's some room to land on Pea Patch Island? Sounds kind of small to me.

36

Welcome to Florida

Let's steer the balloon a little farther south now. While we're here, we might take a side trip to Disney World.

Nicknames: The Sunshine State and the Peninsula State

State motto: In God We Trust

State flower: Orange blossom

State tree: Sabal palm (cabbage palm)

State bird: Mockingbird

State animal: Florida panther

State fish: Sailfish (saltwater) and largemouth bass (freshwater)

State marine mammal: Manatee

State saltwater mammal: Dolphin

State insect: Praying mantis

State gem: Moonstone

State beverage: Orange juice

State shell: Horse conch

State song: "Old Folks at Home" (also known as "Swanee River")

Capital: Tallahassee

Statehood: March 3, 1845, the 27th state

1990 Population: 12,937,926: the 4th largest in population

Area: 58,664 square miles: the 22nd largest state

Neighbors: Georgia, Alabama, Atlantic Ocean and Gulf of Mexico

Florida is a Spanish word meaning "full of flowers." The name was chosen by Ponce de Leon, an early Spanish explorer.

Did You Know?

Florida is the grapefruit and orange growing capital of the nation. If all the oranges grown in Florida in one year were laid in a row, the line would be two million miles long!

What Can You Find in *Tallahassee?*

How many words can you make using the letters in *Tallahassee?* Words must be three or more letters. Do not use words formed by adding *s* at the end. Try to find at least 20 words.

Discussion Question: What If?

What would our country be like today if Ponce de Leon had discovered the Fountain of Youth in Florida?

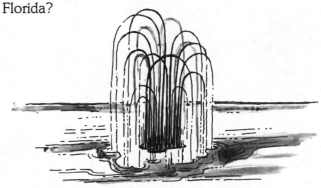

37

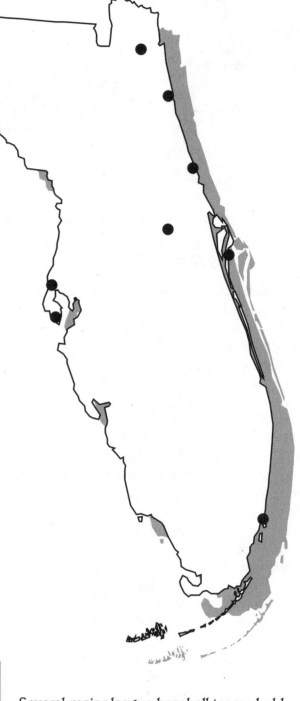

Write the names of the underlined places on the Florida state map.

<u>Tampa Bay</u> is home of one of Florida's professional football teams, the Buccaneers. The other team is the <u>Miami</u> Dolphins. The Gator Bowl college football games are played in <u>Jacksonville</u>.

Florida is a peninsula. A peninsula is land surrounded by water on three sides. The <u>Atlantic Ocean</u> borders Florida on the east.

The <u>Florida Keys</u> are a group of islands off the southern tip of Florida.

Apollo II launched from <u>Cape Canaveral</u> on July 16, 1969, carried the first astronauts to the moon.

Sea World, Epcot Center and Walt Disney World are exciting places to visit near <u>Orlando</u>.

<u>Tarpon Springs</u> on the <u>Gulf of Mexico</u> is a famous sponge fishing center.

<u>St. Augustine</u>, founded in 1565, is the oldest European city in the nation.

At <u>Daytona Beach</u> you'll find the famous auto racetrack, the Daytona International Speedway.

Several major league baseball teams hold spring training near <u>St. Petersburg</u>.

African plants and animals can be seen at Busch Gardens near <u>Tampa</u>.

Europeans discovered Apalachee Indians living in <u>Tallahassee</u> in the 1500s. The name means "old town." Tallahassee became the capital in 1845 when Florida became a state.

Life in the Waters of Florida

Not only is Florida surrounded by water on three sides, it also has thousands of lakes, rivers and swamps. Some of Florida's rivers have rather unusual names, like the Apalachicola, Suwannee, Aucilla, Chipola, Choctawhatchee, Escambia, Kissimmee and Ochlockonee rivers.

With so much fresh water and salt water, marine mammals and birds, reptiles, amphibians and fish are abundant.

Match the names of the sea creatures on the left side of the page with their pictures on the right. Use a dictionary, encyclopedia or other reference book to help you identify these animals.

Alligator

Catfish

Shrimp

Lobster

Crab

Oyster

Coral

Shark

Water moccasin

Florida Swarms with an Abundance of Nature

Type	Number of Species
Trees	350 +
Wild plants	3,500
Mammals	90
Birds	400
Freshwater fish	200
Marine fish	1,200

Select one of these Florida plants or animals. Draw a picture of it and write a short report.

Trees:

Mangrove

Cypress

Coconut palm

Gumbo limbo

Sabal palm

Black tupelo

Flroida fiddlewood

Wild Plants:

Orchids

Spanish moss

Wood lilies

Bougainvillea

Magnolia

Bromeliads

Sawgrass

Mammals:

Manatees

Florida panther

Key deer

Dolphin

Opossum

Raccoon

Porpoise

Birds:

Roseate spoonbill

Snowy egret

Limpkin

Anhinga (snake bird)

Brown pelican

Flamingo

Wood stork

Snail kite

Fish:

Tarpon

Albino catfish

Shark

Pompano

Grouper

Sailfish

Marlin

Barracuda

Reptiles and Amphibians:

Loggerhead sea turtle

Alligator

Indigo snake

Gopher tortoise

Cotton mouth snake

Banded coral snake

Anole

Other Animals:

Lobster

Golden orb spider

Tree snail

Sponge

Coral

The People That Chose to Be Free

About two million years ago, ice moved south during the Ice Age, covering much of what is now the United States. As the ice advanced, the animals moved south in search of a warmer climate. At one time Florida was home to mastodons, saber-toothed tigers, camels, wolves and even lions.

People settled in Florida more than 10,000 years ago, but where they came from is not clear. Some scientists believe the first inhabitants were

descendants of Asians who crossed into Alaska and gradually made their way south. Others believe the early inhabitants may have moved north from Central and South America.

Five main groups of Native Americans lived in Florida when the Europeans began exploring the area: the Ais, the Apalachees, the Calusas, the Tequestas and Timucuas. They hunted, fished, gathered food and farmed.

The Seminoles were members of the Creek tribe who came to

Florida from Georgia and Alabama in the early 1700s. White settlers wanted the land where the Seminoles lived.

Osceola, a leader of the Seminoles, led his people against the U.S. army which had orders from President Andrew Jackson to force the Seminoles to the Indian Territory (Oklahoma). In 1837 Osceola and other chiefs were invited to peace talks at St. Augustine under a flag of truce. The offer was a trick. Osceola was captured and imprisoned at Fort Moultrie where he remained until he died a year later.

In spite of efforts to force the Seminoles to move to reservations, many escaped to the Everglades. The word *Seminole*

means "people that chose to be free." The Seminoles were the only Native Americans that the U.S. government never completely defeated. Technically, the Seminoles are still at war with the United States. No treaty ending the war has ever been signed.

Imagine being a member of Osceola's people. How would you feel when you found out your leader had been tricked and imprisoned? Write a paragraph from the point of view of a friend of Osceola's.

Don't Get Lost in the Everglades

Imagine being in a mysterious swamp like the Everglades, a beautiful but scary and dangerous tropical wilderness. To the Seminoles, the area was called Pa-hay-o-kee, "grassy waters." The Everglades are filled with strange sights, smells and sounds.

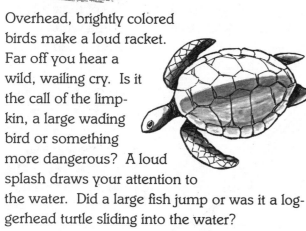

Overhead, brightly colored birds make a loud racket. Far off you hear a wild, wailing cry. Is it the call of the limp-kin, a large wading bird or something more dangerous? A loud splash draws your attention to the water. Did a large fish jump or was it a log-gerhead turtle sliding into the water?

What was that? It sounded like the jaws of an alligator snapping shut. You hear the hum of mosqui-toes, horseflies and other insects. A slithering sound overhead could mean a deadly cotton mouth snake or a harmless ten-foot blue indigo snake. Before you discover what is above, you hear a rustling sound in the thick brush behind you. Could it be a 300-pound wild hog or a family of raccoons?

More sounds come at you from different directions: the bellow of an alligator, the croaking of leopard frogs and bullfrogs and the snarl of a panther. The Everglades, now a pro-tected environment, are filled with strange, mys-terious sights and sounds.

Read more about animals and plants that live in the Everglades. Write a short story about what you think it would be like to travel through a great swamp like the Everglades.

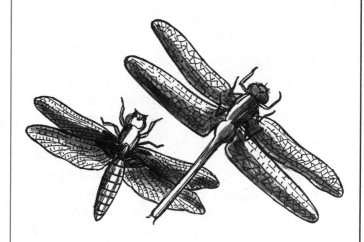

You might also like to read about what kinds of environmental damage has occurred in the Everglades. Has wildlife been affected? Share this information with your class.

Look at that alligator! It must be 15 feet long!

Welcome to Georgia

It's only a short hop, skip and a glide from Florida to the Peach State. Look at all the islands along Georgia's Atlantic coast. There's even one called Blackbeard Island.

Nicknames: Empire State of the South, Peach State and Goober State
State motto: Wisdom, Justice and Moderation
State flower: Cherokee rose
State wildflower: Azalea
State tree: Live oak
State bird: Brown thrasher
State game bird: Bobwhite quail
State fish: Largemouth bass
State insect: Honeybee
State butterfly: Tiger swallowtail
State marine mammal: Right whale
State mineral: Staurolite crystals
State gem: Quartz
State fossil: Shark tooth
State song: "Georgia on My Mind"
Capital: Atlanta
Statehood: January 2, 1788. Georgia was one of the 13 original states and the fourth to ratify the Constitution.
1990 Population: 6,478,216: the 11th largest in population
Area: 58,910 square miles: the 21st largest state. Georgia is the largest state east of the Mississippi River.
Neighbors: Tennessee, South Carolina, North Carolina, Florida, Alabama and the Atlantic Ocean

Six Million Miles of Peanuts!

Georgia leads the nation in the production of peanuts—about two billion pounds a year. There are about 200 peanut pods to a pound. If you placed all those peanuts end to end, they would form a row six million miles long! That's a lot of peanuts.

Georgia is sometimes called the "Goober State." The word *goober* may have come from *nguba* an African word for peanut.

What products made with peanuts do you like to eat?

_____

_____

_____

_____

_____

_____

_____

_____

_____

Discussion Question: What If?

What if the climate of Georgia was more like Wisconsin or Minnesota?

Write the names of the underlined places on the map of Georgia.

Before <u>Atlanta</u> became the capital of Georgia in 1868, the state had four other capitals: <u>Savannah</u>, <u>Augusta</u>, <u>Louisville</u> and <u>Midgeville</u>.

Five states border Georgia: <u>Tennessee</u>, <u>South Carolina</u>, <u>Florida</u>, <u>North Carolina</u> and <u>Alabama</u>. Label their approximate locations.

The <u>Atlantic Ocean</u> forms the southeast border of Georgia.

There is a town in Georgia named <u>Santa Claus</u>.

Several islands are also part of Georgia. Label <u>Ossabaw Island</u>, <u>Blackbeard Island</u>, <u>Jekyll Island</u> and <u>Cumberland Island</u>.

The <u>Appalachian Mountains</u> are found in the northern part of Georgia.

Called "the land of trembling earth," the <u>Okefenokee Swamp</u> lies in southeastern Georgia.

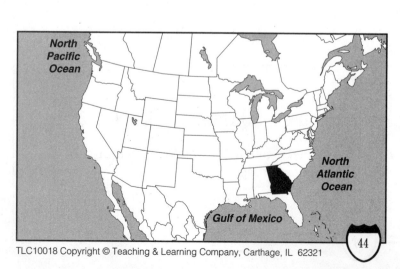

Where the Buffalo Roamed?

Millions of years ago, the southern half of Georgia was covered with water. Farmers have found fossils of fish while plowing land far from the sea.

Little is known about the earliest inhabitants of Georgia. They may have settled in the area about 10,000 years ago. In Putnam County a 100-foot giant eagle made from stones was found. Who built this stone monument? When it was built? These mysteries have never been solved.

Georgia has preserved some of the history of its first settlers.

Kolomoki Indian Mounds and State Park near Blakely is a historic settlement dating from about 800 A.D. There are several burial, temple and game mounds here as well as a ceremonial plaza built by people known as the Mound Builders. There is also a museum depicting Native American cultures of the area.

At the Etowah Indian Mounds near Cartersville, three large mounds and the remains of a fortified settlement from 1000 to 1500 A.D. can be seen.

The culture of the Mound Builders was replaced by other groups who moved into the area. The Muskhogean came from the southwest, conquering and absorbing the earlier residents. Because they often lived near streams, the English called this group the Creek Indians.

The Cherokee, sometimes called the "cave peo-

ple" because they built their homes in hillsides, moved to Georgia from the north.

The Cherokee village of New Echota has been partially restored. This was the last capital of the Cherokee Nation before they were forced to move from Georgia to Oklahoma along the "Trail of Tears."

We usually think of buffalo as living west of the Mississippi River. (American buffalo are really bison, not buffalo.) When Europeans first explored central Georgia, they found grassy plains filled with herds of grazing bison. By 1800, all the bison had all been killed. If you want to see bison in Georgia today, visit the Chehaw Wild Animal Park in Albany.

Protective trails and elevated walkways allow visitors to watch elk, bison, giraffes, elephants, coyotes, foxes, deer and other animals in their natural habitats.

Learn more about one of the sites in Georgia that have been set aside to preserve the culture of the early Americans.

Millions of Trees

Georgia's land is rich and fertile. Forests spread across more than two-thirds of the Peach State. The hills and mountains are covered with pines—longleaf, shortleaf, loblolly, slash, scrub and white pines. Maples, red and white oaks, hickories, birches and beeches grow among the pines.

The southeastern corner of Georgia and part of Florida was called "Land of the Trembling Earth" by Native Americans. Okefenokee Swamp is the second largest freshwater swamp in the United States. Here cypress, willows, cottonwoods and cedars flourish.

You'll also find buckeyes, chestnuts, black, red and sweet gum trees, hemlocks, pecans, yellow poplars, sassafras and sycamore trees in Georgia. Magnolias, dogwoods, wild plums and elderberry trees have beautiful, fragrant blossoms in the spring.

Select one type of tree found in Georgia and learn more about it. How and where does it grow? What products can be made from it? What does it look like? How tall does it grow?

Write your report on the back of this page. Draw a picture of the fruits, flowers and leaves of the tree you selected in the box below.

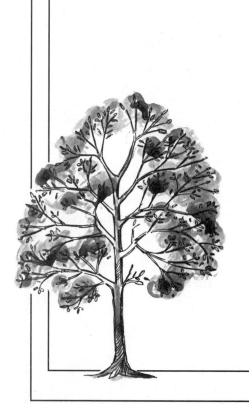

Find Out More About Georgia

Fill in the blanks to answer the assigned questions below.

1. Who was Georgia named after?

_____

2. The "Father of Georgia" was born in London, England. He convinced the king to release prisoners from debtors prison and allow them to settle in the New World. What was his name?

_____

3. Eli Whitney invented a machine for removing seeds from cotton. His machine could clean cotton 50 times as fast as a person and helped make cotton a major crop in Georgia. What was his machine called?

_____

4. What insect was responsible for destroying much of Georgia's cotton crop in the 1920s?

_____

5. Although cotton is still grown in Georgia, two other crops became more important. What are they?

_____ and _____

6. The woman who formed the first U.S. Girl Guides troop in Savannah was born on Halloween in 1860. She soon changed the name to the Girl Scouts. What was her name?

_____

7. What large city in Georgia has the same name as the capital of Maine?

_____

8. Born in Cairo, Georgia, he became the first African American player in the major leagues when he joined the Brooklyn Dodgers in 1947. What was his name?

_____

9. Born in Atlanta, he completed high school and entered Morehouse College when he was only 15. He became a famous Civil Rights leader in the south. In 1963 he gave his famous "I Have a Dream" speech in Washington, D.C. What was his name?

_____

10. What city was called the "Mother City of Georgia"?

_____

11. What marine mammals known as "sea cows" can be seen around Cumberland Island?

_____

12. The world's largest sculpture is carved into the side of Stone Mountain. What three Confederate heroes are shown?

_____, _____

and _____

13. In 1827, gold was discovered in northern Georgia and a gold rush began. Gold coins were minted in Georgia from 1838 until 1861. Where was the mint located?

_____

_____

Please pass the peanuts.

47

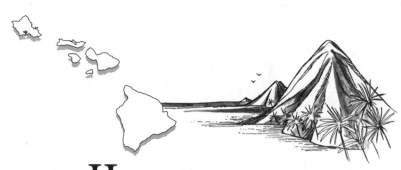

Welcome to Hawaii

The surf's up. Let's head across the Pacific Ocean to the Hawaiian islands, land of volcanoes, rain forests and hula dancing.

Nickname: The Aloha State
State motto: The life of the land is perpetuated in righteousness.
State flower: Hibiscus
State tree: Candlenut (kukui)
State bird: Hawaiian goose (Nēnē)
State song: "Hawaii Pono'ī" (Our Own Hawaii)
Official state languages: English and Hawaiian
Capital: Honolulu
Statehood: Hawaii became the 50th state on August 21, 1959.
1990 Population: 1,108,229: the 41st largest in population. Eighty percent of the people in Hawaii live on the island of O'ahu.
Area: 6,471 square miles: the 4th smallest in area

Discussion Question: What If?

What if you had a chance to travel 2,000 miles in a large canoe to reach the islands of Hawaii? Would you make the trip?

Did You Know?

Both the state and one of the islands are named Hawaii. To avoid confusion, the island of Hawaii is often called the Big Island.

The state of Hawaii is an archipelago—a chain of islands in the Pacific Ocean. The entire chain includes 132 islands and stretches 1,523 miles. Most of the islands are small and unpopulated.

The first people to settle in the Hawaiian Islands came from the Polynesian islands more than 2,000 miles away. They traveled in large canoes, arriving about 300 A.D. Other groups, possibly from Tahiti, arrived five or six hundred years later.

When Captain Cook first arrived in Kaua'i in 1778, he found about 250,000 people living in the Hawaiian Islands. He named them the Sandwich Islands after his patron, the Earl of Sandwich.

Since the first two early groups of settlers came to Hawaii, people from Europe, China, Japan, Korea, Samoa, New Zealand, Tonga and many other countries have chosen to settle in the Hawaiian Islands. As a result, the people have mixed ethnic and cultural backgrounds.

If you think Hawaiian words contain a lot of vowels, you'd be right. When missionaries arrived in Hawaii, they established phonetic spellings for Hawaiian words, using only 12 letters. Hawaiian words are spelled with five vowels: A, E, I, O and U; plus seven consonants: H, K, L, M ,N, P and W.

Name _____   *Hawaii Map Activity*

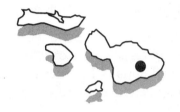

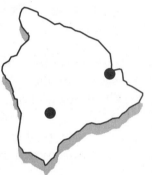

Label these places in Hawaii on the state map above:

Honolulu	Waikiki Beach
Pearl City	Diamond Head
Kailua	Mauna Loa
Hilo	'Aiea
Kāne'ohe	Haleakala Crater

The eight main islands in Hawaii have their own official colors and emblems.
Color the eight main islands their official colors.

Island	Color	Emblem
Hawaii	red	red **lehua** blossom
Kaho'olawe	gray	**hinahina** (threadlike moss)
Maui	pink	**lokelani** flower
Lāna'i	yellow	**kauna'oa** (air plant)
Moloka'i	green	white **kukui** blossom
O'ahu	yellow	**'ilima** flower
Kaua'i	purple	**mokihana** berry
Ni'ihau	white	white **pupu** shell

Pacific Ocean

United States

Mexico

Hawaii

49

TLC10018 Copyright © Teaching & Learning Company, Carthage, IL 62321

The Land of Legends

How did Hawaii get its name? One legend says the islands were named for Hawaii-loa, a Polynesian chief who discovered the islands long ago. The early Polynesian settlers may have named the islands for their South Pacific homeland which was called Hawaiki in ancient times.

According to legend, the Alakoko fishpond was built by the **menehune**, an ancient race of little people who first inhabited Kaua'i. The menehune worked only at night and were rarely seen.

Many popular legends concern Maui, a man with godlike powers who invented the spear and the barbed fishhook and discovered fire. He created a place for people to live by pushing the sky high in the air. He was known as "Maui of a Thousand Tricks."

One day Maui went fishing with a large magic hook. His brothers paddled the canoe but were warned not to watch him. With his magic fishhook, Maui began pulling the Hawaiian Islands from the bottom of the Pacific Ocean. His brothers became curious and turned around to see what he was doing. They broke the magic line, and Hawaii was left only partly emerged. That's why Hawaii is a chain of islands instead of a solid land mass.

Long ago, the sun raced across the sky too quickly and did not leave enough warmth. Maui grabbed the early morning sunbeams and tied them to trees, capturing the sun. The sun begged to be set free. Maui agreed but only if the sun would promise

to move more slowly across the sky in the future. Now the hours of sunlight are longer in Hawaii.

Legends are stories that may be based on truth but have been changed and exaggerated over time. Myths are ancient stories that explain something in nature.

Write your own story about Hawaii. You can use one of the ideas below or make up your own.

- Why do volcanoes on Hawaii erupt?

- How were the Hawaiian Islands formed?

- Why are Hawaiian birds so brightly colored?

- Where did dolphins come from?

- How are coral reefs built?

- About 700 types of fish swim in the waters around Hawaii. Why are there so many kinds of fish?

- Why are some types of birds like the Hawaiian goose, the Hawaiian stilt and several types of honeycreepers found only in Hawaii?

- How did the bird of paradise become a flower?

The Islands of Hawaii

- If the water were drained from the Pacific Ocean, you could see that the Hawaiian Islands are actually the tops of a chain of underwater mountains formed by volcanic activity. Two volcanoes on the Big Island are still very active. When Mauna Loa and Kilauea erupt, fountains of burning lava spout into the air. Mauna Kea and Hualalai on the Big Island and Haleakalā on Maui are called dormant volcanoes. *Dormant* means they haven't erupted for a long time, but scientists believe they could erupt again some time in the future.

- Giant tree ferns grow in the rain forests of Kaua'i, giving this island the nickname Garden Isle. At the center of this nearly round island, Mount Wai'ale'ale makes the record books for the rainiest place on Earth. About 500 inches of rain fall here every year.

- Known as the Forbidden Island, Ni'ihau is an 18-mile long, privately owned cattle and sheep ranch. Few visitors are invited to Ni'ihau.

- Eighty percent of the people in Hawaii live on the island of O'ahu. Called the Gathering Place, this island features many world-famous landmarks including Waikiki Beach, Diamond Head and Pearl Harbor.

- The Friendly Isle of Moloka'i was formed by three volcanoes.

- During the summer harvest, more than a million pineapples a day are taken from Lāna'i, the Pineapple Island. An area of strange shaped lava formations on this island is known as the Garden of the Gods.

- Sugarcane and pineapple grow well on the Valley Island of Maui in the fertile valley between the mountains. Mount Haleakala is the largest inactive volcano crater in the world. The crater is 3,000 feet deep and 22 miles around.

  - Kaho'olawe is the smallest of the eight major islands. No one lives on this barren, windswept island.

- The Big Island of Hawaii is the only one of the islands with active volcanoes. The island contains high mountains, lush valleys and fields, desertlike areas of lava, sand and ash as well as gleaming white sandy beaches, black lava beaches and a green beach of volcanic particles.

Match the names of the islands with their nicknames.

1. Hawaii		Valley Island
2. Maui		Gathering Place
3. Lāna'i		Garden Isle
4. Moloka'i		Big Island
5. O'ahu		Forbidden Island
6. Ni'ihau		Friendly Isle
7. Kaua'i		Pineapple Island

Learn More About Hawaii

Use reference books to find an interesting fact about each of the topics below.

Diamond Head: _____

_____

Pineapples: _____

_____

Bird of Paradise: _____

_____

Hawaiian Goose: _____

_____

The Garden of the Gods: _____

_____

Pearl Harbor: _____

_____

Waikiki Beach: _____

_____

Alaka'i Swamp: _____

_____

Mount Wai'ale: _____

_____

Father Damien: _____

_____

Sugarcane: _____

_____

Macadamia nuts: _____

Mauna Kea: _____

_____

Mauna Loa: _____

_____

Kilauea: _____

_____

Leis: _____

_____

Captain James Cook: _____

_____

Hula: _____

_____

Kamehameha I: _____

_____

Pele, the Fire Goddess: _____

_____

Candlenut Trees: _____

_____

Sandalwood: _____

_____

Queen Lili'uokalani: _____

_____

Haleakala Crater: _____

_____

Iolani Palace: _____

Before we leave, let's stop for some island treats: fresh pineapple, sugarcane and macadamia nuts.

52

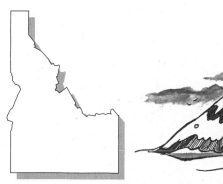

Welcome to Idaho

From the Canadian border in the north, Idaho extends south 483 miles, a land of rugged mountains, deep canyons, roaring waterfalls, deserts and large tracts of wilderness.

Nickname: Gem State

State motto: It Is Perpetual

State flower: Syringa

State tree: Western white pine

State bird: Mountain bluebird

State horse: Appaloosa

State gem: Star garnet

State song: "Here We Have Idaho"

Capital: Boise

Statehood: Idaho became the 43rd state on July 3, 1890.

1990 Population: 1,006,749: the 42nd largest in population

Population density: 12.2 people per square mile

Area: 83,564 square miles: the 13th largest state

Neighbors: Montana, Wyoming, Utah, Nevada, Oregon, Washington and British Columbia

The Story of Coyote

Nez Perce legends tell about Coyote who was part animal, part god. Coyote stole fire for people and taught them how to fish. He lived on top of a mountain. Each night Coyote looked at the sky and studied the stars. One Star seemed to come so close it almost touched the top of the mountain. Coyote wanted to travel in the sky. Each night he asked Star to take him across the heavens, but Star refused. At last, Star agreed so Coyote would stop bothering him. Down

came Star and Coyote jumped up on him. Star moved back up into the sky. As they traveled across the land of the Ice Spirits, Coyote became colder and colder. Finally he lost his grip on Star and fell to Earth. The other coyotes rushed to his aide and discovered he was dead.

They pointed their noses upward and howled at Star. Since then, the coyotes look up at Star every night and howl, mourning the death of their brother.

Write a short poem or story about Coyote or his friends.

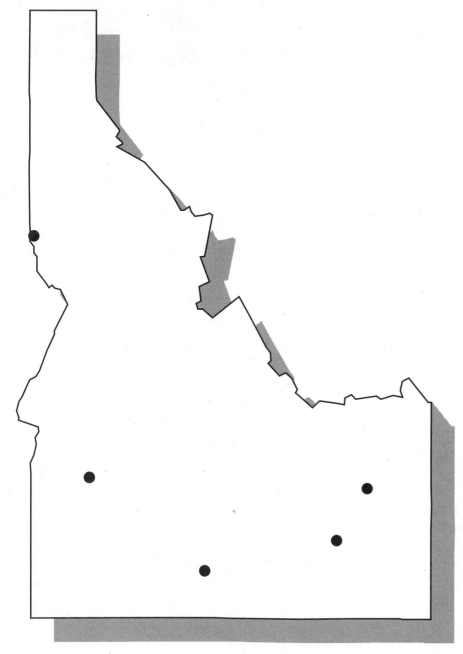

The word *Idaho* was invented by George Willig. He claimed it was a Native American word that meant "gem of the mountains." As far as we know, no such word existed.

1. Which Canadian province forms the northern border of Idaho?

   _____

2. Which two states form Idaho's eastern border?

   _____

3. Which two states are south of Idaho?

   _____

4. Which two states are west of the Gem State?

   _____

Would you like to visit Santa? Would you like to take a trip to Dover, Moscow, Paris or Oxford? You can find places with these names in Idaho.

Label Boise, Pocatello, Idaho Falls, Twin Falls and Lewiston on the state map.

There are lots of places in Idaho named for plants or animals, like Fernwood, Fish Haven, Eagle and Elk City.

Draw the Snake River on the Idaho map.

List some other places in Idaho named for plants or animals.

54

The Nez Perce

Fossil evidence indicates that people have lived in Idaho for more than 13,000 years. By the time white explorers arrived, they found several groups settled in the region including the Shoshone, Paiute and Nez Perce. (*Perce* is pronounced like *purse*.)

The Nez Perce once lived on the land that became Washington, Oregon, Idaho and Montana—an area of more than 150,000 square miles. *Nez Perce* is a French word meaning "pierced nose."

Their homes, called lodges or dugouts, were dug into the ground two to three feet deep. The scooped-out dirt was used to build walls. They cut logs for posts along the sides and middle to support the roof. They cut timbers for rafters and cov-ered the roofs with large mats of cattails sewn together.

Nez Perce villages contained one or more main lodges which could house up to 30 families. Everyone shared the lodge's central cooking fires. At night, young men and women slept in separate smaller lodges. Wives, children, warriors and old people slept in the main lodge.

The Nez Perce built sweat rooms in the sleeping lodges for daily saunas. They heated stones on an outdoor fire, then piled the hot rocks on the floor of the sweat room. Pouring water on the 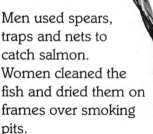rocks produced steam. After sitting in the steam, they dashed to the icy river for an invigorating rinse.

The Nez Perce used digging sticks to gather kouse and camas bulbs. Kouse are bulb-like roots eaten raw that taste like turnips. Camas bulbs are a type of wild lily with blue and white flowers that grow about three feet high. The Nez Perce called them "quamash."

Eaten raw, camas bulbs are crunchy, juicy and sweet. They were dried and stored for winter. After peeling off the outer husks, women piled the bulbs on a bed of grass over hot stones in a fire pit and covered them with another layer of grass. They poured water over the grass to produce steam. Covered with sand, the roots were left to cook all day. When they were ready, the people held a feast. Leftover camas bulbs were shaped into small cakes and dried to pro-vide a nourishing food that lasted a long time without spoiling.

Men used spears, traps and nets to catch salmon. Women cleaned the fish and dried them on frames over smoking pits.

In the mid 1700s, the Nez Perce became expert horse breeders. They developed a sturdy, sure-footed breed known today as the Appaloosa, Idaho's official state horse.

Describe the effects of white settlers on the Nez Perce.

Let's Hear It for Idaho Potatoes!

Fried in a pan or boiled in a pot,
Eaten raw or steaming hot
Idaho potatoes are the best!

How Do You Like Your Potatoes?

- Baked and topped with sour cream and butter?

- Hash browns with eggs and sausage?

- Boiled, mashed and covered with butter or gravy?

- Fried in a skillet with onions?

- French fried and dipped in catsup?

- Scalloped potatoes cooked with ham?

- Potato pancakes?

Chances are you've eaten lots of Idaho potatoes in your lifetime. Potatoes are the state's best known crop. Idaho farmers grow more spuds than any other state, producing 25% of the nation's potatoes.

Although he was born in Illinois, not Idaho, the poet Vachel Lindsay, wrote a poem about potatoes called "The Potatoes' Dance."

Write a cheer to honor your favorite way to eat potatoes or a poem titled "Through the Eyes of a Potato."

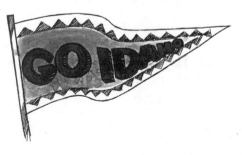

An Idaho Tall Tale

People in most states tell tall tales about how big things are in their state. Known for its large potatoes, one Idaho story tells the tale of a farmer who wouldn't sell a customer 100 pounds of potatoes.

"Why should I cut off part of one potato?" he asked.

Potato People

Draw faces on the "potato people." Add hair, hats or other items to make your potato people unique.

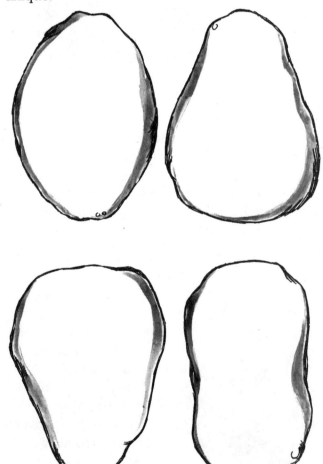

Let's Visit Idaho

Read about these places in Idaho; then answer the assigned questions.

Great earthquakes pushed up the mountains. Volcanoes erupted, spewing ash and pouring lava across the land. Huge glaciers dug deep valleys between the mountains. These natural forces combined to make Idaho a land of contrasts and spectacular scenery. More than 2,000 natural lakes and 16,000 miles of rivers and streams cover the state. Forty percent of the land is covered with forests, with stands of red cedar that date back hundreds of years. Millions of bison once roamed across the grasslands of Idaho.

- Crystal Ice Cave lies deep inside a dormant volcano.

What does *dormant* mean? What can visitors see in Crystal Ice Cave?

- Craters of the Moon National Monument is near Arco, Idaho.

How did this place get such a strange name?

- Minnetonka Cave is a huge sandstone cave near St. Charles.

What unusual sights can be seen there?

- Shoshone Ice Cave is a lava tube that contains spectacular ice formations.

What is a lava tube?

- Sun Valley is popular with people who enjoy alpine skiing.

What is alpine skiing?

- The state capitol in Boise is the only capitol building heated with geothermal hot water.

What does *geothermal* mean?

- The Idaho Historical Museum in Boise contains displays of early pioneer life including a blacksmith's forge and a Chinese apothecary shop.

What is a forge? What is an apothecary shop?

- The Basque Museum in Boise honors the largest Basque community in the U.S.

Who are the Basque? What occupation were they traditionally famous for?

- The Boise Basin Museum in Idaho City is filled with memorabilia of the Old West.

What does *memorabilia* mean?

- The Salmon River is a great place to go white-water rafting.

What is white-water rafting?

- Emerald Creek is one of the few places in the world where star garnets are found.

What does a star garnet look like?

With all the strange rock formations and caves, I feel like we're on another planet.

Welcome to Illinois

As the west winds blow, we'll travel east to visit the Land of Lincoln. There are lots of places to land on the flat prairies of Illinois.

Nicknames: Land of Lincoln, Prairie State and Tall State
State motto: State Sovereignty, National Union
State flower: Violet
State tree: White oak
State bird: Cardinal
State animal: White-tailed deer
State fish: Bluegill
State insect: Monarch butterfly
State mineral: Fluorite
State song: "Illinois"
Capital: Springfield
Statehood: December 3, 1818, the 21st state
1990 Population: 11,430,602: the 6th largest in population
Area: 56,345 square miles: the 24th largest state
Neighbors: Wisconsin, Indiana, Kentucky, Missouri and Iowa

Big Eight

Rank these cities from 1 to 8 based on their population in the 1990 census.

____	Chicago, Illinois	2,783,726
____	Dallas, Texas	1,006,677
____	Detroit, Michigan	1,027,974
____	Houston, Texas	1,630,553
____	Los Angeles, California	3,485,398
____	New York City, New York	7,322,564
____	Philadelphia, Pennsylvania	1,585,577
____	San Diego, California	1,110,549

Honest Abe

How could a man with less than a year of schooling become a lawyer? Who could lose elections for the Illinois legislature and U.S. Senate and still be elected President—twice? No one but Abraham Lincoln, known as "Honest Abe" and the "Illinois Rail-Splitter."

Although he was born in Kentucky and raised in Indiana, people usually think of Illinois as Abraham Lincoln's home state. Lincoln predicted that the nation would either become all slave or all free. "A house divided against itself cannot stand," he said.

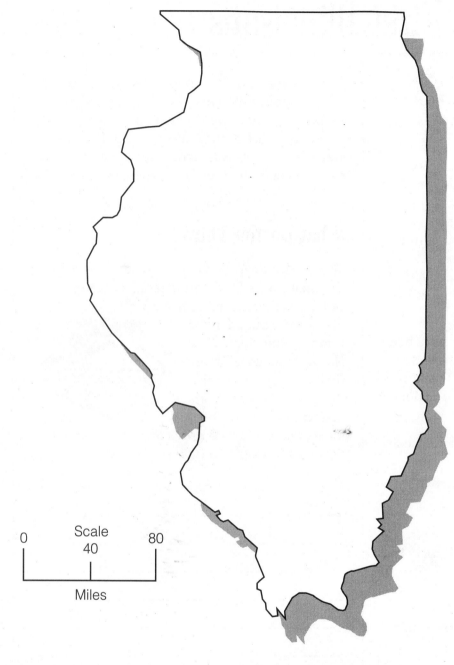

The Mississippi River forms the entire western boundary of Illinois. Color it blue.

Lake Michigan forms the northeast border of Illinois. Color its approximate location blue also.

Label the approximate locations of the five states that border Illinois.

Springfield, the capital, is in central Illinois. Put a star on the map to mark its location.

Draw a circle on the map to show the location of Chicago.

1. Illinois is sometimes called the "Tall State" because of its shape. Use the scale and a ruler. Approximately how far is it from the most northern point to the most southern point in Illinois?

   _____

2. Use the scale and a ruler. How far is it from Springfield to Chicago?

   _____

The First Illinoisans

People have lived in Illinois for about 10,000 years. Little evidence has been found about the culture of first hunters and gatherers.

Between 300 B.C. and 500 A.D. the Hopewell Culture flourished in Illinois and the Midwest. Thousands of earthwork burial mounds were built on sites across the region. Examples of these mounds can be seen at the Dickson Mound State Museum near Lewistown. A museum has been built over part of one mound to display the skeletons, tools, weapons and artifacts of the ancient people in the exact positions where they were buried.

The remains of about 10,000 mounds have been discovered in Illinois. Some of these mounds have been carefully studied by scientists and preserved. Other mounds are found in the middle of cornfields.

The people known as Mississippians flourished in Illinois between 800 and 1500 A.D. They usually built their cities along riverbanks. They too were mound builders, but they built much larger earthen mounds. Many of the 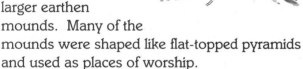 mounds were shaped like flat-topped pyramids and used as places of worship.

We usually think of Native Americans as living in small villages. The size of Monk's Mound, the largest earthwork in the world, indicates a city of as many as 100,000 people. Monk's Mound and 65 other earthen ceremonial and burial mounds are preserved in an 1,800-acre site in southern Illinois called Cahokia Mounds.

In the 1500s, six tribes living in Illinois joined together to form a group called the Illini or Illiniwek. They spoke the Algonquin language and built their homes along streams and rivers. They hunted, fished and grew corn, squash and pumpkins. These people were the Cahokia, Kaskaskia, Michigamea, Moingwena, Peoria and Tamaroa. Illinois was named for the Illini whose name means "the men" or "the superior men."

What Do You Think?

The ancient Egyptians built huge stone pyramids as burial places for their pharaohs (great kings). Gold, silver, gems and other riches were buried in the tombs of the kings. The Native Americans of the midwest also buried their dead with the riches of their culture. Why do you think people believed it was important to bury riches with people who died?

_____

_____

_____

_____

_____

_____

_____

_____

_____

_____

_____

_____

The Windy City

Although the wind often blows in Chicago, that isn't why the city was nicknamed the "Windy City." An eastern writer used the name in the late 1800s. He thought the people of Chicago were "windy" because they bragged so much about their city.

Make up a nickname for the city where you live.

_____

Explain why you chose that name.

_____

_____

_____

_____

The first modern skyscraper was completed in Chicago in 1885 after the Great Chicago Fire. The building was 10 stories tall. Today, a ten-story building doesn't seem very high. Chicago's skyscrapers are much taller.

1. How tall is the Sears Tower?

_____

In his poem "Chicago" written in 1916, Carl Sandburg described the city as . . .

> Hog butcher for the World,
> Tool Maker, Stacker of Wheat,
> Player with Railroads and the
>   Nation's Freight Handler;
> Stormy, husky, brawling,
> City of the Big Shoulders:

Write a poem describing the city where you live.

_____

_____

_____

_____

_____

_____

_____

_____

_____

All About Illinois

Illinois has five professional sports teams. Match the team names with the sport they play.

1. Bears   baseball
2. Black Hawks   basketball
3. Bulls   football
4. Cubs   hockey
5. White Sox   baseball

If you could name four hometown teams, what would you name them?

_____ Baseball

_____ Basketball

_____ Football

_____ Hockey

You can visit the homes of three Presidents in Illinois. In Galena, you'll find the home of Ulysses S. Grant. The log cabin home of Abraham Lincoln is near Decatur, and his home in Springfield has been restored to look as it did in 1860. In Dixon, you can see the house where Ronald Reagan grew up.

6. Of these three Presidents, only one was born in Illinois. Which one?

_____

Some famous people born in Illinois are Walter Payton, Michael Jordan, Walt Disney, Chief Black Hawk, Jack Benny, Jane Margaret Byrne, Richard Daley, George Ferris, Carl Sandburg, Ernest Hemingway, Jane Adams, "Wild Bill" Hickok and Harold Washington.

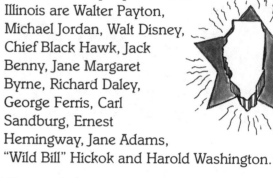

Write a short report about one of these people and why he or she is famous.

7. About 90% of Illinois was covered during the Ice Age. How did this affect the landscape of Illinois?

_____

_____

_____

_____

_____

_____

_____

_____

_____

_____

_____

_____

_____

Now I know why they call Chicago the Windy City.

Welcome to Indiana

Where did the word <u>Hoosier</u> come from? The origin of the word is uncertain, but almost everyone knows Indiana is the Hoosier State.

Nickname: Hoosier State
State motto: Crossroads of America
State flower: Peony
State tree: Tulip poplar
State bird: Cardinal
State stone: Indiana limestone
State song: "On the Banks of the Wabash, Far Away"
Capital: Indianapolis
Statehood: Indiana became the 19th state on December 11, 1816.
1990 Population: 5,544,159: the 14th largest in population
Area: 36,291 square miles: the 38th largest in area
Neighbors: Ohio, Kentucky, Illinois and Michigan

Did You Know?

Between 1900 and 1920, the automobile industry boomed in Indiana. More than 200 different makes of cars were produced including Dusenbergs, Auburns, Stutzes and Maxwells.

Early Indiana

The first people in Indiana arrived about 10,000 years ago. Later cultures rose and fell, leaving little evidence other than large earthen mounds. Some mounds were burial sites. The mounds of later people became centers of worship.

At first, the Native Americans in Indiana were not directly affected by the European colonists who made their home in the New World, but they were soon affected indirectly. When Europeans began settling along the Atlantic coast, they forced thousands of Native Americans to leave their homes and move west. In their push west, the tribes from the east came into conflict with other groups living in Ohio and Indiana. By the early 1700s, Indiana was home to many tribes who settled in the area briefly before being forced to move west again.

The word *Indiana* means "Land of the Indians."

Discussion Question: What If?

What if the Native Americans had joined together, defeated the colonists and started a country of their own? How would this nation be different than the country we know as the United States?

TLC10018 Copyright © Teaching & Learning Company, Carthage, IL 62321

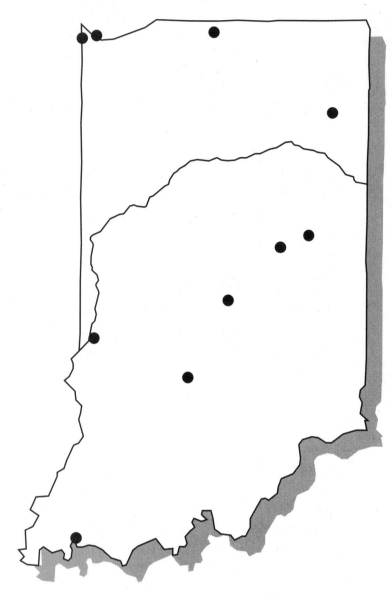

Label the underlined places on the Indiana state map.

Lake Michigan covers 40 miles of the Indiana border on the northwest. Michigan is the state north of Indiana. Label their approximate locations.

The Wabash River is the longest river in the state and forms the southwestern border between Indiana and Illinois. Label their approximate locations.

The Ohio River forms the southern boundary between Indiana and Kentucky. Label their approximate locations.

The border between Indiana and Ohio is a straight line. Label its approximate location.

Indianapolis is the home of the world-famous Indianapolis Motor Speedway.

Not only does the Mesker Park Zoo in Evansville contain more than 400 types of animals, visitors can also tour a reproduction of Columbus's ship, the *Santa Maria*.

The French explorer, LaSalle met with members of the Miami and Illinois tribes in South Bend at a 400-year-old tree called Council Oak Tree.

The remains of 11 earth formations built by the early woodland Indians are located at Mounds State Park near Anderson.

Label these other major cities in Indiana:

Fort Wayne	Gary	Hammond
Muncie	Terre Haute	Bloomington

North Pacific Ocean

North Atlantic Ocean

Gulf of Mexico

64

Indy 15

Use reference books to find the answers to these 15 questions about people and places in Indiana.

1. Fort Wayne was named for:
    A. John Wayne
    B. Mad Anthony Wayne

2. Songwriter from Peru, Indiana, who wrote "Begin the Beguine"
    A. Cole Porter
    B. Ira Gershwin

3. The "Hoosier" poet who wrote "The Old Swimmin' Hole"
    A. Charles Nelson Riley
    B. James Whitcomb Riley

4. Indiana was part of
    A. The Louisiana Purchase
    B. Northwest Territory

5. The first capital of Indiana was
    A. Vicennes
    B. Terre Haute

6. College football team known as the Fighting Irish
    A. Notre Dame
    B. Harvard University

7. Harland Sanders, the Colonel of Kentucky Fried Chicken™ was born in Indiana.
    A. True
    B. False

8. Great Lake that borders Indiana
    A. Lake Erie
    B. Lake Michigan

9. Singer born in Gary, Indiana, who made the album *Thriller*
    A. Michael Jackson
    B. Jessie Jackson

10. Man from Indiana who became Vice President in 1905
    A. Charles Fairbanks
    B. Douglas Fairbanks

11. TV and radio comedian who made Clem Kadiddlehopper famous
    A. Red Buttons
    B. Red Skelton

12. Last name of brothers from Indiana who first made wheelbarrows and wagons, then built cars and trucks
    A. Studebaker
    B. Dodge

13. Wrote *Slaughterhouse Five*, *Cat's Cradle* and *Breakfast of Champions*
    A. Kurt Vonnegut, Jr.
    B. Mark Twain

14. Football team that plays in the Hoosier Dome
    A. Pacers
    B. Colts

15. Popular newspaper correspondent during World War II
    A. Ernie Pyle
    B. Edward R. Murrow

The Indianapolis 500

In the national auto race at Indianapolis, drivers go around and around and around the track 200 times to complete the 500-mile race. In the first Indy 500 race, the winner averaged about 75 miles per hour.

- Use a current almanac to find the top speed attained by a driver in the Indy 500.

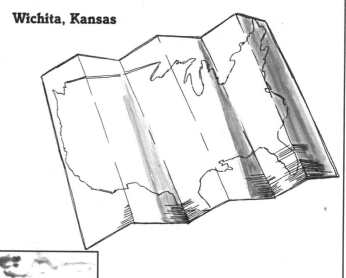

- When was the first 500-mile auto race held in Indianapolis?

- The Indy 500 is held on a holiday weekend. Which holiday?

- What does a checkered flag mean?

- What is a pit stop?

Instead of going around and around, you could visit lots of places if you drove 500 miles from Indianapolis.

Use a ruler and the scale on a U.S. map to find out which of these cities you could visit if you traveled 500 miles in a straight line. Circle the ones that are less than 500 miles away from Indianapolis.

Birmingham, Alabama

Boston, Massachusetts

Charleston, West Virginia

Chicago, Illinois

Cincinnati, Ohio

Cleveland, Ohio

Dallas, Texas

Denver, Colorado

Des Moines, Iowa

Detroit, Michigan

Louisville, Kentucky

Miami, Florida

Memphis, Tennessee

Milwaukee, Wisconsin

Minneapolis, Minnesota

New York City, New York

Pittsburgh, Pennsylvania

St. Louis, Missouri

Washington, D.C.

Wichita, Kansas

I wonder if the drivers get dizzy going around and around so many times?

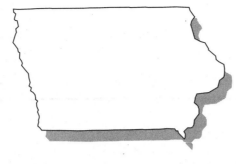

Welcome to Iowa

Let's explore the land where the tall corn grows. Iowa, here we come.

Nicknames: Hawkeye State, Corn State, Corn-Hog State and Land Where the Tall Corn Grows

State motto: Our Liberties We Prize and Our Rights We Will Maintain

State flower: Wild rose

State tree: Oak

State bird: Eastern goldfinch

State stone: Geode

State song: "The Song of Iowa"

Capital: Des Moines

Statehood: Iowa became the 29th state on December 28, 1846.

1990 Population: 2,776,755: the 30th largest in population

Area: 56,290 square miles: Iowa is the 25th largest state

Neighbors: Wisconsin, Illinois, Missouri, Nebraska, Minnesota and South Dakota

Keeping Cool

Until the 1940s, people had no refrigeration in many parts of Iowa. They used an icebox to keep food cool. In the winter, huge chunks of ice were cut from the rivers and stored in icehouses, cool places where ice could be kept all summer. People bought small chunks of ice for their iceboxes. The Icehouse Museum in Cedar Falls demonstrates how the early pioneers once cut and stored blocks of river ice.

Without electricity and refrigerators, what other ways did people use to keep food from spoiling? Name some ways refrigeration has changed people's lives.

Down on the Farm

The Corn State is the nation's number one producer of corn. Iowa ties Illinois for first place as the top soybean-growing state. With all that corn for feed, Iowa has become the number one hog-raising state. The 14,000,000 hogs in Iowa outnumber the people five to one. Beef and dairy cattle, sheep, turkeys and horses are also raised. Oats, rye, alfalfa, wheat, hay, barley and potatoes are other crops grown by the 125,000 Iowans who live on farms.

Name some other products made from soybeans.

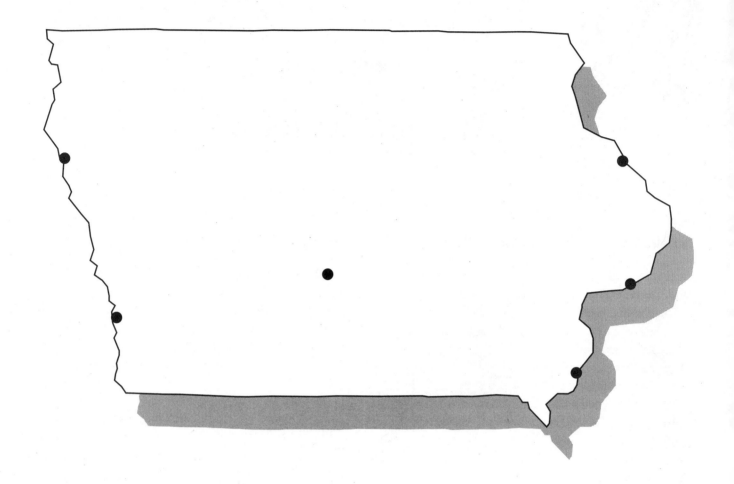

Label the underlined places on the Iowa state map.

The <u>Mississippi River</u> marks the eastern border of Iowa and the <u>Missouri River</u> flows along the western border between Iowa and <u>Nebraska</u>.

The <u>Big Sioux River</u> divides Iowa from <u>South Dakota</u>. Label their approximate locations.

<u>Illinois</u>, <u>Wisconsin</u>, <u>Missouri</u> and <u>Minnesota</u> also share borders with Iowa. Label their approximate locations on the map above.

<u>Des Moines</u> come from the Native American word *moingona* meaning "river of the mounds." This city was first called Fort Des Moines and has been the capital since 1857.

<u>Council Bluffs</u> began as a trading post and fort in the 1820s.

<u>Davenport</u>, founded in 1836, was named for George Davenport, a fur trader.

<u>Sioux City</u> founded in 1854 was named for the Sioux. The world's largest popcorn processing plant is in Sioux City.

Snake Alley in <u>Burlington</u> is said to be the crookedest street in the world.

Founded in 1833, <u>Dubuque</u> was named for Julian Dubuque, Iowa's first white settler.

A Bit of Iowa History

Shallow seas covered Iowa about 500 million years ago. Fossils of starfish and prehistoric amphibians similar to crocodiles have been found in Iowa. A series of glaciers (great mountains of moving ice) covered the land for thousands of years, advancing and retreating, leveling mountains and filling in valleys. When the glaciers finally retreated for the last time, they left fertile soil and gently rolling hills over much of the state. Ancient people who were nomadic hunters settled in Iowa at least 12,000 years ago.

Later peoples who moved to this area built burial mounds in the shape of animals, birds and lizards. One hundred ninety-one mounds can be seen at Effigy Mounds National Monument in northeastern Iowa. Great Bear Mound is 137 feet long and 5 feet high. About 10,000 of these earthen structures can be found throughout Iowa.

Over time other Native Americans settled in Iowa including the Ioway, Omaha, Oto, Missouri, Sioux, Illinois, Ottawa, Mesquakie (Fox) and Sauk (Sac). Many of these people had been pushed west as white settlers claimed more and more of the land east of the Mississippi.

They farmed and built villages along the rivers. They traveled by canoe, fished and hunted deer and bison. While hunting, they lived in tepees—cone-shaped tents made of poles covered with animal skins.

Although the French were the first Europeans to explore the area, and fur traders frequently visited the area, the French didn't settle in Iowa. In

1762 France ceded the land to Spain, then regained it in 1800. Three years later Iowa became a territory of the United States when Napoleon sold the Louisiana Territory for $15 million.

Europeans did not begin settling in Iowa until the early 1800s. When they first arrived, they found marshlands in the north and tall grass prairies in the south and west. Lured by the fertile lands, people from many nations moved to Iowa to farm and raise livestock.

Before the early settlers could begin planting crops, the land had to be cleared and plowed. The prairie grass that covered most of the land had long tangled roots. Plows that worked well on farms in other parts of the country did not work in Iowa. Many farmers hired professionals with enormous plows pulled by teams of oxen to break up the sod (dirt). Some farmers ended up paying more per acre to have it plowed than they did to purchase it in the first place.

At that time few trees grew in Iowa except along the rivers. Without wood for lumber, many early settlers built sod houses. They cut up chunks of earth and used these dirt  "bricks" to build their homes. With walls three-to four-feet thick, sod houses stayed warm in winter and cool in summer.

Write a paragraph about what you think it would be like to build and live in a sod house.

This and That

- Iowa was named for the Ioway Indians. One translation is "beautiful land."

- Iowa's nickname, the Hawkeye State, honors Chief Black Hawk, a Sauk leader who led an unsuccessful resistance against settlers in 1832.

Learn more about Chief Black Hawk and the Sauks who lived in Iowa before white settlers arrived.

- Iowa was a stop on the Underground Railroad for runaway slaves from Missouri seeking freedom in Canada. Although it was against federal law, "conductors" transported slaves from one "station" to the next. Often slaves were hidden in wagons under bales of wheat or piles of corn. Stations were safe houses where the fugitives could find food and shelter.

Learn more about the Underground Railroad in Iowa.

- During a boundary dispute between Missouri and Iowa, a group of Missourians chopped down three hollow trees filled with wild honey in the area claimed by Iowa. The governors of both states called out the militia. By the time the Iowa militia armed with pitchforks and squirrel guns reached the border, the Missouri militia had gone home. The "Honey War" ended without a shot.

What do you think about starting a war over three honey trees?

- Another strange battle called the "Cow War," took place in Iowa in 1931. Farmers protested a program to test dairy cows for tuberculosis. Because infected milk could be fatal to children, diseased cows were to be destroyed. The Great Depression had already caused many hardships to farmers. The state militia was called out and testing was completed with armed guards attending.

- Iowa is one of the leading states for raising hogs. There are almost five times as many hogs in Iowa as there are people.

- An unusual three-story jail was used in Council Bluffs until 1969. Called the Squirrel Cage Jail, the cells were arranged in a circle. The cells had bars but no doors. A jailer turned a hand crank to move the entire structure, bringing the single door on each floor in line with any cell needed.

What would be the advantages and disadvantages of this type of jail?

- Twin sisters, Esther and Pauline Friedman were born in Sioux City in 1918. They both became famous as newspaper columnists. You probably know them better as Dear Abby and Ann Landers.

- Other famous people born in Iowa include Buffalo Bill Cody, Amelia Bloomer, John Wayne, Mamie Eisenhower, Charles Ringling and Herbert Hoover. Hoover was the first President born west of the Mississippi River.

Learn more about one of these famous Iowans.

- Grant Wood grew up on a farm near Anamosa. His painting titled *American Gothic* shows a father and daughter standing in front of a plain Iowa farmhouse.

Study the two people and other details Wood included in the painting. Life was not easy on the Iowa prairie. Describe how this painting makes you feel and what it makes you think of when you look at it.

More to Discover

- People from many different cultural backgrounds settled in Iowa.

- Elk Horn and Kimballton were settled by people from Denmark. A statue of the Little Mermaid from the story by the Danish writer, Hans Christian Andersen, stands in the town square. In 1976, the people of Elk Horn had a windmill brought over from Denmark piece by piece. The mill's 30,000 numbered pieces were reassembled.

Students can enjoy reading *The Little Mermaid* and other stories by Hans Christian Andersen.

Ask students to find out what a windmill is used for and how it works.

- Immigrants from the Netherlands founded the town of Pella, where an annual tulip festival is held every spring. The Historical Village Museum in Pella is a reconstructed Dutch frontier community. The Glockenspiel, a Dutch-style musical clock tower with figures, represents the town's early history.

Discuss festivals in your community that celebrate specific cultures.

- The Amana Colonies are a cluster of seven villages founded in the 1850s by the Community of True Inspiration, a German Protestant sect. Until 1932 the villages had a communal form of government. Work was shared by members of the community and all property was owned by the community.

Explain a communal form of government. Ask students to discuss the advantages and disadvantages of sharing work and owning communal property.

- In Cedar Rapids, the Czech Village displays historic structures, bakeries, restaurants and Old World style markets. The Czech Museum includes a collection of beautiful antique costumes from Czechoslovakia. For many years, Cedar Rapids had the highest percentage of Czechs of any city in the U.S.

- In 1850, Hungarian immigrants founded a colony at New Buda. Other traditions from the Old World are preserved in the Norwegian-American Museum in Decorah. In Stanton, residents celebrate the Swedish Festival of Santa Lucia in December.

Have students locate the countries of Denmark, the Netherlands, Czechoslovakia, Germany, Hungary, Norway and Sweden on a world map.

Discuss the various cultural backgrounds that can be found in your community. Who founded your city? Where did many of the early residents come from? How have they influenced the architecture, trades, music and other aspects of your community?

Visit a cultural museum in your community if one is available.

Hurray for Popcorn!

Iowa is the nation's number one corn-growing state. Some of the corn grown in Iowa is popcorn. The world's largest popcorn processing plant is in Sioux City, Iowa. Chances are you've eaten lots of popcorn, but do you know why popcorn pops?

Native Americans have enjoyed fresh hot popcorn for thousands of years. They introduced this treat to early colonists, supposedly bringing popcorn as a token of friendship to the first Thanksgiving in 1621.

Although most varieties of corn look similar, only one type actually pops. What makes it pop? Believe it or not—water. The kernel actually explodes when the small amount of moisture inside is heated. The heat produces steam. The pressure of the steam inside the corn causes the outside to burst open.

Long ago, people cooked popcorn over glowing coals. Many kernels burned, so they looked for a better way. By laying stones on a hot fire and placing the kernels on top of the stones, fewer kernels burnt. Unfortunately, everyone was kept quite busy chasing the exploding kernels! It would be like making popcorn on the stove in a pan without a cover.

Later, people invented a wire basket to hold the popcorn as they cooked it over an open fire. Popping corn in a closed kettle in oil became the standard method

for over 100 years. Today, many people enjoy the quickness and convenience of microwave popcorn.

October is National Popcorn Poppin' Month. No matter how you pop it, or where you eat it, popcorn remains an all-time favorite American snack every month of the year.

Besides popcorn, which *is* corn, many other products are made from corn, like cornflakes, corn relish, cornmeal, corn chips, corn bread, corn syrup and corn oil.

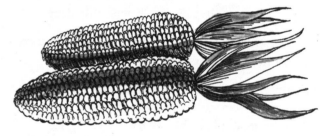

What is your favorite corn product?

_____

Write a short popcorn poem to describe how it tastes, how it smells, how it sounds and how it looks.

Better not get too low over that cornfield; it might be popcorn.

_____
_____
_____
_____
_____
_____
_____

Welcome to Kansas

Tall fields of wheat, sunflowers and corn give Kansas the nickname "Breadbasket of the Nation."

Nicknames: Sunflower State, Wheat State, Jayhawker State, Midway U.S.A. and Breadbasket of the Nation

State motto: To the Stars Through Difficulties

State flower: Sunflower

State tree: Cottonwood

State bird: Western meadowlark

State animal: Buffalo

State song: "Home on the Range"

Capital: Topeka

Statehood: Kansas became the 34th state on January 29, 1861.

1990 Population: 2,477,574: the 32nd largest in population

Area: 82,277 square miles: the 14th largest state

Neighbors: Oklahoma, Colorado, Nebraska and Missouri

Kansas was named for the Native American people known as the **Kansa**. *Kansa* means "people of the south wind."

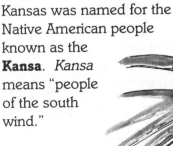

Sing the Kansas State Song

Home on the Range

Oh, give me a home where the buffalo roam,
Where the deer and the antelope play,
Where seldom is heard a discouraging word
And the skies are not cloudy all day.

Home, home on the range,
Where the deer and the antelope play
Where seldom is heard, a discouraging word
And the skies are not cloudy all day.

Tall Tales

People in Kansas tell tall tales about how well corn grows in their state. To pick the corn, two men climb a stepladder and cut off the ears with a crosscut saw. It takes four horses hitched to each ear of corn to drag it to the barn.

Write a tall tale about a crop in your state.

Discussion Question: What If?

What if the capital of the United States was moved to a central location someplace in Kansas?

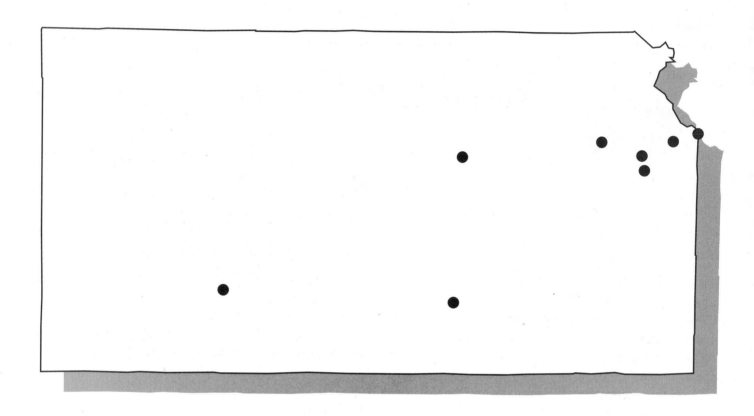

Label the underlined places on the Kansas state map.

<u>Oklahoma</u>, <u>Colorado</u>, <u>Nebraska</u> and <u>Missouri</u> are the four states that border Kansas. Label their approximate locations.

In 1988, archaeologists digging near <u>Bonner Springs</u> along the Kansas River uncovered human bones 15,000 years old.

When Wyatt Earp became Marshall, <u>Dodge City</u> was a wild west town.

<u>Wichita</u> is the largest city in Kansas. With Beech, Boeing, Cessna and Learjet companies centered in Wichita, the city claims the title "Air Capital of the World."

The Huron Indian Cemetery in <u>Kansas City</u> was the Wyandottes burial ground from 1844 until 1954.

The state capital in <u>Topeka</u> was built of native limestone and modeled after the U.S. Capitol in Washington, D.C.

Visitors to <u>Abilene</u> can ride a stagecoach and tour original buildings from the town's early days as a booming cowtown.

In 1884, the Haskell Indian Junior College was founded in <u>Lawrence</u> to provide educational opportunities for Native Americans.

The first library in Kansas opened in <u>Vinland</u> in 1859.

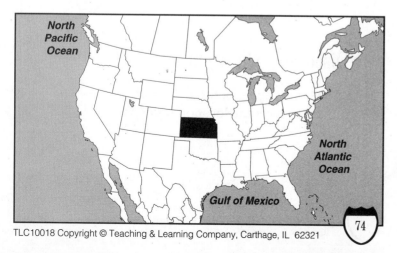

Good Question!

Here are the answers. Use reference books to finish the questions.

1. One of the best known people from Kansas is a fictional character who became popular in the 1939 film *The Wizard of Oz*.

   Who was _____?

2. She wrote *Little House on the Prairie*, a story about growing up in a log cabin in Kansas.

   Who was _____?

3. The "Gallery of Also Rans" in Norton, Kansas, honors a group of people who ran for public office.

   Who are_____?

4. Trees from all 50 states and from 33 countries can be found in this forest near Atchison, Kansas.

   What is the _____?

5. She settled in Kansas in 1899. In 1900 she began her crusade against alcohol by using a hatchet to destroy saloons in major Kansas cities.

   Who was _____?

6. Born in Sedan, Kansas, this famous clown appeared with the Ringling Brothers, Barnum and Bailey Circus. He was known as "Weary Willie," a sad-faced hobo.

   Who was _____?

7. She was a poet, born in Topeka, Kansas, in 1917 who won the Pulitzer Prize in Poetry in 1950 for *Annie Allen*.

   Who was _____?

8. He was born in Wamego, Kansas, founded the Chrysler Corporation and built the Chrysler Building in New York City.

   Who was _____?

9. She was a pilot born in Atchison. In 1932 she became the first woman to fly alone across the Atlantic Ocean. She disappeared while attempting to fly around the world.

   Who was _____?

10. Built in 1865, this fort protected military roads and the men constructing the Union Pacific Railroad.

    What was Fort _____?

Buffalo or Bison?

Millions of bison once roamed across Kansas. Although most people call them buffalo, they are really bison. True buffalo include Asian water buffalo and African buffalo, not the shaggy animals found on the plains of the United States and Canada.

Two different types of bison originally lived in North America. The woods type lived in the woodland areas of Wisconsin and parts of Canada. They were smaller than the plains buffalo that roamed the grasslands west of the Mississippi River. Today's bison are a combination of the two types.

Both male and female bison have horns, although the male's are larger. Cows weigh about 1,000 pounds. Bulls weigh from 1,500 to 2,000 pounds.

Every part of the bison was used by Native Americans. The hides were dried and scraped to make leather clothes and tepees. Bones were used for tools and weapons. The meat was eaten fresh or dried and saved for winter. Spoons were carved from bison horns. Muscle sinews were used for thread and bow strings. Even buffalo droppings were dried and burned for fuel in areas where wood was scarce.

At one time over 30 million bison roamed the plains. Hunting reduced the herds to a mere 500 animals. Herds have slowly been increased by breeding on ranches and refuges. Bison now number between 35,000 to 50,000. They are no longer considered an endangered species.

List several reasons why bison almost became extinct in North America.

_____

_____

_____

_____

_____

_____

_____

_____

_____

_____

_____

_____

_____

_____

About Kansas

Read more about Kansas. Use reference books to answer the assigned questions.

- When the first Spanish explorers arrived in Kansas, they found many groups of Native Americans living in the area. The Kansa (Kaw) lived in the northeast, and the Osage claimed lands in the south. The Wichita roamed the central part of Kansas. The Pawnee were moving in from the north.

Describe the culture of one of these North American groups who lived in Kansas.

- A collection of stone and adobe homes named El Cuartelejo by the Spanish was a Picuris pueblo (village).

Who were the Picuris?

- The cabins and furnishings of a famous abolitionist are preserved at John Brown Memorial State Park.

Who was John Brown?

- Several forts in Kansas have been preserved and restored.

Select one of these Kansas forts: Hays, Larned, Harker, Zarah, Wallace, Leavenworth or Riley. Where is it located? When and why was it built? What is it like today?

- When Wyatt Earp, Bat Masterson, Doc Holliday, Charlie Bassett and Luke Short walked the streets of Dodge City, it was a tough western town.

What would you find if you visited Front Street in Dodge City today?

- Cowboys drove herds of cattle from Texas to the cowtowns of Kansas along the Chisholm Trail.

Show the route of the Chisholm Trail on a map. Why was it named the Chisholm Trail?

- Before the railroads crossed Kansas, people had few choices about how to get from one place to another. They could walk, ride a horse or take a stagecoach.

Describe a stagecoach ride across Kansas.

- The Homestead Act of 1862 and the Timber Culture Act of 1873 promised free land to people who met certain conditions.

What conditions had to be met for people to receive free land under either of these two acts?

- Abilene, Dodge City, Newton, Ellsworth, Wichita, Hunnewell and Waldwell were famous "cowtowns" in the 1800s.

What was a cowtown?

- The original Kansas Dust Bowl was not a college football game.

What was it?

- For many years, the state was known as "Bleeding Kansas."

Why?

TLC10018 Copyright © Teaching & Learning Company, Carthage, IL 62321

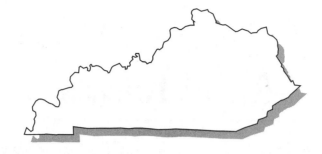

Welcome to Kentucky

From the flat swampy land of western Kentucky, we'll travel east across gently rolling hills to the Appalachian Mountains along the eastern border of the Bluegrass State.

Nickname: Bluegrass State
State motto: United We Stand, Divided We Fall
State flower: Goldenrod
State tree: Kentucky coffee tree
State bird: Kentucky cardinal
State animal: Gray squirrel
State fish: Kentucky bass
State song: "My Old Kentucky Home"
Capital: Frankfort
Statehood: Kentucky became the 15th state on June 1, 1792.
1990 Population: 3,685,296: the 23rd largest in population
Area: 40,395 square miles: the 37th largest state
Neighbors: Ohio, Indiana, Illinois, Missouri, Tennessee, Virginia and West Virginia

Did You Know?

- Kentucky Bluegrass isn't actually blue. The grass itself is a lush, dark green. In the spring, the bluish purple blossoms make lawns and fields of grass look blue.

- Coffee doesn't really grow on Kentucky coffee trees, but the early pioneers did make a drink from the tree's seeds.

- Several Native Americans living in the area had words that sounded similar to *Kentucky*. Translated, the words meant "lands where we live," "meadowlands," "dark and bloody ground," "great meadows" or "land of tomorrow."

- Kentucky's oldest college, in Lexington, is called Transylvania.

- Berea College is dedicated to keeping Kentucky's old-time crafts alive. Besides taking regular college courses, students can learn to make musical instruments, baskets, pottery and dolls.

- Cumberland Falls is the only place in America where a "moonbow" can be seen. A moonbow is like a rainbow, but occurs on clear nights when the moon is full.

- How many times have you heard the song "Happy Birthday" sung? It was written by two sisters in Louisville, Mildred and Patty Hill, who wrote the song in 1893.

Discussion Question: What If?

What would the state's nickname have been if the grass in Kentucky didn't look blue?

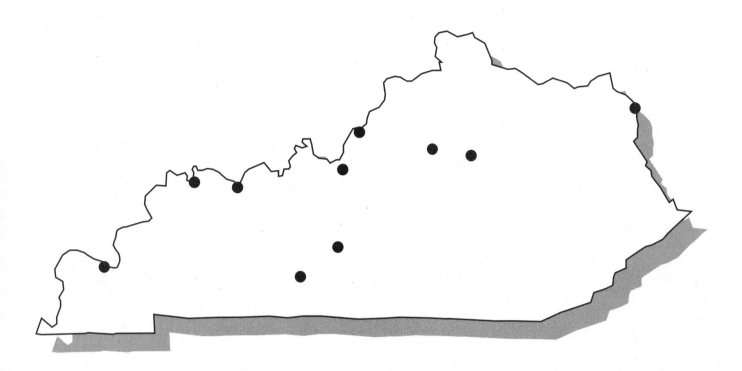

Label the underlined places on the Kentucky state map.

Kentucky contains several land regions. The Eastern coal field is in the Appalachian Mountains and plateaus of eastern Kentucky. Ashland is the largest city in this area.

Louisville, Frankfort and Lexington are in the north-central part of Kentucky known as the Bluegrass region. This area of rolling hills is famous for its horse farms and for growing corn and tobacco. Lexington was the capital until 1793 when it was moved to Frankfort.

Mammoth Cave is in the south-central part of the state called the Pennyroyal region. Rich farmlands cover this area. Robert and George Moses, the founders of Bowling Green, played a game called Bowling on the Green. The town was named for their game.

The Western coal field region lies in the northwest. This hilly area is rich in coal and farmland. Each year a four-day Great Ohio River Flatboat Race is held between Owensboro and Henderson.

Paducah is in the western tip of Kentucky in an area known as the Jackson Purchase. The land includes swamps and lowlands.

About $6 million in gold is stored at the U.S. Gold Depository at Fort Knox.

Label the approximate locations of the seven states that border Kentucky: Ohio, Indiana, Illinois, Missouri, Tennessee, Virginia and West Virginia.

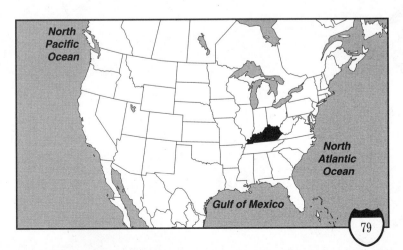

79

At the Races

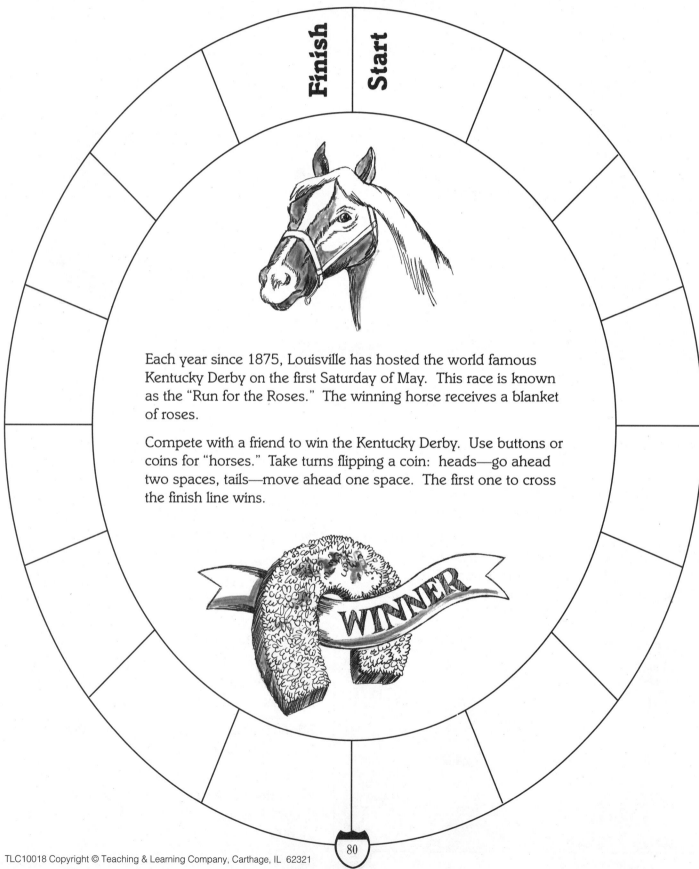

Finish **Start**

Each year since 1875, Louisville has hosted the world famous Kentucky Derby on the first Saturday of May. This race is known as the "Run for the Roses." The winning horse receives a blanket of roses.

Compete with a friend to win the Kentucky Derby. Use buttons or coins for "horses." Take turns flipping a coin: heads—go ahead two spaces, tails—move ahead one space. The first one to cross the finish line wins.

WINNER

In the Early Days of Kentucky

Read about the early days of Kentucky. Answer the assigned questions.

- About 300 million years ago, much of Kentucky was swampland. When the swamp plants died, they formed a thick layer of organic material which eventually turned into coal.

Learn more about how coal was formed, how it is mined and what it is used for.

- The first inhabitants in Kentucky arrived about 15,000 years ago. They hunted huge beavers, mastodons and mammoths.

Describe the prehistoric giant beavers in North America.

- About 1,000 years ago a town stood in far western Kentucky. The Wickliffe Mound Museum contains tools from these ancient people known as the Mississippian Culture.

What kinds of tools did these people make and use?

- Later Native Americans included the Cherokee, Shawnee, Chickasaw and Delaware. They hunted, fished and farmed. One Cherokee story tells how the rabbit challenged the turtle to a race. The turtle knew he couldn't win, so he played a trick on the rabbit.

The race course ran along several ridges. When the rabbit came over the first ridge, he saw the turtle crossing the top ahead of him. He ran faster, but as he came to the second ridge, he again saw the turtle in the lead. He ran as fast as he could, but as he neared the end of the race, he saw the turtle cross the finish line on the last hill.

How do you think the turtle managed to win the race?

Compare this story to the Aesop's fable about the race between the tortoise and the hare.

- In the late 1700s, thousands of settlers moved west to Kentucky. Life for these pioneers was difficult. They built homes from logs, made their own candles, soap and clothing.

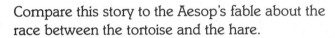

Select one skill pioneers needed, like making candles, soap or butter, spinning, weaving or splitting logs. Use diagrams or pictures to explain how they did this task.

- The Shaker Village at Pleasant Hill was founded by a religious group in 1809.

Who were the Shakers? Why is Shaker furniture valuable?

- By 1839 Kentucky was the leading producer of hemp, tobacco, corn and rye.

Learn more about one of these important Kentucky crops.

More About Kentucky

The official name of Kentucky is the Commonwealth of Kentucky. Pennsylvania is also officially a commonwealth, not a state.

What does the word *commonwealth* mean?

_____

_____

One translation of a Native American word for *Kentucky* means "land of tomorrow."

Why would this saying make a good motto for Kentucky?

_____

_____

_____

_____

It would be difficult to decide which city or town in the U.S. has the most unusual name, but Monkeys Eyebrow would have to be somewhere near the top of the list. So would Loretta Lynn's hometown of Butcher Holler. (Mountain people call narrow valleys, hollows or hollers.)

Look at a map of your state. Make a list of the ten most unusual names of places you can find.

_____

_____

_____

_____

_____

_____

_____

If grass in Kentucky was blue, what color would the sky, trees and flowers be?

Draw a landscape of blue grass and other unusual colors on the back of this page.

The Kentucky Derby is ran each year at Louisville. Two other races make up the Triple Crown.

What are the other two races called?

_____

_____

When and where are they held?

_____

How long is each race?

_____

Robert and George Moses, the founders of Bowling Green, played a game called Bowling on the Green. Find out how it is played.

Make up rules for your own Bowling on the Green game.

_____

_____

_____

_____

_____

_____

_____

_____

_____

Who's Who in Kentucky?

Match the names of these people with their achievements.

1. Daniel Boone

2. Cassius Clay (Muhammad Ali)

3. Jefferson Davis

4. Abe Lincoln

_____ A. Born near Fairview. Married President Taylor's daughter, Sarah. Became president of the Confederacy.

_____ B. Born near Hodgenville. Moved to Illinois when he was about seven. Became 16th President of the U.S.

_____ C. Four-time heavyweight boxing champion born in Louisville.

_____ D. Born in Pennsylvania. He blazed the Wilderness Road through the Cumberland Gap.

Let's Explore Mammoth Cave

Dozens of caverns lie underground in south-central and eastern Kentucky. Mammoth Cave is one of the largest in the world open to the public. *Mammoth* means "large." Three rivers, two lakes and a sea are part of Mammoth Cave.

Caves are "cool" places to explore. The temperature at Mammoth Cave is 54 degrees all year round. Spelunkers are people who explore caves.

Write your answers to the assigned questions on the back of this page.

How large is Mammoth Cave? How many miles of passageways have been explored?

How are limestone caves formed?

How are stalagmites and stalactites formed?

What types of fish can be found in Mammoth Cave? How are they different than most other fish?

What other types of animals live in Mammoth Cave?

Some parts of Mammoth Cave have been named. Describe one of these places in Mammoth Cave: Frozen Niagara, Fatman's Misery, Hindu Temple, Ruins of Karnak, Bottomless Pit, Mummy Ledge or the Snowball Dining Room.

From up here the grass does look blue in Kentucky.

Welcome to Louisiana

Mardi Gras, jazz, bayous, gumbo, crawdads and jambalaya! Let the good times roll as we tour Louisiana.

Nickname: Pelican State
State motto: Union, Justice and Confidence
State flower: Magnolia
State tree: Bald cypress
State bird: Eastern brown pelican
State insect: Honeybee
State gem: Agate
State songs: "Give Me
  Louisiana" and
  "You Are My Sunshine"
Capital: Baton Rouge
Statehood: Louisiana became the 18th
  state on April 30, 1812.
1990 Population: 4,219,973: the
  21st largest in population
Area: 47,752 square miles:
  the 31th largest in area.
  The actual size of
  Louisiana varies
  because of flooding and
  erosion along the coast.
Neighbors: Arkansas, Mississippi, Texas and the
  Gulf of Mexico

Discussion Question: What If?

What if Andrew Jackson and his troops had lost the Battle of New Orleans?

How Many Is XIV?

Louisiana was named in honor of King Louis XIV of France.

What does *XIV* mean? _____
Write the correct numbers next to the Roman numerals.

1. X _____   5. XII _____
2. V _____   6. XL _____
3. XVI _____   7. LXVII _____
4. IV _____   8. XXXII _____

Highs and Lows

The highest point in Louisiana, Driskill Mountain, is only 535 feet above sea level. The lowest point is in New Orleans, five feet below sea level.

What are the highest and lowest points in your state?

A Little Late

The Battle of New Orleans, fought by troops led by Andrew Jackson in January 1815 against the British ended in a major victory for the Americans. What none of the troops knew at the time was that the War of 1812 had ended two weeks before the battle was fought.

Red Stick

The city of Baton Rouge means "red stick" in French. The city was named for the tall red poles that stood at the river's edge.

Name _____   *Louisiana Map Activity*

The Mississippi River forms much of the eastern border of Louisiana. Color the Mississippi River blue.

Texas is west of Louisiana. Label the approximate location of Texas.

Mississippi is east of Louisiana. Label the approximate location of Mississippi.

Lake Pontchartrain is 625 square miles, half the size of the state of Rhode Island. Draw it in and color it blue.

Arkansas is north of Louisiana. Label the approximate location of Arkansas.

The Gulf of Mexico forms Louisiana's southern border. Color its approximate location purple.

Draw a star to show the location of Baton Rouge.

Marsh Island is part of Louisiana. Color it brown.

Label these other major cities in Louisiana:

New Orleans	Shreveport
Lafayette	Lake Charles
Kenner	Monroe
Alexandria	Bossier City

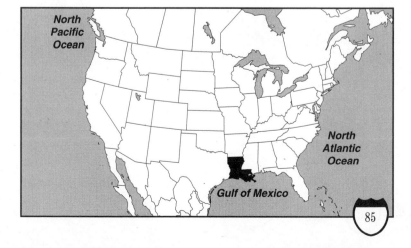

85

Louisiana

- Because the land is so low, flooding is a continuous problem in Louisiana. Levees constructed along the banks of the rivers control flooding.

What is a levee?

- The water in Lake Pontchartrain is brackish.

What does *brackish* mean?

- The Teche, Lafourche, Boeuf, Dorcheat, Dugdemona and D'Arbonne are Louisiana bayous. The word comes from the Choctaw *bayuk*, meaning "creek."

What is a bayou?

- Marshes, swamps and wetlands make up much of the coast of Louisiana. Half of the duck and geese populations in North America spend the winter along the Louisiana coast. Spanish moss and cypress trees, crayfish and alligators, deer, raccoons and nutrias flourish in this area.

Nutrias were brought to Louisiana in 1930. Where were they originally from? What do they look like?

- Louisiana has a humid, subtropical climate. Snow is so rare in the southern part that a park in New Orleans brings in truckloads of snow once a year as a special treat for the children.

Describe the climate of Louisiana.

- New Orleans is called the Crescent City.

Why?

- New Orleans gave birth to a unique American  form of music known as jazz, a combination of traditional African music, spirituals, slave work songs and brass marching bands. Louis Armstrong, one of the world's best known jazz musicians, grew up in New Orleans.

  Listen to recordings of Louis Armstrong and other jazz musicians.

- **Laissez les bons temps rouller!** as they say in Louisiana. Translated into English, it means "Let the good times roll!" The people of Louisiana don't need much of an excuse for throwing a grand party. A good harvest, a saint's day or any holiday is cause for a festival. The most famous celebration in New Orleans is Mardi Gras. People wearing costumes sing and dance through the streets.

Describe the Mardi Gras celebration in New Orleans.

More About Louisiana

Use reference books and encyclopedias to learn more about Louisiana. Write one fact about each of the topics below.

Louisiana parishes: _____

_____

What's unusual about cemeteries in New Orleans?

_____

_____

The Cabildo: _____

_____

French Quarter of New Orleans: _____

_____

Carnival: _____

_____

Brown pelicans: _____

_____

King Louis XIV: _____

_____

Magnolia trees: _____

_____

Mahalia Jackson: _____

_____

Spanish moss: _____

_____

Cypress trees: _____

_____

Treaty of Fountainbleau: _____

_____

Jazz: _____

_____

Lake Pontchartrain: _____

_____

"Fats" Domino: _____

_____

Silt: _____

_____

"Evangeline" (the poem by Henry Longfellow):

_____

_____

The Mississippi Delta: _____

_____

Pitcher plants: _____

_____

Yellow fever: _____

_____

Jelly Roll Morton: _____

_____

Poverty Point: _____

_____

Pompano: _____

_____

Fort Humbug: _____

_____

Oysters: _____

_____

Crawfish: _____

_____

Hernando de Soto: _____

_____

The Houma: _____

_____

_____

The People of Many Cultures

Louisianans are a mix of many cultures and ethnic backgrounds, a true melting pot of people from many countries.

Many Native Americans, descendants of slaves and Hispanics live in the Pelican State. The first white settlers in Louisiana were colonists from France and Quebec and later, people from Spain. Their descendants are known as Creoles.

A 40-mile stretch north of New Orleans is called the German Coast because of the number of German farmers who settled there in the 1720s. Irish and Italian immigrants came to Louisiana in the late 1800s.

In 1755, the British forced nearly 15,000 French colonists to leave Nova Scotia, a land the French called Acadia. Searching for a new home, many died of hunger and disease. About 4,000 survivors made their way to Louisiana. Today Cajuns, people of Acadian descent, are known for their delicious spicy food, lively music and dance.

Compare the exile of the Acadians by the British to the treatment of Native Americans by the U.S. government.

Good Eating in Louisiana

A story is told about a man from Louisiana who died and went to heaven. When he arrived, he asked St. Peter if they served gumbo in heaven. When St. Peter told him no, the man left and went back to Louisiana.

What is gumbo?

Another Cajun specialty is a dish called jambalaya.

What is jambalaya?

Bouillabaisse is one of many delicious Creole dishes.

What is bouillabaisse?

Beignets are a tasty treat found in the French Quarter of New Orleans.

What are beignets?

I get hungry just thinking about all the good eating in Louisiana.

Welcome to Maine

"Oh, Pine Tree State, your woods, fields, and hills, your lakes, streams, and rock-bound coast will ever fill our hearts with thrills. And tho' we seek far and wide, our search will be in vain to find a fairer spot on earth than Maine! Maine! Maine!"

(State song of Maine)

Nickname: Pine Tree State

State motto: The Latin motto, *Dirigo*, means "I direct" or "I lead."

State flower: White pinecone and tassel

State tree: White pine

State bird: Chickadee

State fish: Landlocked salmon

State insect: Honeybee

State mineral: Tourmaline

State song: "State of Maine Song"

Capital: Augusta

Statehood: Maine became the 23rd state on March 15, 1820.

1990 Population: 1,227,928: the 38th largest state

Area: 33,215 square miles: the 39th largest in area

Neighbors: New Hampshire, Quebec, New Brunswick and the Atlantic Ocean

Did You Know?

Although Maine was not admitted as a state until 1820, the people of Maine were actively involved in the Revolutionary War. The colonists felt that many of the laws passed by England were unfair. One example was a law which reserved for the king all white pine trees more than 24 inches in diameter.

Boston wasn't the only place to hold a tea party. The York Tea Party took place in 1774 when colonists from Maine destroyed British tea stored at York, Maine.

British ships often stopped Maine ships at sea and forced the crew to join the British Navy to fight for the king. In protest, the colonists of Maine shut off the lanterns in the lighthouses along the rocky, treacherous coast. Then they hung a lantern around a horse and let it wander up and down the shore at night. Local sailors who knew the area could navigate by moonlight, but the British sailors could not. Those who followed the light from the horse crashed into the rocks and sank.

89

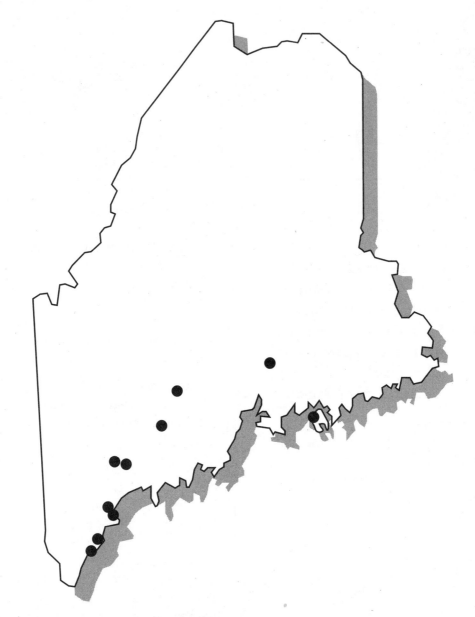

Label the underlined places on the Maine state map.

<u>New Hampshire</u> is the only state that borders Maine. The other borders are formed by <u>Quebec</u>, <u>New Brunswick</u> and the <u>Atlantic Ocean</u>. Label their approximate locations.

The home of the poet Henry Wadsworth Longfellow can be seen in <u>Portland</u>, Maine's largest city.

The majestic granite state capitol building in <u>Augusta</u> was built in 1829.

The Wedding Cake House in <u>Kennebunkport</u> was built by a sea captain for his bride.

A breathtaking view of Maine's rocky coast can be seen from the top of Cadillac Mountain on <u>Mt. Desert Island</u>.

Label these other major cities in Maine:

Lewiston	Bangor
Auburn	South Portland
Biddeford	Waterville

From Moose to Lobster

Answer these questions about the plants, animals, birds and fish that make their homes in Maine.

- Forests of balsam, fir, basswood, beech, hemlock, oak, maple, spruce, birch, willow and pine cover nearly 90% of Maine.

How would your state be different if 90% were woods?

If you live in Maine, how would your state be different if forests covered only 50% of the land?

- Hundreds of different types of animals make their homes in the Maine woods including deer, moose, black bears, bobcats, lynxes, beavers, otters, mink, martens and porcupines.

Draw and describe one type of animal found in Maine.

- Sea mammals like seals, porpoises and even whales live along the Maine coast. The ocean also provides a home for cod, flounder, tuna, halibut, shellfish, clams, oysters and of course, Maine lobsters. Bass, trout and salmon are abundant in freshwater lakes.

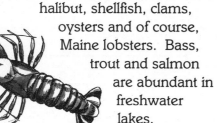

Draw and describe one type of animal found in the ocean, lakes or streams of Maine.

- Maine bird-watchers can spot a wide variety of their feathered friends.

Name some types of birds that can be seen in Maine.

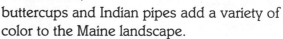

- Mayflowers, lady's slippers, daisies, goldenrod, jack-in-the-pulpits, Canada lilies, buttercups and Indian pipes add a variety of color to the Maine landscape.

Do a color drawing of several plants that grow in Maine.

Long Before Columbus

Long before Christopher Columbus crossed the Atlantic Ocean, the Algonquian people lived in the forests along the coast from Canada south to present day Virginia. They called themselves **Wabanaki**—people of the dawn.

The Algonquian people consisted of a number of tribes related by language and customs. The Algonquians included:

Mahicans	New York
Mohegans and Pequots	Connecticut
Narragansetts	Rhode Island
Wampanoags	Massachusetts
Passamaquoddy, Piscataquis, Kennebec, Penobscots and Abnaki	Maine
Mantauk	Long Island
Delaware	Delaware
Powhatans	Virginia

An ancient legend claims that the Great Father sent a crow to the Algonquian people with a kernel of corn in one ear and a bean in the other. Beans and corn became the two most important crops.

The people also hunted geese, turkeys and deer, fished, gathered wild nuts and berries from the forest and grew corn, beans, squash and pumpkins. They lived in small villages, sharing the work and the food. *Wigwam* is the Algonquian word for house. The frame of a wigwam was built of tall young trees.

The Algonquians shared a common heritage and a common language although it varied somewhat from tribe to tribe. They had similar politics, religion, economics and customs.

Children were expected to help their parents take care of the crops and do other chores. They learned to make arrowheads, bows and arrows. Many of the games they played helped the children learn skills they needed to survive like follow the leader, footraces, swimming and archery contests. They used a long stick for a bat to play a game like baseball. The "ball" was a pinecone.

Many versions of baseball are possible using different objects for a bat and ball.

What are some things you could use for a bat?

What are some objects you could use for a ball?

Besides running around bases to home, imagine another way baseball could be played.

Write the rules to a new baseball game. How are points scored? What is an "out" and an "inning" in your game? How many outs and innings make up a game?

_____

_____

_____

_____

_____

_____

_____

_____

_____

_____

Who's Who?

Use reference books to match the names of these people from Maine with their accomplishments.

1. _____ Founder of the famous outdoor goods store in Freeport

2. _____ Social reformer from Hampden who worked to improve conditions for the mentally ill

3. _____ Painter who lived in Maine as a child. Best known for magnificent seascapes

4. _____ Born in Portland, writer of horror stories including *Carrie, Cujo* and *Christine.*

5. _____ Famous poet born in Portland who wrote "Paul Revere's Ride," "The Village Blacksmith" and "The Song of Hiawatha"

6. _____ Born in Bar Harbor, he became Vice President in 1974.

A. Dorothea Dix

B. Stephen King

C. L.L. Bean

D. Henry Wadsworth Longfellow

E. Nelson A. Rockefeller

F. Winslow Homer

Balloon History

Two British balloonists were the first to cross the Atlantic Ocean in a hot air balloon on July 2, 1987. They left Sugarloaf, Maine, and covered 3,075 miles before landing in Northern Ireland the next day.

Joe Kittinger left Caribou, Maine, in a ten-story tall helium-filled balloon named *Rosie O'Grady's Balloon of Peace* on September 14, 1984. Three days later he became the first successful solo balloonist to cross the Atlantic Ocean when he landed in France.

Discussion Question: What If?

What if airplanes had never been invented and the only way to fly was in a hot air balloon?

Who needs airplanes? Unless you're a bird, hot air balloons are the best way to fly!

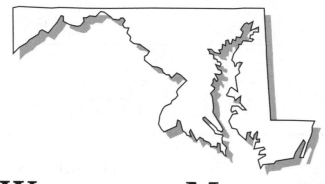

Welcome to Maryland

Let's visit Old Line State and find out about the official state dog, state boat and state sport. Maryland, here we come!

Nicknames: Old Line State and Free State
State motto: Manly Deeds, Womanly Words
State flower: Black-eyed Susan
State tree: White oak
State bird: Baltimore oriole
State dog: Chesapeake Bay retriever
State fish: Rockfish
State insect: Baltimore checkerspot butterfly
State boat: Skipjack
State sport: Jousting
State song: "Maryland, My Maryland"
Capital: Annapolis
Statehood: Maryland was the seventh of the original 13 colonies to ratify the Constitution on April 28, 1788.
1990 Population: 4,781,468: the 19th largest in population
Area: 10,460 square miles: the 9th smallest in area
Neighbors: Pennsylvania, Delaware, Virginia and West Virginia

What's in a Name?

Maryland was named for Henrietta Maria, wife of King Charles I of England. Originally called Anne Arundel Town, the city was renamed Annapolis in honor of Queen Anne.

Who was Baltimore named after?

Sports Spotlight

In 1954, the St. Louis Browns moved to Maryland to become the Baltimore Orioles, Maryland's professional baseball team. People in Maryland also enjoyed watching the Baltimore Colts, until their professional football team moved to Indianapolis in 1984.

Horse racing is another popular sport in Maryland. Every spring, race fans gather at Pimlico Race Course to watch the Preakness Stakes, the second of three races that make up the Triple Crown.

Lacrosse is a popular college sport in Maryland.

What is lacrosse?

Few states have an official state sport, and none have one as unusual as Maryland. Since 1842, Marylanders have held annual jousting tournaments.

What is jousting?

Discussion Question: What If?

If your state had a state sport, what should it be?

Label the underlined places on the Maryland state map.

The border between Maryland and <u>Pennsylvania</u> is called the Mason and Dixon Line. Label Pennsylvania's approximate location.

Maryland's neighbors include <u>West Virginia</u> to the west and <u>Delaware</u> on the east. Label their approximate locations.

The colonists of <u>Virginia</u> and Maryland had frequent disputes about the borders between the two colonies. Label Virginia's approximate location.

The first major monument to George Washington was completed in <u>Baltimore</u> in 1829.

South of <u>Cambridge</u>, thousands of Canada geese winter at the Blackwater National Wildlife Refuge.

The beaches of <u>Ocean City</u> are popular with those who enjoy swimming, sailing, sunbathing and windsurfing.

The octagon wooden dome of Maryland's capitol building at <u>Annapolis</u> was built entirely without nails.

Maryland has only 31 miles of coastline along the <u>Atlantic Ocean</u>.

A skipjack is the traditional wooden sailboat used to dredge for oysters in <u>Chesapeake Bay</u>. The skipjack is Maryland's official state boat.

The wild ponies of <u>Assateague Island</u> may have descended from horses that reached the island during a shipwreck in the 1600s.

The Maryland Colony

King Charles I granted a charter for land along the Chesapeake Bay and north of the Potomac River to Cecil Calvert, the second Lord of Baltimore and a devout Catholic. Calvert hoped to establish a colony where Catholics and Protestants could live together in peace. Led by his younger brother, Leonard, colonists set sail for Maryland in 1633. With the help of the Yaocomaco and other Native Americans, the colonists learned to plant corn and survive in the strange new land.

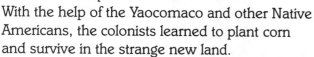

The Pocomoke, Choptank and Nanticoke lived along the Eastern Shore. In southern Maryland, the Anaco, Piscataway, Yaocomaco and Patuxent belonged to the Algonquian-speaking tribes.

Most of these groups numbered only a few hundred. When Europeans arrived in Maryland and other colonies, they brought smallpox, diphtheria, tuberculosis and other diseases. Native Americans had no natural immunities to these diseases and terrible epidemics swept through their villages.

Some of the land claimed for the Maryland Colony was also claimed by the Virginia Colony. The Maryland Colony claimed some of the area being settled by people from the Pennsylvania Colony. These disputes were not settled until after 1767 when two surveyors, Charles Mason and Jeremiah Dixon, determined a straight line, known as the Mason and Dixon Line that became the border between Maryland and Pennsylvania.

During the Civil War, the people of Maryland were divided. Many tobacco planters in southern Maryland and along the Eastern Shore wished to join the Confederate States. Those in the north and western part of the state wanted to remain with the Union. Soldiers from Maryland fought on both sides during the war between the states.

Discussion Questions: What If?

- What if the colonies had not joined together and fought the Revolutionary War?

- What if they had lost the war?

- What if they had chosen to remain independent states after the Revolutionary War?

- What if John Wilkes Booth had missed and Abraham Lincoln had remained the President after the Civil War ended?

- What if Francis Scott Key had not written the "The Star-Spangled Banner"? What would our national anthem be?

- What if there had been no Civil War and the North and the South remained two separate countries?

Advice from Fishermen on Chesapeake Bay

When the wind is from the north,
Sailors don't go forth.
When the wind is from the east,
'Tis neither fair for man nor beast.
When the wind is from the south,
It blows the bait in the fish's mouth.
When the wind is from the west,
Then it's at its very best.

More About Maryland

Use reference books to learn more about Maryland. Write one interesting fact about each of the people and places below.

Frederick Douglass: _____

_____

_____

Babe Ruth: _____

_____

_____

Harriet Tubman: _____

_____

_____

John Wilkes Booth: _____

_____

_____

Francis Scott Key: _____

_____

_____

Billie Holiday: _____

_____

Thurgood Marshall: _____

_____

_____

_____

Shangri-La (Camp David): _____

_____

_____

_____

Fort McHenry: _____

_____

_____

United States Naval Academy at Annapolis:

_____

_____

Blackwater National Wildlife Refuge:

_____

_____

Assateague Island National Seashore:

_____

_____

Antietam National Battlefield: _____

_____

_____

Fort Fredrick: _____

_____

_____

Cranesville Sub-Arctic Swamp:

_____

_____

_____

Let's stop for a taste of the famous Chesapeake Bay oysters.

97

Welcome to Massachusetts

Much of our nation's early history happened in the Bay State. Let's visit the birthplace of Ben Franklin, Paul Revere, John Hancock and many other famous patriots.

Nicknames: Bay State, Old Colony, Puritan State and Baked Bean State

State motto: By the Sword We Seek Peace, but Peace Only Under Liberty

State flower: Mayflower

State tree: American elm

State bird: Chickadee

State fish: Cod

State insect: Ladybug

State horse: Morgan horse

State dog: Boston terrier

State beverage: Cranberry juice

State colors: Blue and gold

State poem: "Blue Hills of Massachusetts"

State song: "All Hail to Massachusetts"

Capital: Boston

Statehood: Massachusetts was one of the 13 original colonies and the sixth to ratify the Constitution on February 6, 1788.

1990 Population: 6,016,425: Massachusetts is the 13th largest state.

Area: 8,300 square miles: Only five states are smaller than Massachusetts.

Neighbors: Vermont, New Hampshire, Rhode Island, Connecticut, New York and the Atlantic Ocean

Did You Know?

- The state's official name is the Commonwealth of Massachusetts.

- The Great Molasses Flood caused a sticky situation in Boston. It occurred when 2.5 million gallons of molasses poured out of a broken tank in downtown Boston in 1919. Twenty-one people were killed and 150 injured.

- Boston was once home to a professional baseball team called the Boston Beaneaters. Today Boston is home to the Bruins (hockey), the Celtics (basketball) and the Red Sox (baseball). The New England Patriots play football outside of Boston in Foxborough.

- Basketball was invented in Springfield, Massachusetts, in 1891 by James A. Naismith.

  What did he use for the first baskets? How was the early game different than the game we play today?

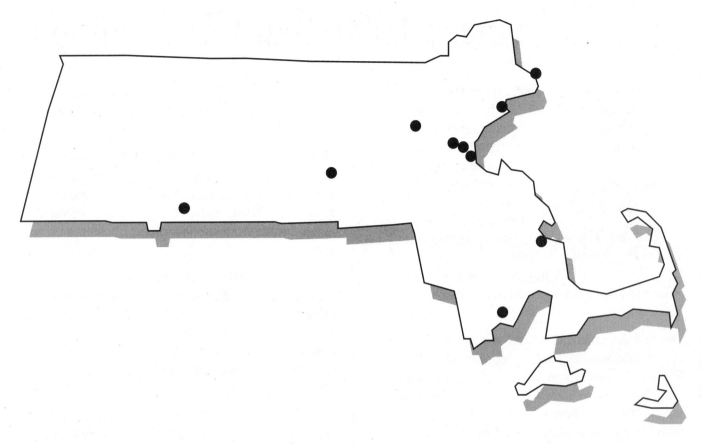

Label the underlined places on the Massachusetts state map.

The first shots of the Revolutionary war were fired at <u>Lexington</u> in 1775.

At nearby <u>Concord</u>, the patriots won their first victory of the Revolutionary War.

<u>Boston</u> is known as the "Cradle of Liberty" because the rebellion against England started there.

Harvard University, Radcliffe College and the Massachusetts Institute of Technology (MIT) are in <u>Cambridge</u>. Founded in 1636, Harvard was the first college in the New World.

<u>Worcester</u> is the second largest city in Massachusetts.

<u>Springfield</u> is home to the Basketball Hall of Fame. Basketball was invented in Springfield.

The Gloucester Fishermen's Memorial in <u>Gloucester</u> honors fishermen who died at sea.

<u>Salem</u> was the first town founded by the Massachusetts Bay Colony in 1628.

The first town settled by the Pilgrims was <u>Plymouth</u>. The Pilgrims spelled it PLIMOTH.

<u>New Bedford</u> was the world's leading port for catching whales in the 1800s.

The southeastern section of Massachusetts that forms a peninsula is known as <u>Cape Cod</u>.

<u>Martha's Vineyard</u> and <u>Nantucket Island</u> are famous islands south of Cape Cod.

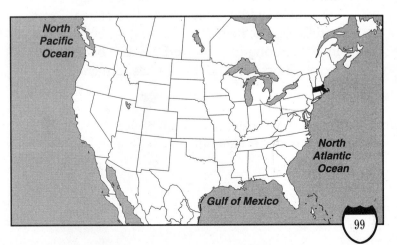

Thanksgiving, a 4,000-Year-Old-Tradition

Giving thanks for a bountiful harvest began long before the Pilgrims landed in the New World. The Egyptians held thanksgiving festivals over 4,000 years ago celebrating with food, music and sports. The ancient Chinese, Greeks and Romans also held harvest festivals. In England, people enjoyed feasting, dancing and playing games at the Harvest Home festival held each fall following the grain harvest.

The first American Thanksgiving, three days of prayer and feasting, was celebrated by the Plymouth colonists in 1621 to give thanks for their first harvest. They had survived a 65-day crossing of the Atlantic Ocean and many hardships in the New World. Most of the first settlers knew little about surviving in the wilderness. About half of them died the first terrible winter in Massachusetts. Without the assistance of several Native Americans, the Pilgrims would never have survived.

When the Pilgrims planned their first thanksgiving festival, they invited Squanto and several other local Indians to join them. Food was prepared for the 50 Pilgrims and the ten expected guests. Much to their dismay, nearly 90 Indians showed up. Realizing there would not be enough food, Chief Massasoit's hunters brought in five deer, insuring plenty of food for all.

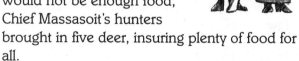

The date of this thanksgiving festival is unknown, as are many details of what they did and ate. The menu probably included wild turkey, corn, fish, fruit and venison. The next year the harvest was poor. A second thanksgiving festival wasn't held until 1623. Again Chief Massasoit brought many guests and much food.

The custom of holding a thanksgiving festival spread as the colonies grew, but no single date was set for the holiday. Some places celebrated in October, some in November. Even within the same settlement, the date changed from year to year.

The first national Thanksgiving holiday, proclaimed by President George Washington, was celebrated on November 26, 1789. The idea of one specific day for Thanksgiving did not take hold at first, however and various communities continued to celebrate Thanksgiving on different days.

In 1863, Sarah Hale, author of the poem "Mary Had a Little Lamb" persuaded President Lincoln to declare Thanksgiving an annual national holiday held on the last Thursday in November. Franklin D. Roosevelt broke the 75-year-old tradition in 1939 when he moved Thanksgiving to the third Thursday in November, to give people more time for Christmas shopping. He thought it would help businesses. Many people 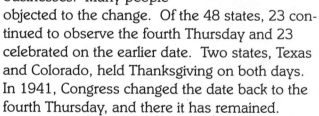 objected to the change. Of the 48 states, 23 continued to observe the fourth Thursday and 23 celebrated on the earlier date. Two states, Texas and Colorado, held Thanksgiving on both days. In 1941, Congress changed the date back to the fourth Thursday, and there it has remained.

How do you celebrate Thanksgiving? Write about your family traditions at Thanksgiving.

Let's Discuss Early Massachusetts

Read about the early history of Massachusetts. As a class, discuss the questions below.

- The first people to settle in Massachusetts arrived about 10,000 years ago. Evidence has been found of an advanced society that lived in Massachusetts around 5000 B.C. They planted corn and squash, made clay pottery and fished with bone hooks. These peo-  ple disappeared about 1000 A.D. when the Algonquian-speaking people moved into the area.

- Lief Erickson and his Vikings may have landed at Cape Cod as early as 1000 A.D.

What if the Vikings had established settlements in Massachusetts long before the Europeans arrived?

- People were not allowed freedom of religion in England in the 1600s. One hundred two Pilgrims left England in September 1620 on the *Mayflower* in search of a place where they could worship in peace. Two months later they reached Cape Cod and established their first town at Plymouth. Others joined the first Pilgrims. By 1640 the Plymouth Colonies included eight towns and about 2,500 people.

- The Puritans founded the Massachusetts Bay Colonies. Salem (1628) and Boston (1630) were the first Puritan settlements. Although they sought freedom of religion for them-selves, the Puritans did not allow others the same rights.

What if people in our country did not have free-dom of religion?

- The Puritans passed the first major public edu-cation law in 1647. Every town of 50 or more home owners had to provide free elementary education. In towns of more than 100 home owners, free secondary education also had to be provided.

How would your life be different if free education was not available?

- Massachusetts also took the lead in requiring compulsory education for children. In 1852 a school attendance law required all children in the state between the ages of 8 and 14 to attend school at least 12 weeks a year. Six of the weeks had to be consecutive.

What do *compulsory* and *consecutive* mean? Would you go to school if you didn't have to attend?

- In 1842, the governor of Massachusetts signed a law making it illegal for children under 12 to work more than 10 hours a day in manufac-turing establishments.

What do you think it would be like for children to work 10 hours a day in a factory?

Who's Who from Massachusetts?

Use reference books to match these descriptions of famous people from Massachusetts with the list of names below.

1. He wrote the Pledge of Allegiance in 1892.

   _____

2. She was arrested and fined $100 for voting in 1872. She worked to change the law so all women would be allowed to vote. She was the only woman to have her picture on a U.S. coin. _____

3. He invented the first sewing machine in the 1840s. _____

4. He helped organize the Boston Tea Party and became known as the "Father of the American Revolution."

   _____

5. He became the first Vice President and the second President of the U.S.

   _____

6. This son of a President became the 6th President of the U.S.

   _____

7. She was the wife and mother of a President.

   _____

8. He was a silversmith. We remember him for his famous "midnight ride" warning the colonists that the British were coming.

   _____

9. This patriot was the first to sign the Declaration of Independence.

   _____

10. She worked for the abolition of slavery and for women's rights. She wrote the words to "The Battle Hymn of the Republic."

    _____

11. He invented the cotton gin.

    _____

12. He gained fame as a patriot, statesman, diplomat and inventor. He wrote *Poor Richard's Almanack*.

    _____

13. He invented the telegraph.

    _____

14. She became a nurse in the Civil War. People called her the "Angel of the Battlefield." She founded the American Red Cross. _____

15. She organized the American Woman Suffrage Association in 1869 in her efforts to gain the right to vote.

16. He was best known for his books *The House of the Seven Gables* and *The Scarlet Letter.* _____

17. His real name was Theodore Geisel, author of *The Cat in the Hat*, *Green Eggs and Ham* and many other books for children.

    _____

18. The 30th President, he served from 1923 to 1929. _____

19. This famous conductor led the Boston Pops Orchestra from 1930 to 1979.

    _____

20. He became the youngest man elected President and founder of the Peace Corps.

    _____

21. He became the 41st President.

    _____

Abigail Adams	John Adams
John Quincy Adams	Samuel Adams
Susan B. Anthony	Clara Barton
Francis Bellamy	George Bush
Calvin Coolidge	Arthur Fiedler
Ben Franklin	John Hancock
Nathaniel Hawthorne	Elias Howe
Julia Ward Howe	John F. Kennedy
Samuel Morse	Paul Revere
Dr. Seuss	Lucy Stone
Eli Whitney	

Follow the Freedom Trail

Beginning at Boston Commons, a trail of red bricks marks the Freedom Trail, a path that leads to 16 of Boston's leading historical places.

Select one of the sites on the Freedom Trail. Write about why that place was important in the early days of Boston.

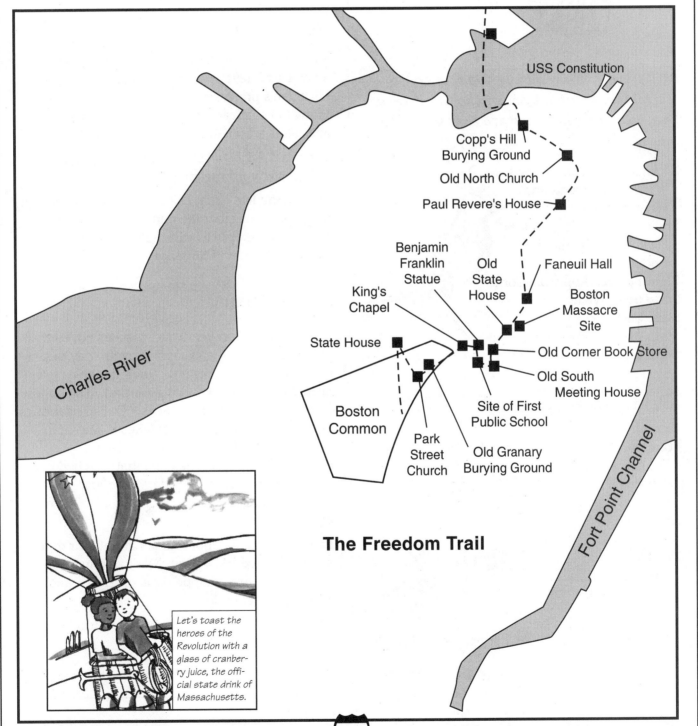

USS Constitution

Copp's Hill
Burying Ground

Old North Church

Paul Revere's House

Benjamin
Franklin
Statue

Old
State
House

Faneuil Hall

King's
Chapel

Boston
Massacre
Site

State House

Old Corner Book Store

Old South
Meeting House

Boston
Common

Site of First
Public School

Park
Street
Church

Old Granary
Burying Ground

Charles River

Fort Point Channel

The Freedom Trail

Let's toast the heroes of the Revolution with a glass of cranberry juice, the official state drink of Massachusetts.

Welcome to Michigan

We'll travel halfway across the country to the Midwest, to visit one of the Great Lakes States, Michigan, the state that looks like a mitten.

Nicknames: Great Lakes State, Water Wonderland and Wolverine State

State motto: If You Seek a Pleasant Peninsula, Look About You

State flower: Apple blossom

State tree: White pine

State bird: Robin

State fish: Brook trout

State gem: Isle Royale green-stone

State stone: Petoskey

State song: "Michigan, My Michigan"

Capital: Lansing

Statehood: Michigan became the 26th state on January 26, 1837.

1990 Population: 9,295,297: the 8th largest in population

Area: 58,527 square miles: the 23rd largest state

Neighbors: Canada; Wisconsin; Indiana; Ohio and Lakes Michigan, Huron, Superior and Erie

Did You Know?

Although it is called the Wolverine State, wild **wolverines** never lived in Michigan. Two of Michigan's professional ball teams are the Detroit **Lions** (football) and the **Tigers** (baseball). Lions and tigers weren't found in Michigan either.

The word *Michigan* came from *Michigama*, a Chippewa word meaning "great lake."

Four of the five Great Lakes border Michigan. To help you remember the names of all five lakes, think of the word HOMES—**H**uron, **O**ntario, **M**ichigan, **E**rie and **S**uperior.

Copper Mining

About two million years ago, glaciers covered all of Michigan. As the glaciers moved, they dug huge holes in the ground. When the holes later filled with water, lakes were formed. The largest holes became the Great Lakes. The smaller ones became thousands of other lakes in Michigan. During the Ice Age, wooly mammoths, mastodons and giant beavers that weighed over 300 pounds lived in Michigan. The first prehistoric people who lived in Michigan 12,000 years ago were hunters.

Ruins of ancient copper mines about four thousand years old have been discovered in the Upper Peninsula. Copper was used to make knives and spear tips.

What products used today are made from copper?

_____

_____

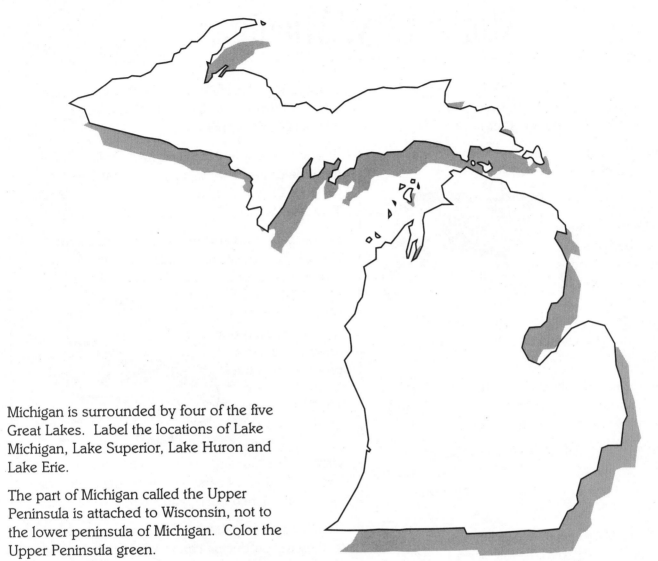

Michigan is surrounded by four of the five Great Lakes. Label the locations of Lake Michigan, Lake Superior, Lake Huron and Lake Erie.

The part of Michigan called the Upper Peninsula is attached to Wisconsin, not to the lower peninsula of Michigan. Color the Upper Peninsula green.

Draw a blue line to show the border between Canada and Michigan. Draw a red line to show the border between Michigan and Wisconsin.

Label the approximate locations of Wisconsin, Ohio and Indiana on the map above.

Draw a small car to show the location of Detroit.

Draw a star at Lansing, the capital of Michigan.

Locate these Michigan cities. Write the number for each city in the appropriate place on the map.

1. Grand Rapids   5. Ann Arbor

2. Flint   6. Escanaba

3. Port Huron   7. Marquette

4. Sault Sainte Marie   8. Dearborn

Several islands are part of Michigan. Label Mackinac Island, Drummond Island, Manitou Island and Beaver Island.

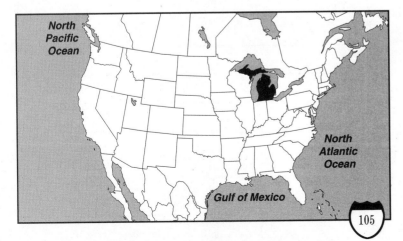

North Pacific Ocean

North Atlantic Ocean

Gulf of Mexico

105

Motor City, Michigan

As you read about Detroit, look for words and names that later became the names of cars. Underline them as you find them.

The first European explorers in Michigan were Frenchmen from Canada who discovered deer, porcupines, beavers, bear, coyotes, badgers, fox, otters, elk, moose, mink, wolves and bobcats in Michigan.  Because the land was rich in furs, the French began trading furs for tools with the Native Americans.

In 1702 Antoine de la Mothe Cadillac led a group of settlers south to establish a fur trading center. As the city grew, it was named Detroit.

The English sent fighting men called Roger's Rangers to take Michigan from the French. Chief Pontiac led the Ottawa against the invasion of English settlers.

When Henry Ford finished building his first automobile on June 4, 1896, he discovered a problem. The car was too big to fit through the doors of the shed where it had been built. Ford took an ax and smashed down the shed wall so he could drive his car out. Henry Ford's 56-room house, called Fairlane, in Dearborn is open to visitors.

Ransom Olds built his first car in Lansing also in 1896. In 1899, he formed the Olds Motor Works in Detroit. In 1901, a new Oldsmobile sold for $695. David Buick founded the Buick

Company in Detroit in 1902. A few years later John and Horace Dodge started the Dodge Brothers Car Company.

At one time you could buy a new Cadillac for less than the cost of a new Ford. The first Cadillac, produced in 1903 sold for $750. The first Model T sold for $875!

By 1905, 77,988 automobiles were registered in the U.S., but most people still considered automobiles as useless, expensive toys. In 1909, a Model T Ford sold for $950. Henry Ford set up his first automobile assembly line for production of the Model T Ford in 1913. He paid his workers a fabulously high wage—$5 a day and was still able to reduce the cost of making his cars. By 1924, the price of a new Model T had been reduced to $290.

Detroit, known as "Motor City," is the nation's leading car-producing center. Oldsmobiles, Fords, Dodges and Buicks are still popular today.

If you could select the name for a car or pickup truck, what would it be?

_____

Why? _____

_____

_____

_____

_____

_____

Learn More About Michigan

To learn more about Michigan, check your encyclopedia, atlas, dictionary or other books about Michigan. Find one interesting fact about each of the topics listed below.

Mackinac Bridge: _____
_____

Mackinac Island: _____
_____

Isle Royale: _____
_____

Flint (the stone, not the city): _____
_____
_____
_____
_____

Copper mining in
Michigan: _____
_____
_____

Holland, Michigan: _____
_____

Tahquamenon Falls: _____
_____

Wolverines: _____
_____

Soo Canal and Locks: _____
_____

Greenfield Village: _____
_____
_____

Iron Mountain: _____
_____
_____

Fort Mackinac and Fort Michilimackinac:
_____
_____

Erie Canal: _____
_____

Charles Lindbergh: _____
_____

Sugar Ray Robinson: _____
_____

Chief Pontiac: _____
_____

John and William Kellogg: _____
_____

Look at all the beautiful waterfalls!

Learn more about one group of Native Americans who lived in Michigan. They were the Ojibwa, Menomoinee, Miami, Wyandot, Ottawa and Potawatomi.

Welcome to Minnesota

You'll find more than gophers in the Gopher State. Timber wolves, moose, deer, elk, bobcats, lynx and black bears live in the northern woods of Minnesota.

Nicknames: North Star State, Gopher State, Land of 10,000 Lakes, Land of Sky-Blue Waters and Bread and Butter State

State motto: The Star of the North

State flower: Showy lady's slipper

State tree: Red pine

State bird: Common loon

State fish: Walleye

State gem: Lake Superior agate

State grain: Wild rice

State song: "Hail Minnesota"

Capital: St. Paul

Statehood: Minnesota became the 32nd state on May 11, 1858.

1990 Population: 4,374,099: the 20th largest in population

Area: 84,401 square miles: the 12th largest state

Neighbors: Wisconsin, Iowa, North and South Dakota, Manitoba, Ontario and Lake Superior

Brrrrrr

Bundle up if you're planning to visit International Falls in the wintertime. Often called the "Nation's Icebox," January temperatures in this northern town range from an average high of 14°F to an average low of -8°F. If people in International Falls want to know the current temperature, all they have to do is take a look at the city's 22-foot high thermometer.

What do people do during the long cold winters of Minnesota? They enjoy skiing, tobogganing, ice skating and hockey. There are more amateur hockey teams in Minnesota than in any other state. The United States Hockey Hall of Fame is in Eveleth, Minnesota.

Ice fishing, snowmobiling, dogsled racing and winter festivals are other favorite pastimes. Ice sculpting, ice skating races, ski jumping and a parade are some of the activities enjoyed at the annual Winter Carnival in St. Paul.

Those who prefer to stay inside can watch the Vikings play football and the Timberwolves play basketball.

Which winter sport do you like best?

_____

Why? _____

_____

Which winter sport would you most like to try?

_____

Why? _____

_____

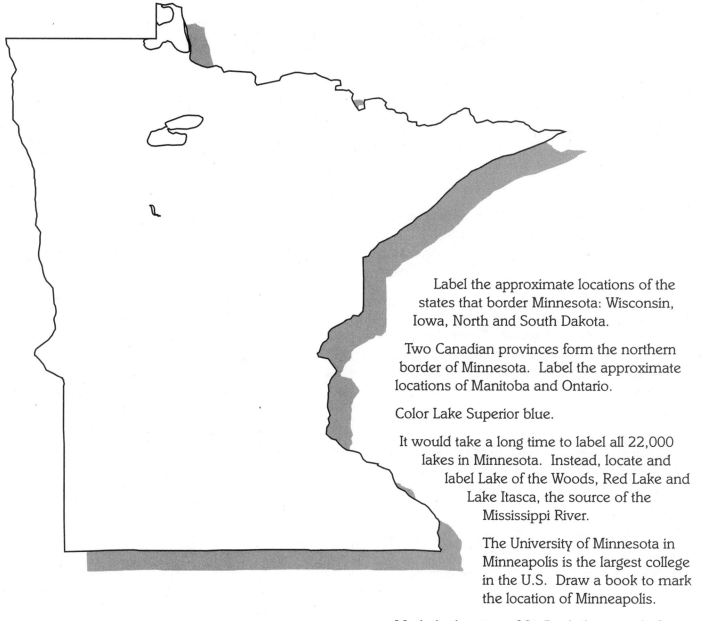

Label the approximate locations of the states that border Minnesota: Wisconsin, Iowa, North and South Dakota.

Two Canadian provinces form the northern border of Minnesota. Label the approximate locations of Manitoba and Ontario.

Color Lake Superior blue.

It would take a long time to label all 22,000 lakes in Minnesota. Instead, locate and label Lake of the Woods, Red Lake and Lake Itasca, the source of the Mississippi River.

The University of Minnesota in Minneapolis is the largest college in the U.S. Draw a book to mark the location of Minneapolis.

Mark the location of St. Paul, the capital of Minnesota, with a star.

Temperatures get pretty cold in International Falls. Mark the location of this shivery city with a snowflake.

Draw a ship to show the location of Duluth, the busiest freshwater port in the U.S.

The Mayo Clinic in Rochester is a world famous medical center. Mark the location of Rochester with the letters *Rx*, the symbol for a prescription.

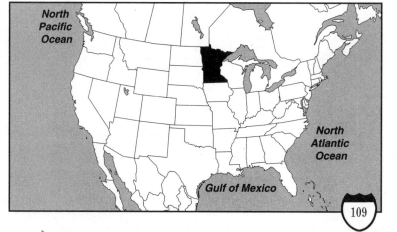

North Pacific Ocean

North Atlantic Ocean

Gulf of Mexico

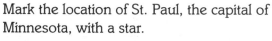

109

Water, Water Everywhere

All of Minnesota except the southeast corner was once covered by mile-thick glaciers that moved back and forth across the state leaving hills and ridges. The highest point in the state is Eagle Mountain (2,301 feet). Low areas filled with water to become lakes and marshes.

Although one nickname for Minnesota is Land of 10,000 Lakes, the number is much higher. There are actually 15,291 lakes in Minnesota. If you count small ponds, the number rises close to 22,000.

More than 25,000 miles of lakes and streams crisscross the state. If all the lakes and streams in Minnesota were laid end to end, they would be long enough to go around the Earth at the equator.

Lake Superior, which forms the northeastern border of Minnesota, covers 31,700 square miles and is the largest lake in the world. Twenty-six states the size of Rhode Island would fit in the area covered by Lake Superior with room left over.

Find 10 interesting names of lakes in Minnesota. Write them below. Circle the name of the lake you like best, and tell why it is your favorite.

1. _____
2. _____
3. _____
4. _____
5. _____
6. _____
7. _____
8. _____
9. _____
10. _____

The Mississippi River begins in north-central Minnesota at Lake Itasca. As it starts its journey to the Gulf of Mexico, the Mississippi isn't very mighty. The Father of Waters begins as a narrow creek, so shallow that children can wade across it.

Label the 10 states that border on the Mississippi River on the map below.

What's in a Name?

- According to legend, Minnesota's lakes were formed by the footprints of Paul Bunyan's companion, Babe, the Blue Ox. When it rained, the footprints filled with water and became lakes. Besides being known as the Land of 10,000 Lakes, Minnesota has several other nicknames.

- Chippewa, Itasca, Jackson and Washington were some of the names suggested when Minnesota became a U.S. Territory. Finally, the name Minnesota was agreed upon. The nickname **Land of Sky-Blue Waters** refers to the origin of the name Minnesota which came from a Dakota word meaning "sky-tinted water."

What name would you have selected for Minnesota?

- Minnesota is known as the North Star State because its northern peninsula, called the Northwest Angle, extends farther north than any other place in the lower 48 states. Although it is part of Minnesota, the Northwest Angle can be reached only by taking a boat across Lake of the Woods or by driving through Canada to get there.

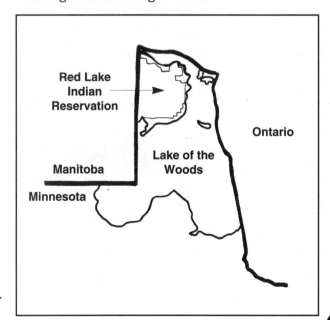

- Although gophers live in Minnesota, that isn't why the state is called the **Gopher State**. Promoters who worked to get state support for their railroad were portrayed as gophers in top hats in an 1859 cartoon.

- Minnesota's abundance of wheat, flour mills and dairy products earned it the nickname **Bread and Butter State**. Soybeans, beef cattle, sheep, poultry, oats, corn, sugar beets and potatoes are other important agricultural products.

Make up another nickname for Minnesota. Explain why you selected that name.

_____

_____

_____

_____

_____

_____

_____

_____

_____

_____

Many Centuries, Many Civilizations

The first people to settle in Minnesota were descendants of those who traveled from Asia to North America by crossing a land bridge in the Bering Sea. Over hundreds of years, these people migrated south and east following herds of mammoth and other game, arriving in Minnesota 8,000 to 10,000 years ago. As the climate warmed, the huge Ice Age animals became extinct. People used their hunting skills to kill elk, moose, deer and bison for food and furs.

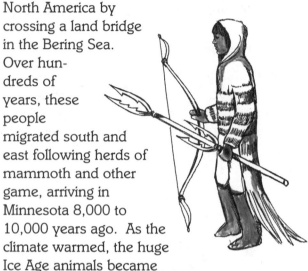

Six thousand years ago people along the shores of Lake Superior discovered copper which they used to make tools and weapons.

A civilization of mound builders developed in Minnesota about 500 B.C. Archaeologists have identified over 10,000 mounds in the state, many of them in the shape of birds, bison, bears and snakes. Other evidence of the early inhabitants include thousands of pictures painted and carved on rocks.

Between 300 B.C. and 100 A.D. people in the southwestern corner of the state began to mine catlinite (pipestone). They carved calumets (peace pipes) from the red rock and traveled long distances to the sacred pipestone quarries.

Vikings may have explored Minnesota as early as 1362, but not all scientists are convinced that the evidence, a stone carved in old Norse letters, is authentic.

By the time French fur traders from Canada began exploring the area around 1660, the Dakota were the dominant group living in Minnesota. Then in the late 1600s, a rival group of Ojibwa (Chippewa) moved into the area, pushed from the east by European settlers. They in turn warred with the Dakota for possession of the land. With guns earned by trading furs with the French, the Ojibwa gradually pushed the Dakotas to the west.

Discussion Questions

History is filled with stories of people who moved into an area and conquered those living there. This happened in Europe, the Americas, Asia, Australia and everywhere else in the world.

Do you think it is right or wrong for people to take over land where someone else lives if they are stronger or have better weapons? How would you feel if people from another country came to the United States and took over?

Who's Who and What's What?

Write the letter of the correct answer in each blank. Use reference books to find the answers.

1. _____ Nicknamed the "Purple People Eaters"

2. _____ Minnesota's professional baseball team

3. _____ Minnesota's professional basketball team

4. _____ A word that means "peace pipe"

5. _____ Actor who played Matt Dillon on the TV series *Gunsmoke*

6. _____ Actress who played Dorothy in the *The Wizard of Oz*

7. _____ Wrote *Main Street* and *Babbitt*

8. _____ Created the cartoon characters Charlie Brown and Snoopy

9. _____ Known as the Twin Cities of Minnesota

10. _____ Legendary companion of lumber-jack Paul Bunyan

11. _____ Site of an unsuccessful bank rob-bery by Jesse James and his gang on September 7, 1876

12. _____ Site of a 45-foot tall musical clock tower called a Glockenspiel with animated per-forming figures

13. _____ Called "laughing waters" in the poem "The Song of Hiawatha" by Henry Wadsworth Longfellow

14. _____ A "best buy" that made Minnesota part of the U.S.

A. Louisiana Purchase

B. Minnesota Twins

C. Judy Garland

D. Minneapolis and St. Paul

E. Minnesota Timberwolves

F. Northfield

G. calumet

H. Gadsen Purchase

I. Mississippi River

J. Babe, the Blue Ox

K. Minnesota Vikings

L. Sinclair Lewis

M. New Ulm

N. Minnehaha Falls

O. Duluth and Superior

P. Charles M. Schultz

Q. James Arness

Let's stop and watch the dog-sleds travel across frozen Lake Phalen.

Welcome to Mississippi

Feel the soft spring breeze as it blows us across Mississippi. Listen to the song of the mockingbird. Take a deep breath and smell the magnolia blossoms and Cherokee roses. Look at the trees in the Mississippi Petrified Forest. Try a taste of Mississippi catfish. There's lots to experience in the Magnolia State.

Nickname: Magnolia State
State motto: By Valor and Arms
State flower: Magnolia blossom
State tree: Magnolia
State bird: Mockingbird
State mammal: White-tailed deer
State water mammal: Bottle-nosed dolphin
State fish: Largemouth bass
State insect: Honeybee
State stone: Petrified wood
State song: "Go, Mississippi"
Capital: Jackson
Statehood: Mississippi joined the Union as the 20th state on December 10, 1817.
1990 Population: 2,573,216: the 31st largest in population
Area: 47,716 square miles: the 32nd largest in area
Neighbors: Louisiana, Arkansas, Tennessee, Alabama and the Gulf of Mexico

A Singing River?

The Pascagoula River makes a strange humming sound. Local legend claims the son of a Pascagoula chief fell in love with a princess from an enemy tribe, the Biloxi. The Biloxi attacked the Pascagoula. Knowing they could not win, the Pascagoula joined hands and walked to the river singing. They drowned in the river, and it is their song that people still hear today.

West Side Story and *Romeo and Juliet* are other tragic stories about two people from different backgrounds who fell in love.

Discussion Question

Why is it sometimes easier for young people to make friends than it is for older people to accept people from different backgrounds or cultures?

Write a short story about two people from different backgrounds who are friends. What happened when they brought the friend home to visit their family? How did their story end?

Name _____   *Mississippi Map Activity*

Label the underlined places on the Mississippi state map.

Four states border on Mississippi: <u>Louisiana</u>, <u>Alabama</u>, <u>Tennessee</u> and <u>Arkansas</u>. Label their approximate locations.

The <u>Mississippi River</u> forms most of the state's western border.

Several islands in the <u>Gulf of Mexico</u> are part of Mississippi. Label the Gulf of Mexico's approximate location.

The lighthouse at <u>Biloxi</u> was painted black after the Civil War by Mississippians who mourned the death of Abraham Lincoln.

A small museum in the house in <u>Tupelo</u> where Elvis Presley was born is open to the public.

Fort Massachusetts on <u>Ship Island</u> was the site of a prison for Confederate soldiers during the Civil War.

According to legend, pirate treasure was hidden on <u>Deer Island</u>. No treasure has been found there.

Winterville Mounds State Historic Site, north of <u>Greenville</u>, was once the center of an ancient Native American culture.

<u>Jackson</u>, the capital and largest city in Mississippi was built on the bluffs of the Pearl River.

<u>Natchez</u> was founded on the Mississippi River in 1716 as a center for trade in furs and bear grease.

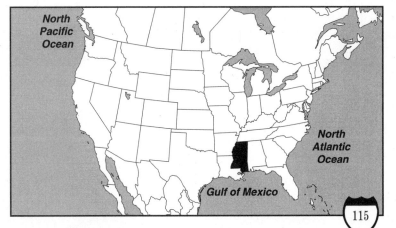

Exploring Mississippi

Read about the early years of Mississippi. Then answer the questions on the right.

In 1541, long before the Pilgrims landed at Plymouth Rock, Spanish explorers, led by Hernando de Soto, searched through Mississippi and other areas looking for gold. Finding none, they left.

More than 140 years passed before the next group of explorers became interested in Mississippi. The French explorer, LaSalle, traveled down the Mississippi River from Canada, claiming all of the land for France. He named the area Louisiana in honor of King Louis XIV.

As the French began building forts along the Mississippi River, the English started trading with the Chickasaw, Choctaw and Natchez. They brought many wonderful new tools and other items never seen by the Native Americans. They also brought diseases and war.

The Choctaw and Chickasaw became British allies in wars against French and Spanish claims to the territory. Later, they helped the American colonists against the Creek and fought with Andrew Jackson at the Battle of New Orleans.

Once Mississippi became a state, settlers moved in by the thousands, taking over the land by trickery, bribery and force.

Finally, the Native Americans of Mississippi, like those of many other states, were forced to move from their home to the Indian Territory in Oklahoma. Few survived the forced march, blizzards, hunger and diseases they encountered along the Trail of Tears.

1. What was the name given by the French to all the land along the Mississippi River?

   _____

2. Name two groups of Native Americans living in Mississippi when Europeans began exploring the area.

   _____

   _____

3. People from which country were the first Europeans to explore Mississippi?

   _____

   _____

4. What were the Spanish explorers looking for in Mississippi, Alabama, Georgia and Florida?

   _____

   _____

5. The French reached Mississippi by traveling down the _____ River from _____.

6. The Choctaw and Chickasaw fought under his leadership at the Battle of New Orleans. When _____ became President, he enforced the Indian Removal Act, forcing them to leave their homes in Mississippi and travel to the Indian Territory in _____.

116

More About Mississippi

Use reference books to answer the assigned questions about Mississippi.

- Pecan, sweet gum, bald cypress, tupelo and magnolia trees flourish in Mississippi.

Draw the leaves and flowers or fruit of one of these trees in the box below.

- Liberty Hall, Rowan Oak and Waverly Plantation are restored antebellum mansions in Mississippi.

What does *antebellum* mean?

- Cotton was once "king" in Mississippi. Other crops are much more important today.

List some crops important to Mississippi farmers today.

- Giant prehistoric logs that have turned to stone are found in the Mississippi Petrified Forest.

What does *petrified* mean? How does wood become petrified?

- Early travelers followed the Natchez Trace from Nashville, Tennessee, to Natchez, Mississippi.

What does the word *trace* mean?

- The National Fish Hatchery in Tupelo maintains 15 huge ponds.

What types of fish are raised there? What happens to the fish raised there?

Mississippi Musicians

Use reference books to find out what kind of music these Mississippi musicians are best known for.

    A. Rock and Roll

    B. Blues

    C. Country and Western

1. _____ Bo Diddly
2. _____ Bobbie Gentry
3. _____ B.B. King
4. _____ Charlie Pride
5. _____ Elvis Presley
6. _____ Jimmie Rodgers
7. _____ Ike Turner
8. _____ Conway Twitty
9. _____ Muddy Waters
10. _____ Tammy Wynette

I'd like to spend a little time on Deer Island looking for buried treasure.

Welcome to Missouri

If you enjoy spelunking, Missouri is a great place to explore caves. More than 5,000 caves have been discovered in Missouri. Twenty-four caves are open to the public.

Nicknames: Show Me State and Gateway to the West

State motto: The Welfare of the People Shall Be the Supreme Law

State flower: Hawthorn

State tree: Dogwood

State bird: Bluebird

State insect: Honeybee

State mineral: Galena

State stone: Mozarkite

State musical instrument: Fiddle

State song: "Missouri Waltz"

Capital: Jefferson City

Statehood: Missouri became the 24th state on August 10, 1821.

1990 Population: 5,117,073: the 15th largest in population

Area: 69,697 square miles: the 19th largest state

Neighbors: Iowa, Illinois, Kentucky, Tennessee, Arkansas, Oklahoma, Kansas and Nebraska

About Missouri

- Missouri was named for the Missouri Indians. The name means "people of the big canoe."

- The Missouri River was called "the Big Muddy." The Mississippi River is known as the "Father of Waters."

How did these two rivers get their nicknames?

- Sometimes the names of cities can be confusing—take Kansas City for example.

What two states have a city named Kansas City?

- The fiddle is Missouri's state musical instrument.

What would you choose as the official musical instrument for your state? Why?

- Missouri is nicknamed the "Show Me State."

How did Missouri get this nickname?

Discussion Question: What If?

What if the U.S. had not bought the Louisiana Purchase and all the land west of the Mississippi River never became part of the United States?

Name _____   *Missouri Map Activity*

Missouri is divided into four major land regions. 50,000 miles of rivers and streams crisscross the state. Label the Mississippi, Missouri and Osage rivers.

The area north of the Missouri River is the Glaciated Plains. This part of Missouri was once covered by glaciers. Color this section red.

No glaciers covered the region in western Missouri between the Missouri and Osage rivers known as the Osage Plains. Color this area yellow.

The smallest region is the Alluvial Plain in the southeastern corner of Missouri. The Mississippi River left thick layers of mud and sand when it flooded. Cotton, rice and soybeans grow well here. Color this area green.

The Ozark Highlands are the largest region in the south, central part of Missouri. Color this area blue.

Locate and label these major cities in Missouri:

St. Louis	Kansas City
Springfield	Independence
St. Joseph	Columbia
Florissant	Hannibal
University City	

Label the approximate locations of the eight states that border Missouri: Iowa, Illinois, Kentucky, Tennessee, Arkansas, Oklahoma, Kansas and Nebraska.

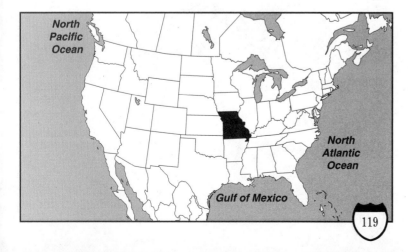

The Mail Must Go Through

San Francisco newspapers carried this ad in March, 1860:

> Young skinny wiry fellows not over eighteen. Must be expert riders willing to risk death daily.
> Orphans preferred.

Can you figure out what job these young men were being asked to fill?

Here's another hint: They rode from St. Joseph, Missouri, to San Francisco, California, a distance of nearly 2,000 miles in a record 10 days.

If you haven't figured it out yet, here's one more clue: In spite of the dangers from the weather and hostile tribes, only one bag of mail was lost by these riders.

Who were these first mail carriers?

_____

These young men, some only 14 and 15 years old, worked for the Pony Express. The first run was made on April 3, 1860. Relay stations were set up along the route. As one exhausted rider rushed in, the next rider grabbed the bags of mail and galloped off for the next station on a fresh horse.

Some young men who accepted the challenges of this job later became quite famous. "Buffalo Bill" Cody became a rider for the Pony Express at the age of 14. Another Pony Express rider was "Wild Bill" Hickok.

Mail service by Pony Express was quite expensive. It cost $5.00 per half ounce to send letters and $3.50 for a ten-word telegram.

Once the transcontinental telegraph was completed in October 1861, messages could be sent in a few seconds, and the Pony Express was no longer needed.

Delivery of mail today involves a lot less danger and excitement than it did in the days of the Pony Express.

Write an ad for a modern day mail carrier describing the duties and hazards of the job.

_____

_____

_____

_____

_____

_____

_____

Compare your ad to the one at the top of the page.

Compare the cost and time of sending a letter across the country by Pony Express to mailing a letter to China today.

The Early Settlers of Missouri

The first people known to settle permanently in Missouri were the **Bluff Shelter People** who lived in shallow caves along steep hillsides. Over thousands of years these people learned to grow crops, hunt and fish. They made pottery and formed tools from wood, stone and bone. They traveled the rivers of Missouri in birchbark canoes.

About 2,000 years ago, the people of the Hopewell Culture dominated in Missouri and other parts of the Midwest. They lived in towns surrounded by high wooden fences. They buried their dead in mounds built in the shapes of birds and animals. One mound near Caruthersville is 400 feet long, 250 feet wide and 35 feet high.

The people of the Hopewell Culture were eventually replaced by those known as the Mississippians who built flat-topped pyramids. These people carried on extensive trading with other groups as far away as the Rocky Mountains in the west and the Atlantic coast on the east.

By the time the French began exploring the area in the 1690s, three major groups of Native Americans lived in Missouri—the Missouri, the Iowa and the Osage. By the mid 1800s, most Native Americans had been forced to move west.

Learn more about one of these early Native American peoples who lived in Missouri.

A Question of Land

After the government made the Louisiana Purchase from France in 1803, people were encouraged to move west. Land could be purchased for very little money and thousands traveled west to start a new life.

Conflict between Native Americans and European settlers occurred continuously from the Atlantic coast to the Pacific Ocean. Why? Mostly because of land. The Native Americans had it. The settlers wanted it.

Imagine moving to Missouri in 1810. You believe you have a right to settle on the land. After all, the government bought it from France, and you bought 40 acres from the government.

Discussion Questions

How would you feel about anyone who tried to burn your farm and force you off your land?

Now imagine you are a member of a tribe who has lived on this land for hundreds of years. The land belongs to your people, not to France or the U.S. government. Your people have always traveled, hunted and fished where they pleased. Now settlers are taking over your land.

How would you feel about settlers who took your land? What would you do to defend your land?

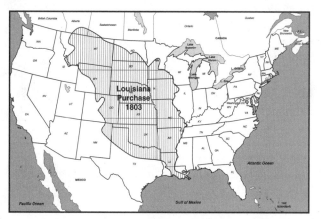

Learn More About Missouri

To learn more about Missouri, check your encyclopedia, atlas, dictionary or read other books about Missouri. Find one interesting fact about each of the places and people listed below.

Arrow Rock State Historical Site: _____

_____

_____

Fort Osage: _____

_____

Gateway Arch: _____

_____

Pony Express Stables Museum: _____

_____

_____

Trail of Tears State Park: _____

_____

Missouri River: _____

_____

Fantastic Caverns: _____

_____

Jesse James Home: _____

_____

_____

Mark Twain Cave: _____

_____

_____

St. Louis World's Fair: _____

_____

Missouri Compromise: _____

_____

Samuel Clemens: _____

_____

Harry Truman: _____

_____

Dale Carnegie: _____

_____

Jesse James: _____

_____

Carry Nation: _____

_____

Joyce Hall: _____

_____

T.S. Eliot: _____

_____

Dizzy Dean: _____

_____

_____

Yogi Berra: _____

_____

_____

Chuck Berry: _____

_____

_____

It must have been spooky for Tom and Becky when they were lost in the caves near Hannibal, Missouri.

122

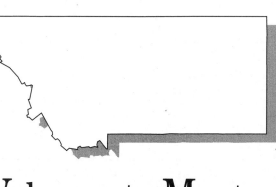

Welcome to Montana

West, then north to the Canadian border we'll find Big Sky Country, the state of high mountains and vast plains. Keep your eyes open for grizzly bears, the state animal of Montana.

Nicknames: Treasure State, Big Sky Country, Land of the Shining Mountains and the Last Best Place

State motto: Gold and Silver

State flower: Bitterroot

State tree: Ponderosa pine

State bird: Western mead- owlark

State animal: Grizzly bear

State fish: Black-spot- ted cutthroat trout

State gems: Sapphire and agate

State fossil: Duck-billed dinosaur

State song: "Montana"

Capital: Helena

Statehood: Montana became the 41st state on November 8, 1889.

1990 Population: 799,065: the 44th in population

Area: 147,046 square miles: Montana is the fourth largest state.

Neighbors: North and South Dakota; Idaho; British Columbia; Alberta and Saskatchewan, Canada

Did You Know?

- *Montana* means "mountain" in Spanish.

- Montana has only about five people per square mile. The cattle population of the state is about three times larger than the people population. There are even more deer, elk, antelopes and bears in Montana than there are people.

- There's gold in Montana: A gold nugget weighing about two pounds was found near Butte, Montana, in 1989.

- The tyrannosaurus rex skeleton on display at the New York American Museum of Natural History was found in Montana. Fossils of triceratops, pterosaurs and other dinosaurs have also been discovered here.

- Warm chinook winds blow across Montana in late winter and early spring, helping to melt the snow. The Blackfeet call these winds the "snow eater."

- Winters can get down-right chilly in Montana. The temperature dipped to -70°F at Rogers Pass on January 20, 1954. A high temperature of 117°F was also recorded in Montana.

Discussion Questions: What's in a Name?

What do you think each of the four nicknames for Montana means? Which nickname for Montana do you think is best? Make up a new nickname for your state.

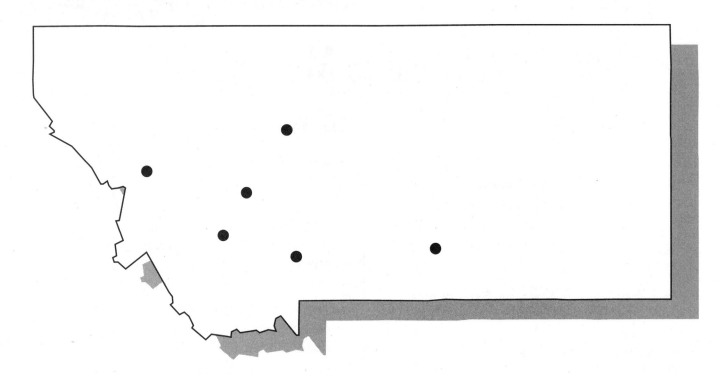

Scale

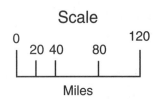

Miles

Label these places on the Montana state map:

Billings   Helena   Great Falls
Missoula   Butte   Bozeman

Label the approximate locations of North and South Dakota, Wyoming, Idaho and Canada.

How long is the northern border of Montana?

How far is it from Billings to the northwest corner of the state?

How long is the eastern border of Montana?

Is Helena north or south of Butte?

Is Bozeman east or west of Billings?

Which city is farther north: Great Falls or Missoula?

Which city is farther west: Billings or Great Falls?

Is Montana north or south of Colorado?

Which state is farther west: Montana or Utah?

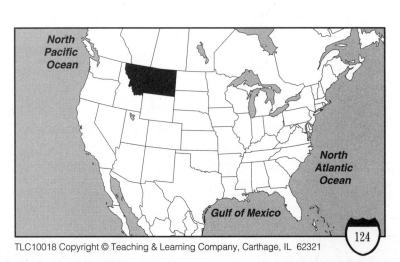

More to Discover

On a rainy day when students can't get outside, teach them to play a game enjoyed by the Crows and other Native Americans. The equipment needed is simple and inexpensive. Gather it in advance and wait for a rainy day.

You'll need six peach or plum pits, dried, a small flat wooden bowl or basket, a marker, paper and a pencil. Almonds in the shell would also work. If these are not available, students could use buttons or shapes cut from cardboard.

Have students color one side of the peach or plum pits with a marker. Divide the group into two teams with the same number of students on each team. One student can be the scorekeeper for both teams. If you have a large class, consider dividing the class into several teams.

To play, hold the bowl or basket with the peach pits in one hand. With a slight toss, flip the pits into the air and catch them again in the bowl. Each pit that lands with the marked side up counts one point. Pits must land in the bowl to count. Pits that land with the marked side down do not count.

Students from both teams take turns tossing the pits. When everyone on both teams has had ten turns, the team with the highest score wins.

Some version of this game was played by most groups of Native Americans. The game was taken very seriously when played for high stakes, like bows, arrows or ponies.

More About Montana

Read these facts about places in Montana. Answer the assigned questions.

• Helena, the capital of Montana, began as a mining town in 1864.

1. What was the town's original name?

• Garnet and Granite are two of the ghost towns in Montana.

What is a ghost town?

• There are about 50 glaciers in Glacier National Park. Iceberg Lake contains icebergs, even in the middle of summer.

What is a glacier? What is an iceberg?

• Butte, Montana, was named for Big Butte, a nearby volcanic mountain.

What does the word *butte* mean?

• Yellowstone National Park is partly in Montana and partly in two other states.

2. What other two states contain part of Yellowstone National Park?

• At Pictograph Cave State Historical Site near Billings, visitors can follow a trail that leads to drawings in a cave made about 2,000 years ago. Eight thousand-year-old tools have also been found in the cave.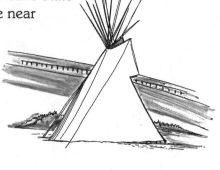

What are pictographs?

• Petrified wood can be found along the Yellowstone River.

What is petrified wood?

• Pompey's Pillar was named for the son of a famous Shoshone woman.

3. What was her name?

• Custer Battlefield National Monument marks an important battle between the U.S. and the Native Americans of Montana.

Describe the battle known as Custer's Last Stand.

• Wind and water carved many strange shapes in the sandstone rocks at Medicine Rocks State Park.

Why were these rocks called "Medicine Rocks"?

• Unusual columns of rock at Makoshika State Park are called hoodoos.

Draw or describe these columns of rock.

• Medicine Lake Refuge and Charles Russel Refuge are two natural wildlife preserves in Montana. Unusual fish, called paddlefish, live in the Charles Russel Refuge.

Draw or describe a paddlefish. What other animals and birds can be found in these wildlife refuges?

• The Nez Perce, fleeing through Montana to Canada, met with U.S. troops only 30 miles from their destination, at Bears Paw Battlefield in 1877. They were defeated during a four-day battle with U.S. troops. Their leader made a famous speech when he surrendered: "The little children are freezing to death. My heart is sick and sad. From where the sun now stands, I will fight no more forever."

4. What was the name of the Nez Perce chief who said these sad words?

A Bit of Montana History

Read about Montana. Select one of the underlined items for a report. Include drawings and pictures from magazines in your report.

Many different tribes lived in Montana before white settlers arrived. The <u>Arapaho</u>, <u>Blackfeet</u>, <u>Crow</u>, <u>Cheyenne</u> and <u>Assiniboine</u> lived on the eastern plains. They hunted the huge herds of bison that roamed the plains. The Sioux also traveled from the Dakotas to hunt in Montana.

In the Rocky Mountains the <u>Kutenai</u>, <u>Shoshone</u>, <u>Salish</u> and <u>Bannock</u> hunted for deer and bear, fished and gathered berries.

Captain <u>Meriwether Lewis</u> and Captain <u>William Clark</u> were sent west by Thomas Jefferson to explore the land that had been obtained from France through the <u>Louisiana Purchase</u>. <u>Sacagawea</u>, a Shoshone woman who knew the wilderness trails and passes, and her French Canadian husband went with the explorers as guides.

At first, the riches of <u>fur trapping and trading</u> brought people to Montana. When <u>gold</u> was discovered, thousands rushed to the Treasure State to seek their fortune. Some found gold, others found <u>silver</u> and <u>copper</u>.

Ranchers drove huge herds of Texas cattle to Montana to graze on the grassy plains. Other ranches began raising large herds of sheep.

As more people arrived in Montana, thousands of bison were killed. The settlers claimed land where the Native Americans had hunted and fished for centuries. Food became scarce. They suffered from smallpox and other diseases. Some groups fought to save their way of life.

In 1875 the Native Americans of Montana were ordered onto a reservation. Under the leadership of <u>Sitting Bull</u> and <u>Crazy Horse</u>, they defeated <u>General Custer</u> and his troops at the <u>Battle of Little Big Horn</u>. Although they won that battle, they lost the war. By 1880 nearly all Native Americans in Montana lived on reservations.

At first, Montana was important for mining, <u>cattle</u> and <u>sheep</u> ranching. Major <u>oil fields</u> were discovered in the 1950s and <u>coal</u> mining became important in the 1970s. Gold, silver, copper, oil and coal have made Montana a Treasure State of natural resources.

Have you ever seen so much blue sky? No wonder they call Montana Big Sky Country.

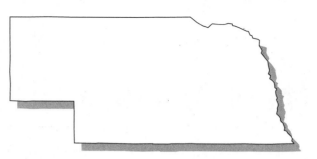

Welcome to Nebraska

If we follow the Platte River across Nebraska, we'll be traveling along the same route taken by thousands of pioneers heading for Oregon, California and Utah.

Nickname: Cornhusker State
State motto: Equality Before the Law
State flower: Goldenrod
State tree: Cottonwood
State bird: Meadowlark
State insect: Honeybee
State rock: Prairie agate
State fossil: Mammoth
State song: "Beautiful Nebraska"
Capital: Lincoln
Statehood: Nebraska became the 37th state on March 1, 1867.
1990 Population: 1,578,385: the 36th largest in population
Area: 77,355 square miles: the 15th largest state in area
Neighbors: South Dakota, Iowa, Missouri, Kansas, Colorado and Wyoming

Did You Know?

Fossil evidence suggests that Nebraska once had a tropical climate. In addition to weird rock formations in Toadstool Park, scientists discovered fossils of saber-toothed tigers, camels, rhinoceroses, turtles and crocodiles.

Agate Fossil Beds National Monument near Harrison, one of the richest sources of fossils in the U.S., includes the remains of 20 million-year-old mastodons and huge pigs.

Father Edward Flanagan established Boys Town in 1917 as a home and school for boys. Based on his belief that "there is no such thing as a bad boy," he helped thousands of neglected and troubled boys. Today the school is home to about 400 boys and girls. A movie called *Boys Town* was made in 1938 and a sequel, *Men of Boys Town*, was made three years later.

Built in 1819, Fort Atkinson was the earliest military post west of the Missouri River. The outside walls measured 455 feet by 468 feet. (A football field is 300 feet long.) More than 1,000 soldiers were stationed there at a time. Fort Atkinson became the site of Nebraska's first school, farm, library, sawmill and hospital.

Measure out an area about the size of Fort Atkinson near your school. What do you think it would be like for 1,000 soldiers to live in that space?

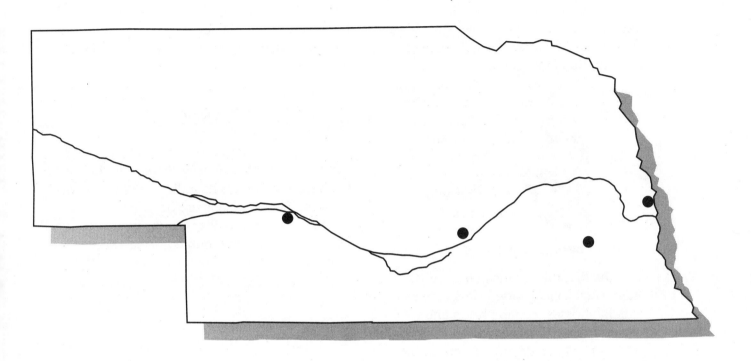

Label the underlined places on the Nebraska state map.

Nebraska has 11,000 miles of rivers and streams that empty into the <u>Missouri River</u>. The Missouri River forms the eastern boundary of Nebraska.

The <u>Platte River</u> is so shallow in some places it is only a foot deep. In summer, parts of the river may dry up.

<u>South Dakota</u>, <u>Iowa</u>, <u>Missouri</u>, <u>Kansas</u>, <u>Colorado</u> and <u>Wyoming</u> border Nebraska. Label their approximate locations.

The Orpheum Theater in <u>Omaha</u> is the home of the Omaha Symphony Orchestra, Opera and Ballet.

<u>Lincoln</u> became the capital of Nebraska in 1867 when it joined the Union as the 37th state. A 400-foot domed tower tops the state capitol building.

The Stuhr Museum of the Prairie Pioneer at <u>Grand Island</u> contains a huge display of an operating steam train and 60 restored buildings called "Railroad Town."

<u>North Platte</u> was the home of Buffalo Bill's Wild West Show and Rodeo.

Only a Small Part of History

The earliest people settled in the area that became Nebraska about 12,000 years ago. Over the centuries, various cultures grew, flourished and died out. By the time Europeans began exploring the area, they met the Pawnee, Oto, Omaha, Ponca and Missouri living in Nebraska. The Sioux, Arapaho and Cheyenne were nomadic hunters who followed the huge herds of bison across the Great Plains.

When people think of the American Indians of the past, they usually picture the Plains Indians of the 1800s, riding horses, hunting bison and attacking wagon trains. This idea of how Native Americans lived has been greatly influenced by television and movies. This image is only a small part of the history of people who lived in the area for 12,000 years.

Fossil remains show that horses once lived in the United States but died out millions of years ago. Until Spanish explorers arrived in the New World in the 1500s and 1600s, none of the Native Americans had ever seen a horse. As they captured and bred horses of their own, the way of life of many tribes changed. They could follow the huge herds of bison that filled the Great

Plains. Although attacks on wagon trains occur frequently in the movies, Indian attacks of the heavily armed wagon trains that crossed the plains were rare.

Discussion Questions

Why do you think people who make television shows and movies usually show only this part of the history of the Plains Indians? Why do you think the Plains Indians are usually the ones shown, rather than other groups who lived in villages without horses, hunted, fished and farmed?

THE TRUE STORY OF THE PLAINS INDIANS

Early Nebraska

Few people settled in Nebraska in the early years, but many passed through on their way west. In 1854, the population of Nebraska Territory included only 2,732 whites. (Native Americans and African Americans were not included in the early census.) Between 1843 and 1858, about 500,000 pioneers crossed Nebraska in covered wagons. Known as the Great Platte River Road—the route along the Platte and North Platte Rivers became part of the Oregon Trail, the Mormon Trail and the California Trail.

Nebraska comes from the Oto word *Nebrathka* used to describe the Platte River. It means "flat water." Flowing westward across the state, the Platte is sometimes a mile wide and quite shallow. Parts of the river may even dry up in the summer. Settlers called it the "mile-wide, inch deep river."

Nebraska has very little forested land—only about 2%. This includes many areas that have been planted within the last 100 years. Much of the land is prairie where about 200 types of grasses grow.

In 1865 the Union Pacific Railroad began laying track at Omaha as part of the transcontinental rail-

road. They needed to build over 600 miles of track westward across a land with few trees. Crews traveled long distances, cutting every tree they could find to use for railroad ties. A state with few trees to begin with, had even less by the time the railroad was completed.

With few trees available to build log cabins, the early settlers adapted a style of home used by many Native Americans. Many early homes in Nebraska were made of sod (a layer of soil with a thick growth of grass and weeds). Cut into

blocks to form walls, sod houses kept out the cold in winter and were fairly cool in summer. One problem with sod houses occurred when it rained.

Can you imagine traveling more than 1,000 miles in a covered wagon? I get tired riding 50 miles in the car to Grandma's house.

Discussion Questions

What do you think it would be like to live in a sod house during a heavy rainstorm? What else might have been a problem for those living in sod houses?

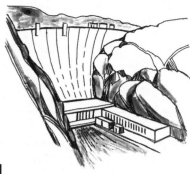

Welcome to Nevada

As we head south across Idaho, we come to the Silver State of Nevada. Nevada is a Spanish word meaning "snowy" or "snow-clad." Isn't that a strange name for a state that is mostly hot, dry desert?

Nicknames: Sagebrush State, Battle Born State and Silver State

State motto: All for Our Country

State flower: Sagebrush

State trees: Single-leaf piñon and bristlecone pine

State bird: Mountain blue-bird

State animal: Desert bighorn sheep

State song: "Home, Means Nevada"

Capital: Carson City

Statehood: October 31, 1864, the 36th state

1990 Population: 1,201,833: the 39th largest in population

Area: 110,561 square miles: the 7th largest state

Neighbors: Idaho, Oregon, California, Arizona and Utah

Resources: Nevada is the nation's leading producer of gold, magnesite and mercury, a leader in silver production and the world's largest producer of turquoise.

Home, Means Nevada

Read the chorus of Nevada's state song:

Home, means Nevada.
Home, means the hills.
Home, means the sage and the pines.

Think about your state. What does *home* mean to you? Write a short song or poem about the state you call home.

_____

_____

_____

_____

_____

_____

_____

_____

_____

_____

_____

Discussion Question: What If?

What if Nevada had no deserts?

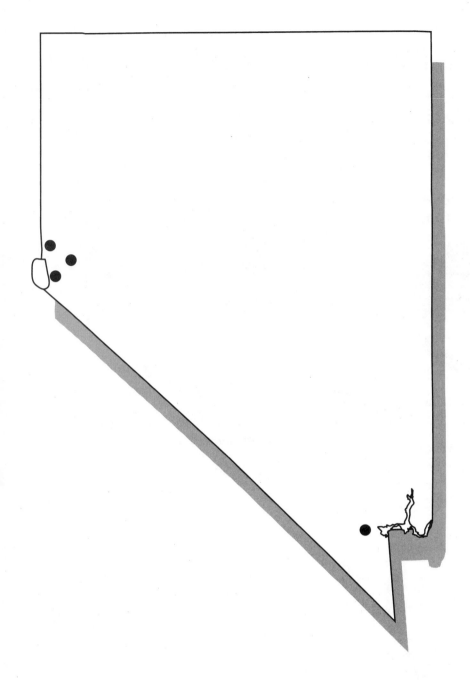

Label the underlined places on the map of Nevada.

<u>Lake Tahoe</u>, on the Nevada-California border, is the largest and second deepest alpine lake in North America.

<u>Lake Meade</u>, the largest man-made lake in the U.S., was formed when Hoover Dam was built in the 1930s.

Many buildings from the mining boom era are preserved in <u>Virginia City</u>, nicknamed the "Liveliest Ghost Town in the West."

<u>Reno</u> started out as a dusty, rough town. Today it is a popular resort and ski center.

<u>Carson City</u> was named for Kit Carson.

Nevada is bordered by <u>Idaho</u>, <u>Oregon</u>, <u>California</u>, <u>Arizona</u> and <u>Utah</u>. Label their approximate locations on the map above.

<u>*Las Vegas*</u> means "the meadows" in Spanish.

Nevada includes some towns with unusual names like Babbit, Bunkerville, Carp, Cherry Creek, Imlay, Jean, Jiggs, Midas, Valmy and Zephyr Cove. How many of these places can you locate on the map?

North Pacific Ocean

North Atlantic Ocean

Gulf of Mexico

133

The First People of Nevada

Archaeologists have found evidence of people living in Nevada 12,000 years ago. The remains of these people were discovered with the bones of extinct prehistoric animals.

About 3,000 years ago, people called Basket Makers lived near Lovelock Cave in northern Nevada. They were skillful weavers who made beautiful baskets and sandals from tree bark and plant fibers. Although they left no written records, these early people were known as the Anasazi. Their name came from a Navajo word meaning "the ancient ones."

Around 500 A.D. the Anasazi began to mine salt and turquoise and trade with their neighbors. They built pit houses by digging a large round hole a few feet deep. They built slanted walls and flat roofs from tree limbs, bark and dirt. To enter and leave their homes, they used ladders.

Two hundred years later the Anasazi became Nevada's first farmers when they built dams for irrigation and grew cotton, corn, beans and squash. Their homes were flat-roofed clay buildings. Some buildings had as many as 100 rooms. About 1150 A.D. the Anasazi disappeared from Nevada. Where they went and why they left are mysteries scientists are still trying to solve.

Learn more about how the Anasazi built their pit houses. Draw an Anasazi pit house below. Describe what you think it would have been like to live in a pit house.

Spirit Dancers

By the 1850s most Native Americans had been affected by the advance of white settlers. Many had lost their lands and their traditional way of life. They were forced to flee to less desirable places or to live on reservations where they had little food and much sickness.

Wovoka, a Paiute living in Nevada, had visions in 1887 and 1889 while in a trance. He said he visited the land of the dead and returned with a message from the Great Spirit. He wanted all Native Americans to join in a ritual dance called the Spirit Dance. This would allow their ancestors to return to life in a world where game was plentiful and all lived happily together in the old way. Soon the whites would be swept away by a great flood and the people would be free.

News of Wovoka's vision spread quickly among the Arapaho, Cheyenne and Oglala Sioux. Sixty thousand members of more than 30 different tribes joined in Wovoka's dance.

Called the "ghost dance" religion by whites, they feared the Indians would unite and rebel. In 1890 the U.S. Army captured a group of Sioux Ghost Dancers and ordered them to give up their weapons. Some refused. What became known as the Wounded Knee Massacre followed. Many of the people wore shirts decorated with eagles, buffalo and morning stars. They believed these symbols of powerful spirits would protect them from the soldiers' bullets. Three hundred Sioux men, women and children were killed by the soldiers. Belief in the Spirit Dance ended.

Write a paragraph to answer one of these questions:

Why do you think so many different people from different tribes accepted Wovoka's vision?

Why do you think whites feared the "ghost dancers"?

_____

_____

_____

_____

_____

_____

_____

_____

_____

_____

_____

_____

_____

_____

_____

_____

Nevada, a Land of Natural Wonders

Millions of years ago, the Pacific Ocean covered much of Nevada. Nevada's mountains and deserts resulted from glaciers moving across part of the state and from powerful earthquakes and volcanic eruptions. Nevada has many strange and beautiful landscape features. People have also changed the landscape of Nevada.

Learn more about these places in Nevada. Write a few sentences to describe each place.

The Valley of Fire: _____

_____

_____

_____

Cathedral Gorge: _____

_____

_____

_____

Hoover Dam: _____

_____

_____

_____

_____

Lake Meade: _____

_____

_____

_____

_____

Pyramid Lake: _____

_____

_____

_____

Lunar Crater: _____

_____

_____

_____

Paradise Valley: _____

_____

_____

_____

Great Basin National Park: _____

_____

_____

_____

Lehman Caves: _____

_____

_____

_____

Berlin-Ichthyosaur State Park:

_____

_____

_____

_____

Look, there's Lunar Crater. Are you sure we haven't landed on the moon?

136

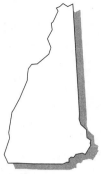

Welcome to New Hampshire

We'd better steer clear of Mount Washington as we head for New Hampshire. The winds on that mountain are the strongest on Earth.

Nicknames: Granite State, White Mountain State, Switzerland of America and Primary State
State motto: Live Free or Die
State flower: Purple lilac
State tree: White birch
State bird: Purple finch
State animal: White-tailed deer
State amphibian: Red-spotted newt
State insect: Ladybug
State mineral: Beryl
State gem: Smoky quartz
State rock: Granite
State song: "Old New Hampshire"
Capital: Concord
Statehood: New Hampshire was one of the 13 original colonies and the ninth state to ratify the Constitution on June 21, 1788.
1990 Population: 1,109,252: the 40th largest in population
Area: 9,297 square miles: the 7th smallest state
Neighbors: Quebec, Maine, Massachusetts, Vermont and the Atlantic Ocean

- New Hampshire was named for the county of Hampshire in England.

- The oldest family farm in our country is in Dover, New Hampshire. Members of the Tuttle family have worked the farm since 1632. How many years has the farm been in the family?

Chief Passaconaway

Many legends surround Chief Passaconaway. The Pennacook people claimed he could change himself into fire. They believed he could turn trees green in winter. When the English settlers arrived, he lost his powers. Passaconaway said it was because their magic was stronger than his. He became a peacekeeper between his people and the white settlers.

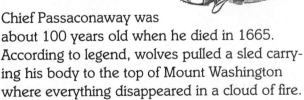

Chief Passaconaway was about 100 years old when he died in 1665. According to legend, wolves pulled a sled carrying his body to the top of Mount Washington where everything disappeared in a cloud of fire.

Make up another legend about Chief Passaconaway that his people might have told about him.

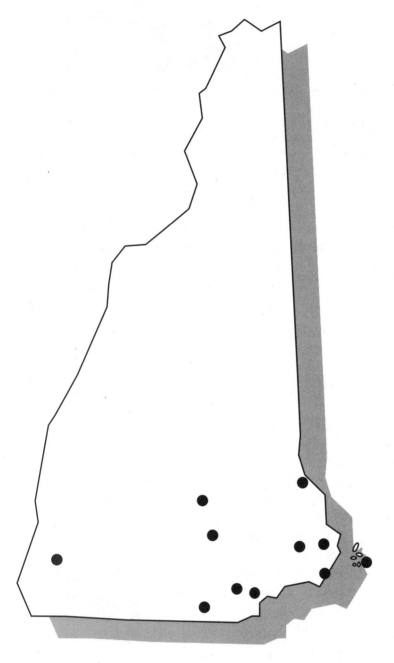

Label the underlined places on the New Hampshire map.

New Hampshire has only 18 miles of coastline along the Atlantic Ocean.

The state's four oldest cities are Portsmouth, Exeter, Dover and Hampton.

The Canadian province of Quebec forms part of New Hampshire's border.

Maine, Massachusetts and Vermont are the three states that border the Granite State. Label their approximate locations on the map to your left.

Manchester, Nashua and Concord are the three largest cities in New Hampshire. Manchester, originally called Derryfield, was settled in 1722. Concord, founded in 1727, was first named Pennycook.

The Isles of Shoals are a few miles offshore. Three of these islands are part of New Hampshire. The other six are part of Maine.

The home of Robert Frost, the poet, is in Derry.

No one knows who built the place near North Salem called Mystery Hill. It is filled with stone walls, passageways, chambers and carvings.

Along the side roads near Keene are several old covered bridges.

North Pacific Ocean

North Atlantic Ocean

Gulf of Mexico

138

From A to Z

Many birds, animals, trees and plants live in New Hampshire. Forests cover 80% of the state. Pine, spruce, fir and cedar as well as maple, birch, oak, ash and hickory trees grow here. In the fall, shades of red, yellow, orange and brown cover the forest. In spring, the bright blossoms of apple and cherry trees, dogwoods and other plants produce bright splashes of color. Seals and dolphins live off the coast of New Hampshire. Water birds nest in the area.

Use each of the letters from A to Z to complete the names of animals and birds found in New Hampshire. Cross out the letters as you use them.

```
A B C D E F G H I J K L M
N O P Q R S T U V W X Y Z
```

1. B E A __ E R S
2. B __ A C K   B E A R S
3. B L U E   __ A Y S
4. B O B C __ T S
5. C H I P M __ N K S
6. __ U C K S
7. E A S T E R N
    C __ Y O T E S

8. E L __
9. F I __ C H E S
10. __ O X E S
11. __ R O U S E
12. L I __ A R D S
13. L Y N __
14. M __ N K
15. __ O O S E
16. M U __ K R A T S
17. O __ O S S U M S
18. O S P R E __ S
19. O __ T E R S
20. G E __ S E
21. P __ E A S A N T S
22. P O __ C U P I N E S
23. R A __ B I T S
24. R A C __ O O N S
25. S H R E __ S
26. S __ U I R R E L S

About New Hampshire

Use an encyclopedia or books about New Hampshire to answer the assigned questions below.

1. This rock formation in the White Mountains of New Hampshire looks like an old man's head. It has been New Hampshire's official emblem since 1945. What is it called?

   _____

2. The _____ Mountains of New Hampshire are part of the Appalachians. Many of the peaks are covered with snow much of the year. Sunlight reflecting off the rocks makes the mountains look white even in summer.

3. Relics of early settlers in New Hampshire over 9,000 years old have been found at Lake Winnipesaukee. *Winnipesaukee* means

   _____

   _____

   _____

4. The first warship to fly the American flag was the _____ built in New Hampshire in 1777. It was commanded by John Paul Jones.

5. Why is New Hampshire nick-named the Primary State?

   _____

   _____

   _____

   _____

   _____

   _____

6. Not only is it the highest peak in New England, it also has the most remarkable weather. Scientists work year-round at a weather station where the temperature can drop to -30°. Winter winds blow at 60 mph or more. A world record for the strongest wind ever measured on Earth was recorded here on April 12, 1934. The winds reached 231 miles per hour. What is the name of this mountain?

   _____

7. For a short time, part of northern New Hampshire was an independent country. In the 1800s, both the U.S. and Canada claimed the area. In 1832, the people formed their own country and called it _____. Ten years later the Webster-Ashburton Treaty was signed, and the land became part of the U.S.

8. Who or what are the New Hampshire Reds?

   _____

   _____

   _____

9. New Hampshire is also nicknamed the Granite State. Describe what granite looks like and what it is used for.

   _____

   _____

   _____

   _____

   _____

   _____

   _____

That mountain looks like an old man's face. Maybe that's why they call it the Old Man of the Mountain.

Welcome to New Jersey

Wow! Look below at the Great Falls of the Passaic River. A billion gallons of water crash over a 77-foot cliff every day.

Nicknames: Garden State and Cockpit of the Revolution

State motto: Liberty and Prosperity

State flower: Purple violet

State tree: Red oak

State bird: Eastern goldfinch

State animal: Horse

State insect: Honeybee

State dinosaur: Hadrasaurus

State song: None

Capital: Trenton

Statehood:
New Jersey became the third state to ratify the Constitution on December 18, 1787. Although it is not an island, New Jersey was named for the English Isle of Jersey.

1990 Population: 7,730,118: the 9th largest in population. New Jersey averages about 995 people per square mile, the highest of the 50 states.

Area: 7,787 square miles: the 5th smallest in area. New Jersey could fit inside Alaska 75 times.

Neighbors: New York, Delaware, Pennsylvania and the Atlantic Ocean

New Jersey, Home of the Hadrasaurus

In 1858 dinosaur bones were discovered at Haddonfield, New Jersey. Often called the "duck-billed" dinosaur, the hadrasaurus was about 30 feet long.

Draw a picture of a hadrasaurus, New Jersey's state dinosaur.

Many actors, musicians and singers were born in New Jersey. Learn more about one of these people:

Count Basie	Sarah Vaughan
Frank Sinatra	Dionne Warwick
Paul Simon	Bruce Springsteen
Bud Abbott	Lou Costello
Jack Nicholson	Meryl Streep
John Travolta	

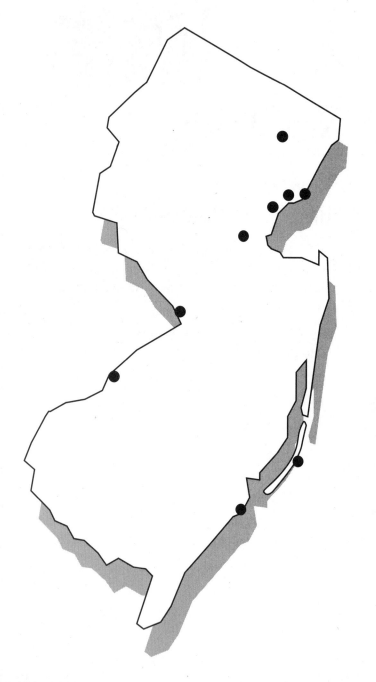

Label the underlined places on the New Jersey map.

Atlantic City is a popular resort town in New Jersey.

Long Beach Island and Absecon Island are two of the islands that are part of New Jersey.

The Delaware River separates New Jersey from Pennsylvania and Delaware to the west and south. Label their approximate locations on the New Jersey map.

The Hudson River forms most of the northern border between New Jersey and New York. Label their approximate locations on the map above.

The Atlantic Ocean forms the eastern border of New Jersey.

Trenton became the capital of New Jersey in 1790.

Edison was named for the inventor, Thomas A. Edison.

Label these New Jersey cities: Newark, Jersey City, Paterson, Elizabeth and Camden.

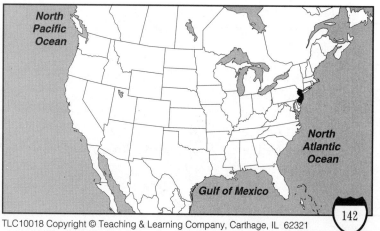

142

All About New Jersey

Fill in the blanks with words from the word bank. Check reference books if you need help finding the answers.

1. An unusual museum in Lyndhurst is the _____ which shows how recycling can stop pollution.

2. The _____ has soup bowls dating back 2,500 years.

3. The first motion pictures showed events like people dancing, circus acts and a man sneezing. _____, New Jersey, became the nation's first movie capital.

4. The first motion picture that told a story was _____. It was made in New Jersey in 1903.

5. _____ operated the country's first successful electric telegraph near Morristown in 1838.

6. Born in Elizabeth, New Jersey, her books are popular with many students. _____ wrote *Tales of a Fourth Grade Nothing, Deenie* and *Blubber*.

7. Another New Jersey author wrote *The Last of the Mohicans*. Who was he?

   _____

8. What New Jersey author wrote *The Red Badge of Courage*, a novel about the Civil War?_____

9. Four states are smaller than New Jersey. What are they?

   _____

   _____

   _____

10. What is the capital of New Jersey?

    _____

11. Who was the early Dutch explorer in New Jersey who sailed on a river later named for him? _____

12. A Frenchman, _____, was the first European known to explore the New Jersey area.

13. What three states border New Jersey?

    _____

14. About 20,000 Lenni-Lenape tools, pipes and clay pots can be seen in the

    _____.

15. New Jersey is nicknamed the

    _____.

16. The Lenni-Lenape lived in dome-shaped houses called a _____.

Word Bank

New York
Stephen Crane
Henry Hudson
Giovanni da Verrazano
Connecticut
Delaware
Trenton
Hawaii
Judy Blume
Gone with the Wind
Snow White
Nutmeg State
Thomas Edison
Woodruff Indian Museum

Pennsylvania
The Great Train Robbery
Trash Museum
Campbell Museum
James Fenimore Cooper
Iowa
Samuel B. Morse
Fort Lee
Rhode Island
Christopher Columbus
Garden State
wigwam
hogans

The State Without a Song

New Jersey does not have a state song. It's up to you to write one. You could write words that fit a familiar melody, like "Are You Sleeping?," "Row, Row, Row Your Boat" or "This Land Is Your Land."

If your song doesn't fit a melody, write only the words. Your song could rhyme or not.

Here are some words and phrases you might want to include in your song:

New Jersey   Trenton
Meadowlands   Garden State
Atlantic Ocean   Islands
Atlantic City   Princeton
Rutgers   Menlo Park
Fort Lee   Coastline
Monopoly   Tomatoes
Blueberries   Cranberries
Peaches   Orchids
Underground Railroad
Isle of Jersey
One of 13 original colonies
Great Falls of the Passaic River
Land of industry and invention,
     farms and forests

Write other words or phrases you could use in your New Jersey state song.

_____

_____

_____

_____

_____

Write the first draft of your song below. Make as many changes as you'd like. Write your final copy on another piece of paper.

_____

_____

_____

_____

_____

_____

_____

_____

_____

_____

_____

_____

_____

_____

_____

_____

_____

_____

_____

_____

_____

_____

New Jersey News

New Jersey has been the birthplace of many inventions and the manufacturing and developing site of products that have changed our lives, like the phonograph, electric lights, transistors, weather satellites, Colt revolvers, steamboats and steam engines.

New Jersey is the nation's leading manufacturer of medicines, soaps and cleaners and the number two producer of chemicals.

Traffic would be even worse without the "cloverleaf." The first one was built in New Jersey in 1929.

The world's first drive-in movie theater opened near Camden, New Jersey, in 1933.

John Stevens built our country's first steam locomotive in 1825. It went 12 miles an hour. People can run faster than that.

One of the largest clocks in the world ticks in Jersey City. The minute hand is 26 feet long.

The Lenni-Lenape, early settlers in New Jersey, lived in dome-shaped houses called wigwams. They were peaceful hunters and farmers. They gave food to strangers who stopped at their villages. Out of respect, other tribes called them "Our Grandparents."

It takes a lot of people to keep the Garden State blooming. About 40,000 people farm in New Jersey. Orchids, roses, ornamental shrubs and other flowers are important money-making crops. New Jersey is also one of the nation's leading producers of tomatoes, blueberries, cranberries, spinach and peaches. Farms and forests cover two thirds of New Jersey.

The Pinelands are a 1.3 million acre undeveloped wilderness which covers about 20% of New Jersey. Nearly 13% of the state is covered with wetlands or marshes, including the Great Swamp, the Hackensack Meadowlands and the bogs and salt marshes of the Pinelands.

Several teams play at the Meadowlands Sports Complex in East Rutherland, New Jersey, including the New York Giants, the New York Jets (football), the New York Nets (basketball) and the New Jersey Devils (hockey).

On November 6, 1869, Rutgers beat Princeton 6 to 4 in the first college football game ever played.

The New York Nine beat the Knickerbocker Baseball Club at the first baseball game ever played. The score was 23 to 1 in Hoboken, New Jersey, on June 19, 1846.

In its state constitution in 1776, New Jersey became the first state to allow women to vote. In 1807, that right was taken away. Women in New Jersey were not allowed to vote until more than 100 years later.

Have you ever played Monopoly™? More than 150 million Monopoly™ games have been sold in 23 different languages. Charles Darrow invented the game in 1930 and named the streets after those in Atlantic City, his favorite vacation spot.

New Jersey had two capitals for a number of years. Burlington became the capital of West New Jersey in 1677, and Perth Amboy also became the capital of East New Jersey in 1686. Trenton become the capital in 1790.

Industry, farming, forests, major league sports! New Jersey has it all!

Welcome to New Mexico

Let's hurry to New Mexico. Maybe we'll be in time for the annual International Balloon Fiesta. Albuquerque holds the world's largest hot air balloon rally every fall.

Nickname: Land of Enchantment
State motto: It Grows as It Goes
State flower: Yucca flower
State tree: Piñon
State bird: Roadrunner
State animal: Black bear
State fish: New Mexico cutthroat trout
State insect: Tarantula hawk wasp
State gem: Turquoise
State fossil: Coelophysis
State vegetables: Chili pepper and pinto bean
State cookie: Biscochito
State song: "O, Fair New Mexico"
Capital: Santa Fe
Statehood: New Mexico became the 47th state on January 6, 1912.
1990 Population: 1,515,069: the 37th largest in population
Area: 121,593 square miles: New Mexico is the fifth largest state.
Neighbors: Colorado, Oklahoma, Texas, Arizona, Utah and Mexico

New Mexico was named for Mexico and originally called Nuevo Mejico.

A Long Ride

Three men from Albuquerque, New Mexico, were the first to complete a transatlantic crossing in a balloon. Starting from Presque Isle, Maine, they traveled 3,200 miles in their balloon the *Double Eagle II* to land in Miserey, France, in 1978. The journey took 137 hours and 18 minutes.

Describe the sights and sounds you would see if you took a balloon ride over your community. Draw a picture of your community as it would look while riding over it in a hot air balloon.

Discussion Question: What If?

What if everyone in New Mexico spoke Spanish?

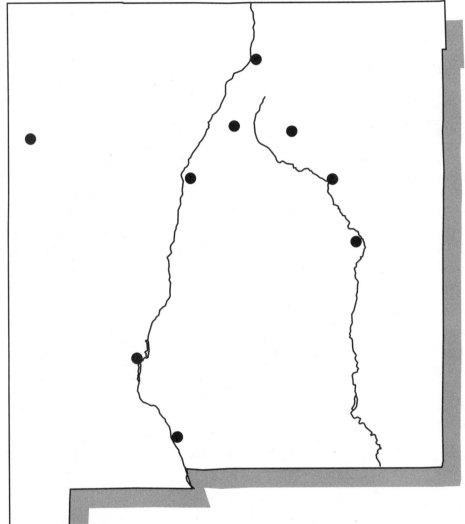

Label the underlined places on the New Mexico map.

<u>Albuquerque</u> is the largest city in New Mexico and the only one with a population of over 100,000.

<u>Santa Fe</u> is the highest of the 50 state capitals and the oldest capital in the country.

<u>Gallup</u> is known as the "Indian Capital of the World."

The Theodore Roosevelt Rough Riders' Memorial and Museum is located in <u>Las Vegas</u>, New Mexico.

More than 100 art galleries can be found in the small city of <u>Taos</u>.

Sheriff Pat Garrett killed Billy the Kid at <u>Fort Sumner</u>.

In 1950 the town of Hot Springs changed its name to <u>Truth or Consequences</u>.

<u>Las Cruces</u> means "the crosses" in Spanish.

<u>Colorado</u>, <u>Oklahoma</u>, <u>Texas</u>, <u>Arizona</u> and <u>Utah</u> border New Mexico. Label their approximate locations on the map above.

Draw a green line to show the New Mexico-Mexico border.

Trace the Rio Grande in blue and the Pecos River in red.

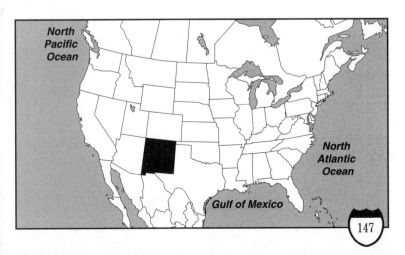

North Pacific Ocean

North Atlantic Ocean

Gulf of Mexico

147

A Long, Long Time

Scientists know that people have lived in New Mexico for a long, long time. Ears of corn dating from 3000 to 2000 B.C. have been found in Bat Cave. When 10,000-year-old spearheads were discovered in Folsom, people were impressed with how long people had been living in New Mexico. In the Sandia Mountains archaeologists discovered cave dwellings at least 20,000 years old. But in 1990, Dr. Richard MacNeish made an even more startling discovery. He found tools in the Orogrande Caves dating back 55,000 years. This is the oldest evidence of humans found anywhere in the Americas.

The people known as the Anasazi received their name from a Navajo word meaning "the ancient ones." The earliest evidence shows they were skillful weavers. They wove beautiful baskets and sandals from tree bark and plant fibers. They were a nomadic people, sometimes called the Basket People.

Later as they learned to farm, they built pit houses by digging a large round hole a few feet deep. They built slanted walls and flat roofs of tree limbs, bark and dirt. A fireplace in the center allowed smoke from cooking fires to escape. To enter and leave their homes, they used ladders.

When the Spanish first explored New Mexico, they found the Pueblo people, descendants of the Anasazi, as well as the nomadic Navajo and Apache.

Turquoise has long been cherished by the Native Americans of the Southwest, although they did not begin using it extensively for jewelry until the late 1800s. It is found in rock deposits in Arizona, New Mexico, Colorado and Nevada.

Apache medicine men wore turquoise. The Pueblos buried turquoise with their dead. Turquoise was used as ornaments and decorations in building and sometimes as money. In Pueblo Bonito, more than 50,000 pieces of handworked turquoise were found in one chamber.

Many of the early American legends include beliefs about turquoise, a gift from First Man. The Zunis said that turquoise was taken from the blue of the heavens, a gift of the sky and a protection from evil. They believed the beautiful blue stones had many powers—victory, good fortune and friendship. Turquoise was even considered a love charm. They believed turquoise guarded the wearer from harm.

The ideal color of turquoise is a cool sky blue. Most turquoise also has some variation of green in it. Spider-web turquoise has delicate black lines running through it.

Make up a story about turquoise, where it came from and what powers it has.

More to Discover

Encourage your students to learn more about New Mexico by exploring the topics and answering the questions below. Assign questions to different students or groups of students. Ask them to write short reports, do illustrations or share the information with the class in oral reports.

- What is adobe? How is it made? What is it used for?

- What is a kiva? What is a sipapu? What is a petroglyph?

- Why was Geronimo a famous Apache leader?

- What happened at Los Alamos?

- Describe a piñon tree.

- Describe what visitors see at Carlsbad Caverns.

- What was the Sante Fe Trail?

- Much of the early Americans' culture and history has been preserved in New Mexico. Ask students to describe what they could see at these places:

  Aztec Ruins National Monument

  Bandelier National Monument

  Chaco Culture National Historic Park

  Gila Cliff Dwellings National Monument

  Petroglyph National Monument

- The volcanos at Capulin Volcano National Monument have been dormant for about 10,000 years. What are volcanoes? How did volcanoes affect New Mexico?

- Describe these three land formations found in New Mexico: butte, mesa, canyon.

- How did a secret code formed from the Navajo language help the U.S. in World War II?

- How was New Mexico's largest lake, Elephant Butte Reservoir, formed?

- Javelinas live in New Mexico. What is a javelina? What does it look like?

- New Mexico's state fish is the cutthroat trout. How did this fish get its name? What does it look like?

- Dinosaur bones from tyrannosaurus rex and coelophysis were found in New Mexico. Learn more about one of these two dinosaurs.

- Select one of these New Mexico animals for a report: roadrunner, coyote, tarantula, jackrabbit, mountain lion, pronghorn.

- Prairie dogs are members of the squirrel family. Describe a prairie dog "town."

- The Pueblo people are descendants of the Anasazi. Learn more about the Zuni, Acoma, Hopi or Taos people of New Mexico.

149

Visit the Land of Enchantment

Design a travel poster to encourage people to visit New Mexico. You can use words, pictures from magazines or drawings for your poster.

How blue the sky looks in New Mexico, Land of Enchantment.

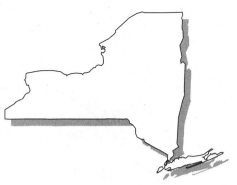

Welcome to New York

It's a long ride from New Mexico which borders on Mexico to New York which borders on Canada. There's so much to see. Where should we begin our tour of the Empire State?

Nickname: Empire State
State motto: Ever Upward
State flower: Rose
State tree: Sugar maple
State bird: Bluebird
State animal: Beaver
State fish: Brook trout
State insect: Ladybug
State gem: Garnet
State fruit: Apple
State song: "I Love New York"
Capital: Albany
Statehood: New York was one of the 13 original colonies and the eleventh to ratify the Constitution on July 26, 1788.
1990 Population: 17,990,455: the second largest in population
Area: 49,108 square miles: New York is the 30th largest state.
Neighbors: Pennsylvania; New Jersey; Connecticut; Massachusetts; Vermont; Quebec and Ontario, Canada; and the Atlantic Ocean

About New York

1. New York City was the capital of the U.S. from 1785 to 1790. What city became the country's next capital? _____

2. Which state has a larger population than New York? _____

   New York is home to nine professional teams. Name the sports played by these teams:

3. Yankees and Mets _____

4. Bills, Giants and Jets _____

5. Sabres, Islanders and Rangers _____

6. Knicks _____

   The highest peak in New York is Mount Macy, 5,344 feet above sea level.

7. How much higher than a mile is Mount Macy? _____

   Like Christopher Columbus before him, Henry Hudson, also searched for a shorter route to Asia. Instead of China, Hudson found New York. Although Hudson was English, he had been hired by the Netherlands. Based on his explorations along the Hudson River, the Dutch claimed parts of New York, New Jersey, Connecticut and Delaware.

8. What was the Dutch name for *New York*?

   _____

   When the English gained control of the area, they renamed it New York for James, the Duke of York and Albany.

   New York has cities named Alabama, Cuba, Florida, Greece, Mexico, Peru, Poland and Wyoming.

   Look at a map of New York. List some other cities with unusual names.

151

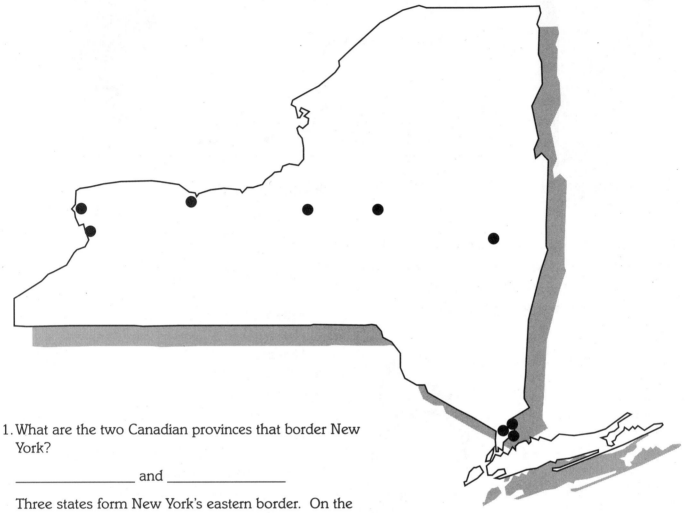

1. What are the two Canadian provinces that border New York?

   _____ and _____

   Three states form New York's eastern border. On the map above, label the approximate locations of Vermont, Massachusetts and Connecticut.

   On the map above, label the approximate locations of Pennsylvania and New Jersey, New York's neighbors to the south.

2. What are the two Great Lakes that border New York?

   Lake _____ and Lake _____

   Draw a star to show the location of Albany, the capital of New York.

   Draw a circle around the area that is New York City.

   Color Long Island green.

   Color the Atlantic Ocean blue.

   Put the number of each of these major cities in New York on the map above in the correct place.

   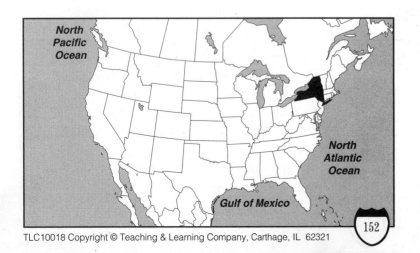

   1. Buffalo   6. New Rochelle
   2. Rochester   7. Mount Vernon
   3. Yonkers   8. Schenectady
   4. Syracuse   9. Niagara Falls
   5. Utica

The People of the Longhouse

During the Ice Age, most of New York was covered with glaciers, moving mountains of ice up to two miles thick. The glaciers carried rich soil across the state and created deep valleys which filled with water and became lakes. Prehistoric mastodons and mammoths roamed the state.

The first nomadic hunters reached New York about 11,000 years ago. Thousands of years later, many groups of Algonquian-speaking people and various groups of Iroquois settled in this area.

According to legend, the Iroquois waged war against each other until the Peacemaker came to Hiawatha in a canoe made of white stone. Together, the mysterious stranger and Hiawatha convinced the five tribes to stop fighting and make a pact known as the Great Law of Peace. Many features of the U.S. Constitution are similar to the Iroquois system of government.

The Mohawks, Oneida, Seneca, Onondaga and Cayuga called themselves **haudenosaunee**, "people of the longhouse." Many families lived together in one house which could be up to 200 feet long. Small tree trunks and saplings were used to build the frames. The walls and roof were covered with tree bark.

The Iroquois hunted, fished and farmed. They believed that all living things had souls that went on to another life after death. Women played an important role in tribal matters. They arranged marriages and approved or denied divorces. Children took their names from their mothers, not their fathers. When a man married, he moved into his wife's longhouse.

Describe life in an Iroquois longhouse.

_____
_____
_____
_____
_____
_____
_____
_____
_____
_____
_____
_____
_____
_____
_____
_____
_____
_____

A Look at the "Big Apple"

Read these facts about New York City. Write a report about one of the underlined places. Include pictures from magazines or illustrations in your report.

About 7.3 million people live in the Big Apple. Only nine states have more people than New York City. About 4 million people ride the subways of New York City every day. New York City is divided into five sections called boroughs. They are <u>Manhattan</u>, <u>Queens</u>, the <u>Bronx</u>, <u>Brooklyn</u> and <u>Staten Island</u>.

<u>Grand Central Terminal</u> is the world's largest railroad station.

When the <u>Empire State Building</u> opened in 1931, it was the world's tallest building.

The <u>World Trade Center</u> is the world's largest office center.

At <u>Carnegie Hall</u>, home of the New York Philharmonic Orchestra, concerts are given by many well-known musicians.

The <u>Metropolitan Museum of Art</u> is the largest art museum in the U.S.

The <u>Statue of Liberty</u> was a gift to the United States from France. It stands on <u>Liberty Island</u>.

Over 17 million immigrants to the United States entered the country at <u>Ellis Island</u>.

People who enjoy plays go the area of the city known as <u>Broadway</u>.

Thousands of people gather at <u>Times Square</u> to celebrate New Year's Eve.

Ballet and opera lovers attend performances at the <u>Lincoln Center for the Performing Arts</u>.

Lincoln Center also houses the <u>Julliard School of Music</u>.

The country's largest science museum is the <u>American Museum of Natural History</u>.

New York City has about 2,100 bridges, more than any other U.S. city. The <u>Brooklyn Bridge</u> was completed in 1883.

<u>Central Park</u> covers 840 acres in the middle of Manhattan.

<u>Fifth Avenue</u> is the place to shop if you're in New York City.

Another famous street is <u>Wall Street</u>, home of the <u>New York Stock Exchange</u>.

Who's Who from New York?

Use reference books to find the names of these famous New Yorkers. Choose the answers from the word bank.

1. Who was the author of *Rip Van Winkle* and *The Legend of Sleepy Hollow*?

   _____

2. Which New York writer is best known for his book *Moby Dick*?

   _____

3. Who wrote *The Wizard of Oz* and other books about Oz?

   _____

4. Which New York writer and illustrator's best known book is *Where the Wild Things Are*?

   _____

5. Which First Lady worked to help the poor while her husband, Franklin, was President?

   _____

6. A New York man invented a vaccine named after him that prevented polio. Who was he?

   _____

7. She was called "Grandma Moses" because she didn't begin painting until she was about 80 years old. What was her name?

   _____

8. Which New York Yankee made the record book with 23 home runs with the bases loaded and played in a record 2,130 straight games?

   _____

9. Sandy Koufax and Warren Spahn were great athletes. What sport did they play?

   _____

10. Which basketball player born in 1947 totaled 38,387 points during his career with the help of his famous "sky-hook"?

    _____

11. Who was the 13th President of the U.S. born in Locke, New York?

    _____

12. Which composer received a Pulitzer Prize for a musical comedy, *Of Thee I Sing*? He also wrote *Rhapsody in Blue*, *An American in Paris* and *Porgy and Bess*.

    _____

13. Born in New York City in 1882, he served as the city's mayor from 1934 to 1945. An airport was named for him. What was his name?

    _____

14. Which artist born in 1894 was best known for his illustrations for the cover of the *Saturday Evening Post* magazine?

    _____

15. The 26th President of the U.S. was born in New York City. He commanded the Rough Riders in Cuba during the Spanish-American War. What was his name?

    _____

16. The 32nd President was born in Hyde Park, New York. Who was the man known for his policy called the New Deal?

    _____

Word Bank

Herman Melville	baseball
Maurice Sendak	Jonas Salk
Norman Rockwell	George Gershwin
Lou Gehrig	Washington Irving
Frank Baum	Eleanor Roosevelt
Theodore Roosevelt	Fiorello LaGuardia
Millard Fillmore	Anna Moses
football	Abe Lincoln
Kareem Abdul-Jabbar	Franklin D. Roosevelt

The Rest of New York

New York City has much to offer. The state of New York also has many other interesting places worth visiting.

- Not everyone in New York lives in a big city. More than 100,00 New Yorkers live and work on farms.

Unscramble these letters to find important crops grown in New York:

1. PEALPS	5. RERIESCH
2. APERS	6. NABES
3. TELCUTE	7. BAGCABSE
4. RONC	8. STOPATOE

- If you'd like to see a state capitol building that looks like an old castle, visit Albany. The Dutch settled here in 1624. Albany became the capital of New York in 1797.

  9. What was the Dutch name for Albany?

- If you want to see a real castle, travel along the St. Lawrence River to the Ten Thousand Islands. There are more than 1,800 small islands here. On Heart Island, George Boldt built a 120-room castle as a gift for his wife.

Write a short story about what it would be like to live in your own castle.

- Like baseball? Visit the National Baseball Hall of Fame in Cooperstown.

- If you like the outdoors, you'll enjoy Adirondack Park which covers about 9,000 square miles and has 750 miles of hiking trails and hundreds of lakes.

10. Which lake in the Adirondack Mountains was the site of the 1932 and 1980 Winter Olympic Games?

- West of the Hudson River, the Catskill Mountains are a vacationer's paradise. Dozens of luxury hotels and resorts are located here. Visitors enjoy camping, hiking, fishing, swimming, golfing and skiing.

- Slavery was outlawed in New York in 1827. About 10,000 slaves were set free 34 years before the Civil War began.

- The Women's Rights National Historic Park is the site of the first Women's Rights Convention held in 1848. More than 300 people met in Seneca Falls to discuss the social condition of women.

- The Corning Glass Center depicts the 3,500-year-old history of glassmaking.

How is glass made? Why is Corning, New York, an important glassmaking center?

- In the western part of the state, the Niagara River forms the New York-Canada border. Every year 15 million people visit the two huge falls and many smaller ones that make up Niagara Falls, one of the most spectacular natural sights in the world.

Learn more about the spectacular Niagara Falls. Write a story about what it might be like to visit these great waterfalls. Describe the feel of the water spray and the thunderous sound of the falls. Illustrate your story.

Welcome to North Carolina

Don't get confused as we head south. Even though it was called *"Old North State"* and has the word <u>north</u> in its name, North Carolina is one of the southern states along the Atlantic Ocean.

Nicknames: Tar Heel State and Old North State
State motto: To Be Rather Than to Seem
State flower: Flowering dogwood
State tree: Pine
State bird: Cardinal
State mammal: Gray squirrel
State reptile: Turtle
State insect: Honeybee
State gem: Emerald
State shell: Scotch bonnet
State song: "The North State"
Capital: Raleigh
Statehood: November 21, 1789. North Carolina was one of the 13 original states and the twelfth to ratify the Constitution.
1990 Population: 6,628,637: the 10th largest in population
Area: 52,669 square miles: the 28th largest state
Neighbors: Virginia, South Carolina, Georgia, Tennessee and the Atlantic Ocean

Vanished

Early English explorers in the New World reported that Roanoke Island would be a good place to establish a colony. Six hundred men landed there in 1585 to establish the first English settlement but returned to England a year later.

Another group of 100 settlers landed at Roanoke Island in July 1587. On August 18, 1587, Virginia Dare was the first English child born in America. Shortly after, Governor White went back to England for supplies. He could not return to Roanoke until 1590. He found the letters *CRO* carved on one tree and the word *CROATOAN* carved on another but no trace of the colonists. The Croatoans were a group of Native Americans who lived nearby. Historians have never learned the fate of the "Lost Colony."

What do you think might have happened to the people on Roanoke Island? Be creative with your answer.

_____

_____

_____

_____

_____

_____

Discussion Question: What If?

What if the Roanoke settlers had flourished?

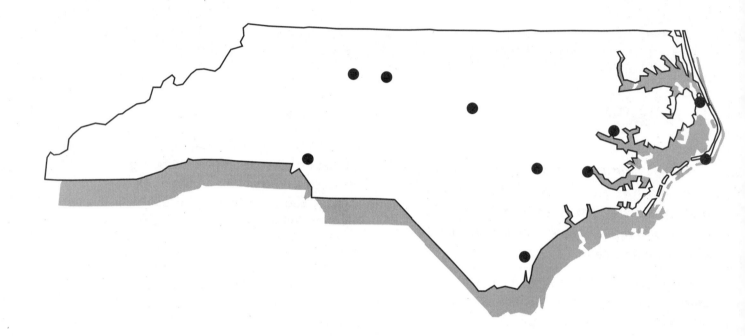

Write the names of the underlined places on the North Carolina map.

The capital city of <u>Raleigh</u> was named for Sir Walter Raleigh.

The city of <u>Bath</u> was named for Bath, England.

<u>New Bern</u> was named for Bern, Switzerland.

Nearly 100 battles were fought in North Carolina during the Civil War. The biggest battle took place at <u>Bentonville</u>, March 19-21, 1865.

A popular tourist attraction in <u>Wilmington</u> is the retired battleship *USS North Carolina* anchored at the city's waterfront.

In 1960, four African American college students sat at a "whites only" lunch counter in <u>Greensboro</u>. They refused to leave. "Sit-ins" became a way to fight for Civil Rights.

The towns of Winston and Salem were separate cities until they joined in 1913 to become <u>Winston-Salem</u>.

<u>Charlotte</u>, North Carolina's largest city, was named for Queen Charlotte, wife of King George III.

The first two English settlements began on <u>Roanoke Island</u>. Neither were successful.

At <u>Cape Hatteras</u> you'll find the tallest lighthouse in the United States.

<u>Virginia</u>, <u>South Carolina</u>, <u>Georgia</u>, <u>Tennessee</u> and the <u>Atlantic Ocean</u> form the borders of North Carolina. Label their approximate locations on the map above.

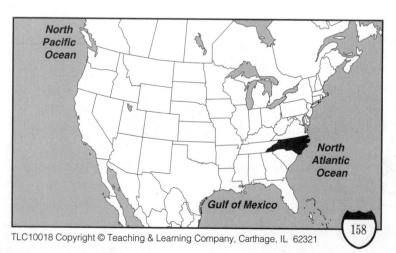

The First North Carolinians

Millions of years ago, most of eastern North Carolina was covered by the ocean. Mammoths and mastodons lived on the land. The first people arrived here about 10,000 years ago. They hunted and fished. Later they learned to grow corn, beans and squash. Evidence suggests that people in this area may have been the first to use pottery.

In the 1500s when European explorers arrived, about 35,000 people lived in the area that became North Carolina. They belonged to about 30 different groups. The Cherokees lived in the Blue Ridge and Smoky Mountains. The central part of the state was home to the Cheraw, the Keyauwee, the Waxhaw and the Catawba who lived along the Catawba River. The Tuscaroras, Pamlico and Coree lived along the coastal plain. The Croatoans (Hatteras) and Roanokes lived along the coast and the Outer Banks.

Some of the people lived in wigwams made of wooden poles covered with bark and clay. They made clothing from animal skins and used small bones as fishhooks. Shells were used as a form of money.

Native Americans in this area held planting and harvesting festivals. They celebrated with feasts and games. For one game, tree poles were sunk into the ground as goalposts. Two teams used sticks to send a deerskin ball towards each other's goals.

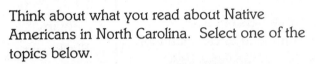

Think about what you read about Native Americans in North Carolina. Select one of the topics below.

- What modern games sound similar to the one played by the early Americans? How are they alike?

- What if people used shells for money today? Write a short story about going to the store with a pocket full of shells.

- Imagine living in a wigwam. What would be the advantages? What would be the disadvantages?

- How was a wigwam constructed? Draw the steps to make a wigwam.

- Select one of the groups of Native Americans who lived in North Carolina and write about their customs.

Great Smoky Mountains National Park

The Great Smoky Mountains are part of a larger range, the Appalachians, which extend from Canada southwest through the United States as far south as Alabama and Georgia.

The name Smoky Mountains comes from a Cherokee word *shagonigei* which means "blue smoke place." A blue smoky haze almost always blankets the mountains. The haze is formed by water vapor and natural plant oils released into the air by the forests that cover the mountains.

Early settlers cut trees for building and to clear land for crops. In the early 1900s when timber became valuable, lumber companies cut millions of trees. By the 1930s, about 70% of the area had been stripped. The once-beautiful mountains were bare and ugly. Few birds or animals lived there.

John D. Rockefeller contributed $5 million and Tennessee and North Carolina each contributed $2 million to buy land.

In 1934, the Great Smoky Mountains National Park was set up on a half million acres of wilderness in Tennessee and North Carolina. To rebuild the land, no logging or hunting was allowed. Today, the mountains, once stripped bare, are again covered with trees. More than 60 species of mammals, 200 types of birds, 100 kinds of trees and 1,500 species of flowering plants can be found in the park.

Visitors enjoy camping, fishing and hiking. The park includes almost 900 miles of hiking trails and 270 miles of roads. Dozens of log houses, churches, barns, mills and school buildings are preserved in the park. Some of these historic buildings are "living museums" where the skills of our pioneer ancestors are demonstrated for visitors.

Write the names of these plants and animals you might see as you hike through the Great Smoky Mountains National Park. Use the list in the box to help identify them.

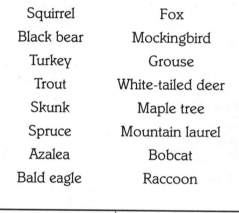

Squirrel	Fox
Black bear	Mockingbird
Turkey	Grouse
Trout	White-tailed deer
Skunk	Maple tree
Spruce	Mountain laurel
Azalea	Bobcat
Bald eagle	Raccoon

Bits and Pieces

- North and South Carolina were named in honor of King Charles I of England. *Carolina* comes from the Latin word *Carolana* meaning "Land of Charles."

If you could name a place after yourself, what would you call it? Make up a name that means "Land of . . . (your name)."

- Pirates in North Carolina? That's right. Pirates were a problem in both North and South Carolina until 1718. They hid in the Outer Banks, a region of sandbars and islands along the coast. When a ship passed, the  pirates raised their flag and attacked. Blackbeard, Stede Bonnet, Anne Bonney and Mary Read had their headquarters here.

- The Venus flytrap grows in the wild in only two states: North and South Carolina. This unusual plant captures insects with its leaves, then produces a liquid that turns the insects into food it can eat.

Learn more about the Venus flytrap or other plants that grow wild in North Carolina.

- Like to holler? You might want to attend the annual National Hollerin' Contest in Spivey's Corner held in June. If you don't want to yell, you could enjoy the music, dancing and barbecue.

- During the Civil War, it was said that troops from North Carolina stuck to their posts as if held by tar. That's one explanation of why North Carolina is called the Tar Heel State. One of the first industries in North Carolina was making tar.

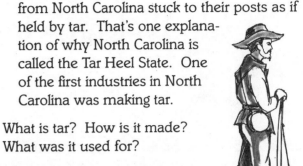

What is tar? How is it made? What was it used for?

- Most people have heard of the Boston Tea Party, but have you ever heard of the revolutionary tea party held in North Carolina? In 1774 women in North Carolina protested the English tax on tea and pledged not to use British products. This became known as the Edenton Tea Party.

- Presidents James Polk and Andrew Johnson and First Lady Dolly Madison were born in North Carolina.

Name some other famous people from this state.

- Wilbur and Orville Wright made history near Kitty Hawk in 1903 when they flew the first powered, heavier-than-air plane. They didn't fly very high, or very far, or very fast, or for very long, but they did fly!

How has the invention of the airplane changed our lives?

Nothing could be finer than to be in North Carolina in the morning.

Welcome to North Dakota

North Dakota is a lot farther north than North Carolina. We'll travel to the Canadian border to visit the geographic center of North America.

Nicknames: Flickertail State, Peace Garden State, the Sioux State and the Rough Rider State

State motto: Liberty and Union, Now and Forever, One and Inseparable

State flower: Wild prairie rose

State tree: American elm

State bird: Western meadowlark

State fish: Northern pike

State fossil: Teredo petrified wood

State drink: Milk

State grass: Western wheatgrass

State march: "Spirit of the Land"

State song: "North Dakota Hymn"

Capital: Bismarck

Statehood: North Dakota became the 39th state on November 2, 1889.

1990 Population: 638,800. North Dakota is the fourth smallest state in population.

Population density: 9.2 people per square mile

Area: 70,702 square miles: the 17th largest state

Neighbors: Minnesota, South Dakota, Montana, Saskatchewan and Manitoba

Did You Know?

- The world's largest buffalo stands on a hill overlooking Jamestown, North Dakota. The 60-ton steel and concrete bison rises 26 feet high.

- Important North Dakota crops include spring wheat, flaxseed, sunflowers, barley, pinto beans, rye and sugar beets.

- Usually we don't think of clay as a natural resource, but in North Dakota clay is mined and made into bricks and ceramic products. Salt is mined from deposits left by a salt sea that once covered the state.

- Named for the President who was a great conservationist, Theodore Roosevelt National Park covers 70,000 acres of North Dakota badlands and prairie.

What types of birds, animals, plants and trees live in this national park?

- North Dakota is nicknamed the Flickertail State. A flickertail sounds like a type of bird, but it's not.

What is a flickertail?

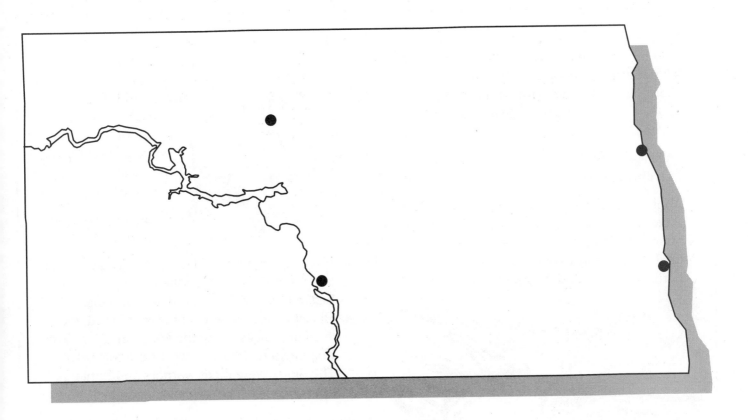

On the map above, label the approximate locations of the three states that border North Dakota: Minnesota, South Dakota and Montana.

On the map above, label the approximate locations of the two Canadian provinces north of North Dakota: Saskatchewan and Manitoba.

According to the 1990 census, only four cities in North Dakota had more than 20,000 people.

Match the population figure with the correct city:

1. Bismarck	34,544
2. Fargo	49,425
3. Grand Forks	49,256
4. Minot	74,111

Label these four cities on the North Dakota state map.

More or Less?

What is the population of your city? _____

How many more (or less) people live in your city than in Bismarck, the capital of North Dakota? _____

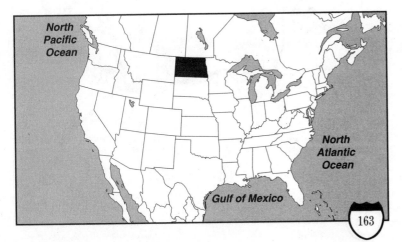

Early North Dakota

- Millions of years ago, North Dakota was covered by a salt sea. When the sea dried up, it left deposits of limestone, sandstone and shale. Combined with the remains of plants and sea animals, oil and lignite coal were formed.

What is lignite coal? How is lignite coal different than anthracite coal?

- About a million years ago, the climate in North Dakota became colder. Year after year more snow fell. Winters became longer and longer until glaciers formed over the land. As they partially melted and froze, over and over, the

powerful sheets of ice and snow moved across the state like a gigantic bulldozer.

How did the glaciers affect the topography (surface features of the land) of North Dakota?

- When the climate finally warmed, the glaciers retreated and people began moving into the area. Some knives, dart points and stone tools are evidence of the early nomads who hunted the great mammoths and mastodons.

What does the word *nomad* mean?

- Five major groups of Native Americans lived in the North Dakota area when Europeans first began to settle the area. The Mandans, Hidastsas and Arikaras hunted, farmed and lived in villages along the Missouri River. The Chippewa had moved west from Minnesota. The Sioux were great warriors and hunters of the Plains.

Why did the Chippewa move to North Dakota from Minnesota?

Horses were not native to North America. How did the Sioux and other tribes obtain horses?

How did horses change the way the Plains Indians lived?

At the Center of the Continent

A stone monument near Rugby, North Dakota, marks the geographic center of the entire North American continent. From Rugby, it is about 1,500 miles to the **Arctic Ocean** on the north, the **Gulf of Mexico** on the south, the **Atlantic Ocean** on the east and the **Pacific Ocean** on the west.

Label these four places on the map below.

More About North Dakota

- Temperature differences from winter to summer in North Dakota are among the most extreme of any place on the continent. Winters tend to be long and cold. Summers are usually short and hot. Because there are few trees and no mountains, the wind blows almost all the time across the plains of North Dakota causing dust storms and blizzards.

Why would the lack of mountains and forests cause the state to be windy?

- North Dakota has four nicknames: the Flickertail State, the Rough Rider State, the Peace Garden State and the Sioux State.

Explain how North Dakota received one of its four nicknames.

- In some ways, North Dakota is very different from its neighbors.

Select one topic listed below. Compare and contrast North Dakota with South Dakota, Montana, Minnesota, Saskatchewan or Manitoba.

- Climate
- Wildlife
- Topography (land forms)
- Agricultural products
- Manufacturing
- Natural resources
- Economy
- Early settlers

Isn't it great to be at the very center of the whole continent?

Welcome to Ohio

Let's head east to the Buckeye State, birthplace of seven U.S. Presidents.

Nicknames: Buckeye State, Mother of Presidents and Mother of Inventors

State motto: With God, All Things Are Possible

State flower: Scarlet carnation

State tree: Buckeye

State bird: Cardinal

State insect: Ladybug

State stone: Flint

State fossil: Isotelus (trilobite)

State drink: Tomato juice

State song: "Beautiful Ohio"

Capital: Columbus

Statehood: Ohio became the 17th state on March 1, 1803.

1990 Population: 10,847,115: the 7th largest in population

Area: 41,330 square miles: Only 15 other states are smaller.

Neighbors: Pennsylvania, Indiana, Michigan, West Virginia, Kentucky and Lake Erie

Did You Know?

- Ohio has cities and towns that begin with every letter of the alphabet—even *J*, *Q*, *X* and *Z*.

- The country's first antislavery newspaper, the *Philanthropist,* was published in 1817 in Point Pleasant, Ohio.

- *Ohio* is from an Iroquois word meaning "something great" or "beautiful."

- Cleveland, Ohio, became the first U.S. city with electric street lights in 1879.

Slow Reading

Don't forget to return your library books, or you could face a large fine. A book taken from the Cincinnati library in 1823 was returned by the borrower's grandson 145 years later. Luckily he did not have to pay the overdue fine. It would have been $2,264!

1. What year was the book returned?

2. If a library charged 10 cents a day for each day a book was overdue, how much would the fine be for a book overdue exactly 50 years? (Don't worry about leap years.)

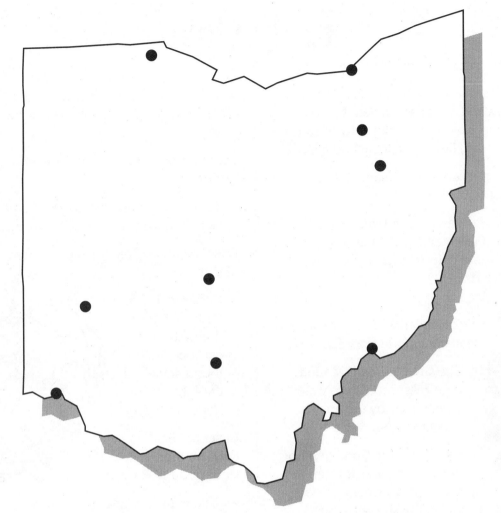

Write the names of the underlined places on the Ohio map.

<u>Columbus</u> is the capital and largest city in Ohio.

<u>Cleveland</u> was named for Moses Cleaveland who founded the city. Due to a spelling error by a newspaper in 1831, the first "a" in *Cleaveland* was omitted. *Cleveland* has been spelled that way ever since.

Organized in 1869, the <u>Cincinnati</u> Red Stockings (the Reds) is baseball's oldest professional team.

The National Football League (NFL) began in <u>Canton</u> in 1920.

Have you ever heard anyone say "Holy Toledo"? They could be talking about <u>Toledo</u>, Spain, or Toledo, Ohio.

<u>Akron</u> means "high point" in Greek.

<u>Chillicothe</u> became the capital of Ohio in 1803.

<u>Marietta</u>, the oldest city in Ohio, was founded in 1788.

James Ritty of <u>Dayton</u> invented the cash register in 1879.

Five states border Ohio: <u>Pennsylvania</u>, <u>Indiana</u>, <u>Michigan</u>, <u>West Virginia</u> and <u>Kentucky</u>. Label their approximate locations on the map above.

Early Ohio

- Millions of years ago, Ohio was covered with shallow seas and swamps. When the water receded, Ohio was left with deposits of sandstone, shale, salt, limestone, coal and oil.

Write a short report about how sandstone, shale, limestone, coal or oil was formed.

- The first people who lived in Ohio arrived about 10,000 years ago. They left little except some chipped flint knives and spearheads.

Use diagrams to show how knives, spearheads or arrowheads are made from flint.

- The Great Serpent Mound near Hillsboro, Ohio, was constructed by the ancient Adena people.

How long is the Great Serpent Mound? Why was it given that name? Draw or make a clay model in the shape of this mound.

- At Fort Ancient, three miles of walls enclose nearly 100 acres of land. This earthwork ceremonial site was built about 2,000 years ago.

Who built Fort Ancient? Why would a group build a wall three miles long?

- The Hopewell people lived in the Ohio Valley from about 100 B.C. to 500 A.D. At Mound City Group National Monument 23 prehistoric Hopewell burial mounds have been preserved.

Describe the Hopewell culture.

- Tecumseh and Tenshwatawa tried to unite several groups to fight against the white settlers.

Give an oral report about these two Shawnee brothers.

- Zoar Village was built in 1817 by a group of Germans who sought religious freedom.

Describe life in Zoar Village as it was in the 1800s.

- Between 1825 and 1865 more than 2,000 escaped slaves found shelter at the John Rakin house in Ripley.

Describe this "station" on the Underground Railroad.

- Ohio is nicknamed the "Buckeye State."

What is a buckeye? Describe it and draw a picture of it.

- The isotelus (trilobite) is Ohio's state fossil.

Describe a trilobite and draw a picture of one.

- Ohio had two other capitals before Columbus became the capital in 1816.

Where were the first two capitals? Why was the capital moved?

Name These Famous Ohioans

1. Who was the first American to orbit the Earth on February 20, 1962?

   _____

2. The first person to set foot on the moon was born in Ohio. What was his name?

   _____

3. Who wrote *Make Way for Ducklings* and *Time of Wonder*?

   _____

4. Considered one of the world's greatest inventors, he held patents for the incandescent electric lamp and the phonograph. He also invented wax paper and a talking doll. Who was he?

   _____

Seven U.S. Presidents were born in Ohio. Who were they? Their initials should give you a clue.

5. U.S.G. _____

6. R.B.H. _____

7. J.A.G. _____

8. B.H. _____

9. W.M. _____

10. W.H.T. _____

11. W.G.H. _____

12. Two brothers invented the first successful self-propelled airplane. Who were they?

    _____

13. Harriet Beecher Stowe lived in Cincinnati in the mid-1800s. What was the name of her famous book?

    _____

14. A writer of popular Westerns, was born in Zanesville, a town named for his great

great grandfather. Who was he?

   _____

15. Phoebe Moses was a sharpshooter who traveled with Buffalo Bill's Wild West Show. What was her nickname?

   _____

16. Born in Geneva, Ohio, he founded the Olds Motor Works in Detroit, Michigan, in 1899. What was his name?

   _____

17. Who directed many popular movies including *Jaws*, *E.T.* and *Raiders of the Lost Ark*?

   _____

Sports Spotlight

1. What are Ohio's two major league baseball teams?

   _____ and _____

2. What are Ohio's two professional football teams?

   _____ and _____

3. What is Ohio's professional basketball team?

   _____

4. Where is the Football Hall of Fame located?

   _____

5. This athlete grew up in Ohio and starred on the Ohio State University Track Team. He won the 100- and 200-meter races and the long jump competition at the 1936 Olympics. Who was he?

   _____

Wouldn't it be great to find a fossil of a trilobite!

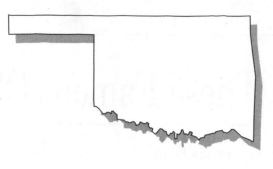

Welcome to Oklahoma

We won't have any trouble traveling across Oklahoma, where the wind comes sweepin' down the plain.

Nicknames: Sooner State, Boomer State, Land of Six Countries and America's Frontier Lake State

State motto: Labor Conquers All Things

State flower: Mistletoe

State wildflower: Indian blanket

State tree: Redbud

State bird: Scissor-tailed flycatcher

State animal: American bison

State fish: White bass or sand bass

State rock: Barite rose rock

State song: "Oklahoma!"

Capital: Oklahoma City

Statehood: Oklahoma became the 46th state to join the Union on November 17, 1907.

1990 Population: 3,145,585: the 28th largest in population

Area: 69,956 square miles: the 18th largest state

Neighbors: Kansas, Colorado, Arkansas, Missouri, Texas and New Mexico

Did You Know?

- The word *Oklahoma* came from two Choctaw words meaning "red people."

- At the top of Poteau Mountain, in Heavener Runestone State Park, a stone stairway leads down into a small valley where a 12-foot high, 10-foot wide runestone is encased in a glass shelter. The runes (letters) may have been carved by Norse explorers. Not all scientists agree, but the runes may be the date November 11, 1012 A.D. Two other inscriptions found nearby may be translated as November 11, 1017, and November 24, 1024.

- Some famous Oklahomans include Ralph Ellison, Woody Gutherie, Mickey Mantle, Will Rogers and Jim Thorpe.

- Rome may not have been built in a day, but some cities in Oklahoma were. In March 1889, Benjamin Harrison announced that two million acres of land would be opened to white settlers at noon on April 22. When noon arrived, 50,000 settlers rushed across the Oklahoma border to claim land. Overnight, Oklahoma City became a tent city of 10,000 and Gutherie acquired a population of 15,000 in a single day.

What's in a Name?

Explain how Oklahoma received one of its nicknames: Sooner State, Boomer State, Land of Six Countries or America's Frontier Lake State.

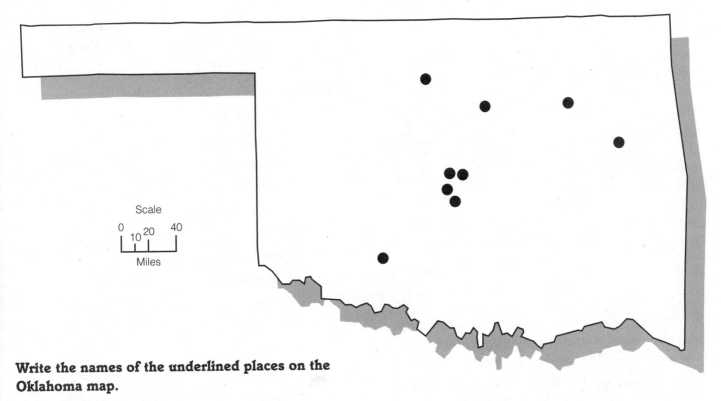

Write the names of the underlined places on the Oklahoma map.

Kansas, Colorado, Arkansas, Missouri, Texas and New Mexico border Oklahoma. Label the approximate locations of these states on the map above.

The Red River forms the southern boundary between Oklahoma and Texas. Draw a red line along the Red River.

The National Cowboy Hall of Fame and Western Heritage Center in Oklahoma City house John Wayne's collection of guns, knives, saddles, art and kachina dolls. Put a star on the map to show the location of Oklahoma City.

Visitors to the Wichita Mountains Wildlife Refuge near Lawton can watch herds of bison and longhorn cattle.

A large collection of modern Native American art is housed in the Five Civilized Tribes Museum in Muskogee. Label Muskogee.

The "panhandle" is the long, thin strip of land in northwest Oklahoma that looks like the handle of a pan. The Panhandle was once known as No Man's Land. Color the panhandle green.

Use the map scale to determine the width and length of the panhandle.

Width: _____

Length: _____

Label these other major cities in Oklahoma:

Norman	Enid	Midwest City
Stillwater	Moore	Tulsa

Many People, Many Thousands of Years

The earliest inhabitants of Oklahoma were known as Clovis Man, people who shared the land with mammoths, giant bisons, small horses and camels about 11,600 years ago. They were replaced by a group known as the Folsom Culture, 10,000 years ago, and then followed by those of the Plano Culture.

Over the centuries, Oklahoma's climate gradually changed, and the animals that lived there also changed. Those who lived in Oklahoma after the Ice Age were known as the Paleo People. They hunted and gathered food which they stored in caves where they lived during the winter.

About 800 A.D. the Mound Builders flourished in eastern Oklahoma. Between about 1200 and 1350, their civilization dominated the area, carrying on trade with groups far to the east and south.

By the time Europeans explorers arrived, Oklahoma was home to the Kiowa, Comanche, Plains Apache, Caddo, Wichita, Pawnee, Quapaw and Osage.

Beginning in 1804, the first of many laws were passed designed to remove all Native Americans living anywhere east of the Mississippi River. More than 60 tribes were forced to move west to the Indian Territory of Oklahoma.

Today, more people descended from Native Americans live in Oklahoma than in any other state except California.

Select one of these topics for a report:

- Clovis Man
- Plainview Man
- Folsom Man
- Paleo People
- Mound Builders
- Kiowa
- Comanche
- Plains Apache
- Caddo
- Wichita
- Pawnee
- Quapaw
- Osage
- Kachina dolls
- Trail of Tears
- Indian Removal Act
- Five Civilized Tribes
- One of the "nations" in Oklahoma

The Natural World of Oklahoma

- Rocky Mountain elk and deer roam free in the Wichita Mountains Wildlife Refuge near Lawton. Here visitors can watch herds of bison and longhorn cattle, and even visit a prairie dog town.

- Oh, give me a home where the kangaroos roam, where the yaks and the ostriches play . . . . Those aren't the words to the Oklahoma state song, but they could be. Some unusual animals roam free in Oklahoma's 400-acre Arbuckle Wilderness including llamas, yaks, gnus, giraffes, lions, ostriches, kangaroos, antelope and bighorn sheep.

- You'll also find antelopes, rabbits, coyotes, armadillos, horned lizards and opossums in Oklahoma. The name *armadillo* comes from a Spanish word meaning "little armored one." Although they look something like scaly lizards, armadillos are mammals. Female armadillos always give birth to four identical quadruplets.

What do armadillos eat? How do they protect themselves? How large are they when fully grown?

Something to Crow About

- As many as 10 million crows arrive at the world's largest crow roost in Fort Cobb Recreation Area every October.

- Once hunted for its long tail feathers, the scissor-tailed flycatcher is now protected by state law.

- Almost every type of bird that lives between the Rocky Mountains and the Mississippi River makes its home in Oklahoma.

Unscramble the names of these birds found in Oklahoma:

1. lube yajs	5. darcnails	9. vodes
2. lowwasls	6. borins	10. looreis
3. rowparss	7. liqua	11. greets
4. rohens	8. worcs	12. rudnoarners

Look at that roadrunner go! No wonder Wile E. Coyote could never catch it.

173

Welcome to Oregon

From the Pacific coast, across mountains, canyons and lush green valleys, we'll visit Oregon, the Pacific Wonderland.

Nickname: Beaver State
State motto: She Flies with Her Own Wings
State flower: Oregon grape
State tree: Douglas fir
State bird: Western meadowlark
State animal: Beaver
State fish: Chinook salmon
State insect: Oregon swallowtail butterfly
State gem: Sunstone
State rock: Thunder egg (geode)
State dance: Square dance
State song: "Oregon, My Oregon"
Capital: Salem
Statehood: Oregon became the 33rd state on February 14, 1859.
1990 Population: 2,842,321: the 29th largest in population
Area: 97,073 square miles: the 10th largest state
Neighbors: Washington, Idaho, Nevada, California and the Pacific Ocean

Rich in Resources

Oregon produces more than 170 different crops including wheat, cranberries, hazelnuts, apples, pears, cherries, sugar beets and peppermint. Although salmon are the most valuable catch, tuna, flounder, oysters, rockfish and sturgeon are also important to the commercial fishing industry. The Beaver State is rich in other natural resources: gold, silver, iron, copper, bauxite and timber.

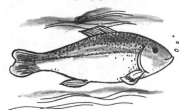

Oregon leads the nation in lumber production. To preserve the ecology, logging companies must plant trees to replace the ones they cut. In more than two million acres of forest, logging is not permitted. Conservationists object when trees in "old-growth" forests are cut.

What is an old-growth forest? Why do conservationists object? Why would lumber companies want to cut trees in old-growth forests?

Discussion Question: What If?

If you could visit Oregon, what site would you most like to see? Why? If you live in Oregon, what is your favorite place to visit? Why?

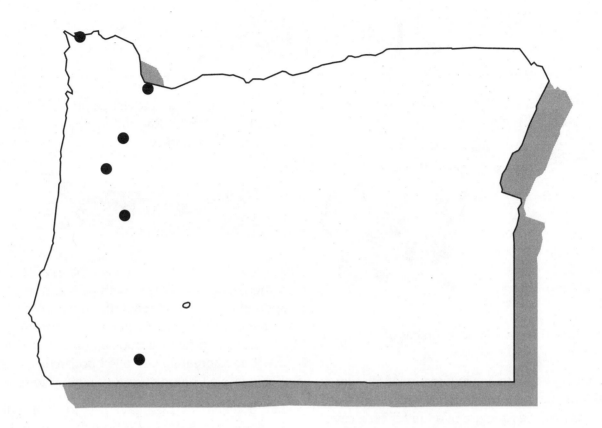

Label the underlined places on the Oregon state map.

The <u>Columbia River</u> forms most of the border between Oregon and <u>Washington</u>. Label the approximate location of Washington on the map above.

The <u>Snake River</u> flows along the northern border between Oregon and <u>Idaho</u>. Carved by the Snake River, Hells Canyon, the deepest gorge in North America, dips 8,000 feet in some places.

<u>California</u> and <u>Nevada</u> border Oregon on the south. Label their approximate locations on the map above.

The <u>Pacific Ocean</u> forms the west coast of Oregon.

<u>Crater Lake</u>, the deepest lake in the nation, lies in the crater of an extinct volcano. It was formed about 6,000 years ago when an eruption blew the top off Mount Mazama. The water in this lake, is extremely blue.

<u>Astoria</u> began as a trading post in 1811. It became the first permanent settlement in Oregon.

When the capital was moved to <u>Salem</u> in 1852, it was a small village. For a time, <u>Corvallis</u> became the capital; then it was changed again, back to Salem.

The Willamette River flows through the center of <u>Portland</u>, a city known for its beautiful parks and gardens. Washington Park includes a five-acre Japanese Garden. Ten thousand rose bushes bloom in the Rose Test Garden. The 5,000-acre Forest Park contains 30 miles of hiking trails.

<u>Medford</u>, located in a fruit-growing region, holds a Pear Blossom Festival every April.

<u>Eugene</u> was named for its first white settler, Eugene F. Skinner.

Early Oregon

John Day Fossil Beds National Monument contains the fossilized bones of animals that lived in eastern Oregon 30 million years ago. Displays at the visitors center include remains of three-toed horses, giant pigs and saber-toothed cats.

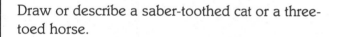

Draw or describe a saber-toothed cat or a three-toed horse.

The earliest people to live in Oregon left no written records, no large mounds, no great temples or villages. A faded picture of a hunter on a cave wall at Fort Rock is one of the few pieces of evidence left by people who lived in Oregon as long ago as 13,000 B.C. Another unusual find included 70 sandals made from woven cord and sagebrush bark.

By the time white settlers arrived in Oregon, about 38,000 people from nearly 100 different tribes lived there. The five major groups were the Klamaths, Modocs, Paiutes, Nez Perce and Chinooks.

The Klamaths and Modocs lived in pit houses in the Klamath Mountains and along the shore of Lake Klamath. The land of the Paiutes received little rain. Food was often a problem, and they struggled to survive. The Nez Perce lived in northeastern Oregon. They, like the people of the Great Plains, became great horsemen.

The Chinooks lived and fished along the coast near the Columbia River. They traveled the coastal waters and swift rivers in cedar canoes.

Food was plentiful. They became excellent fishermen, catching salmon with nets and traps, spearing them or shooting them with bows and arrows. To celebrate important events, the Chinooks and other groups along the northwest coast, held great feasts called potlatches. *Potlatch* is a Chinook word meaning "to give."

At a potlatch, the host gave gifts to all his guests. By doing this, he showed how wealthy and important he was.

What types of gifts did the Chinooks give to guests at a potlatch?

What events were important enough to hold a potlatch?

Write an invitation to a potlatch. What gifts could you give to people at your potlatch?

More About Oregon

Use reference books to learn more about Oregon. Answer the assigned questions below.

• Oregon is divided by
the Cascade
Mountains that
run north to
south.
Oregon's climate is very different west of the mountains than it is on the east side of the Cascades.

How do the Cascade Mountains affect Oregon's climate?

• Millions of migratory birds
visit Oregon as they follow
the Pacific flyway.

What is the Pacific flyway?

• John McLoughlin is known as the Father of Oregon. Why?

• Lava Lands is a geological wonderland of volcanic formations including Lava Butte, a 500-foot cinder cone, Lava River Cave, a one-mile long lava tube and the world's largest forest of lava-cast trees.

What are lava-cast trees?

• Oregon Caves National
Monument contains limestone
rock formations known as
Paradise Lost, the River Styx,
Petrified Garden and Banana
Grove.

Describe one of these natural rock formations.

• John Jacob Astor organized the American Fur Company in 1808.

What was the purpose of the American Fur company?

• To encourage people to move to Oregon, Congress passed the Oregon Donation Land Law in 1850.

What was the Oregon Donation Land Law?

• Many people in New England and the Midwest were struck with Oregon Fever in the 1850s.

What was Oregon Fever?

• Along some sections of the Oregon Trail, ruts left by the wheels of covered wagons can still be seen. The Oregon Trail began in Independence, Missouri, and led thousands of settlers to Oregon and Washington, a distance of about 2,000 miles.

Show the Oregon Trail on a map. If a group of settlers left Independence on April 1 and averaged 12 miles a day, when would they arrive at the end of the trail?

I'd like to watch some of the sea lions and humpback whales that live along the Pacific coast.

Welcome to Pennsylvania

Although the Liberty Bell hasn't rung since it cracked in 1835, we can see this symbol of the U.S. in Philadelphia, the City of Brotherly Love.

Nicknames: Keystone State and Quaker State

State motto: Virtue, Liberty and Independence

State flower: Mountain laurel

State tree: Eastern hemlock

State bird: Ruffed grouse

State animal: White-tailed deer

State dog: Great Dane

State fish: Brook trout

State insect: Firefly

State song: None

Capital: Harrisburg

Statehood: Pennsylvania was the second of the 13 original colonies to become a state on December 12, 1787.

1990 Population: 11,881,643: the 5th largest in population

Area: 45,302 square miles: the 33rd largest state

Neighbors: New York, New Jersey, Delaware, Maryland, West Virginia and Ohio

Did You Know?

- The official name of the state is the Commonwealth of Pennsylvania.

- When Ben Franklin was 17, he was apprenticed to a printer. He ran away from his master in Boston and became a prominent writer, inventor and diplomat in Philadelphia. He established the first circulating library in the colonies and formed America's first volunteer fire department.

- Although Boone County and Booneville, Kentucky, were named for him, Daniel Boone was a Quaker, born in Pennsylvania.

- In 1769, a 69-mile stone-surfaced road was completed between Philadelphia and Lancaster. To pay for the project, which cost nearly half a million dollars, travelers paid tolls at gates, called pikes, along the road. The toll collector turned the pike to let travelers continue on their way. The word *turnpike* came to mean "a toll road."

- Philadelphia carpenters staged the first strike in 1791. They demanded that their workday be shortened to 12 hours.

What Can You Find in *Pennsylvania*?

How many words can you make using the letters in the word *Pennsylvania*?

- Words must be three or more letters.

- Words made by adding *S* to the end do not count.

- Proper nouns may be used.

Letters to use: A A E I L N N N P S V Y

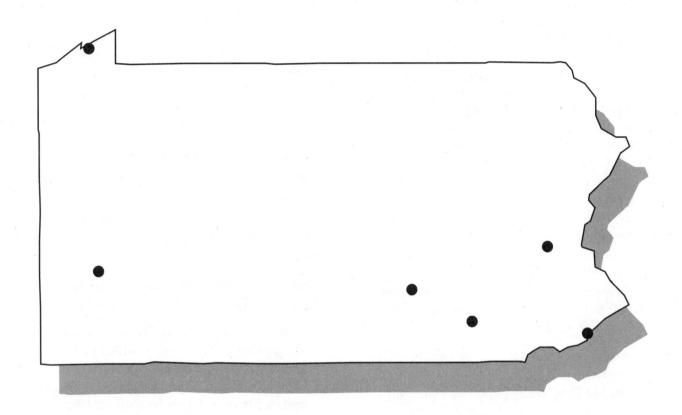

Label the underlined places on the Pennsylvania state map.

Lake Erie forms the northwest boundary of Pennsylvania. Label its approximate location on the map above.

The Delaware River separates Pennsylvania from New Jersey.

Delaware, Maryland and West Virginia border Pennsylvania on the south. Label their approximate locations on the map above.

New York is Pennsylvania's neighbor to the north and east. Label its approximate location on the map above.

Ohio is west of Pennsylvania. Label its approximate location on the map above.

Philadelphia is from a Greek term meaning the "City of Brotherly Love." In 1799, the capital of Pennsylvania was moved from Philadelphia to Lancaster.

Originally the site of a British fort, Fort Pitt eventually became the city of Pittsburgh.

The city of Erie grew on the site of Fort Presque, built by the French in 1753.

The state capital was moved to its present location in Harrisburg in 1812.

The Liberty Bell Shrine at Allentown commemorates the time the famous bell was hidden at Zion United Church of Christ during the Revolutionary War.

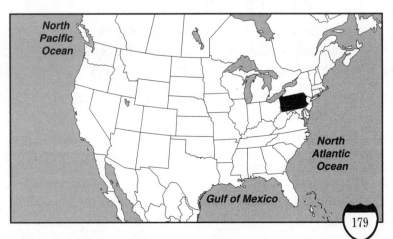

The Pennsylvania Colony

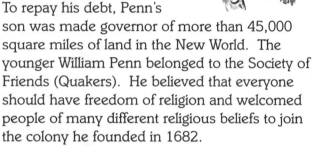

The name *Pennsylvania* means "Penn's Woods." The name was given by King Charles II of England in honor of Admiral William Penn. The king owed Penn a large sum of money. To repay his debt, Penn's son was made governor of more than 45,000 square miles of land in the New World. The younger William Penn belonged to the Society of Friends (Quakers). He believed that everyone should have freedom of religion and welcomed people of many different religious beliefs to join the colony he founded in 1682.

A group who sought religious freedom, known as the Pennsylvania Dutch, didn't come from the Netherlands. They immigrated from Germany. The word *Deutsch* means "German." These Pennsylvania Germans—Mennonites, Amish and other conservative religious groups—are known for their simple lives. They do not have tele-

phones or electricity in their homes. Although many are farmers, they do not own automobiles or tractors. They use horse-drawn plows in the fields and travel in horse-drawn buggies.

Discussion Questions

How would your life be different if your family chose not to have electricity, telephones or cars?

- The British government left the Pennsylvania colonists pretty much alone for nearly 100 years. In 1765, the British Parliament passed the first of a series of laws requiring the colonists to pay taxes on certain items. They resented "taxation without representation."

What does taxation without representation mean?

- Delegates from 12 colonies met in Philadelphia in 1774. They agreed to boycott British products "until all obnoxious acts (laws) shall be repealed."

What is a boycott? Why did the colonists think it would convince the British to repeal the taxes?

- By the time the Second Continental Congress met in May 1775, several battles had been fought between colonists and British troops. After meetings and discussions, the delegates declared their independence from Britain. As the great bell in the State House rang, the Declaration of Independence, written by Thomas Jefferson, was publicly proclaimed in Philadelphia at noon on July 8. Ever since, the bell has been called the Liberty Bell.

Imagine hearing the Declaration of Independence read as you stand before the State House in Philadelphia in 1775. How would you feel?

- During the Revolutionary War, the Liberty Bell was hidden beneath the floorboards of a church in Allentown.

On December 6, 1790, Philadelphia became the nation's capital until 1800 when the center of government moved to Washington, D.C.

- What if the nation's capital had remained in Philadelphia?

Who's Who?

Use reference books to identify these famous people from Pennsylvania.

____ 1. Fifteenth President of the United States

____ 2. Marine biologist and author, known for the book *Silent Spring*

____ 3. Played 18 seasons with the Pittsburgh Pirates, won 4 batting titles and selected to All-Star team 12 times

____ 4. Founder of the company known for its "57 Varieties"

____ 5. Poet and novelist, wrote a well-known short story "The Devil and Daniel Webster"

____ 6. Composer who wrote "My Old Kentucky Home" and "Jeannie with the Light Brown Hair"

____ 7. Inventor and engineer who built the first successful steamboat

____ 8. Opera singer, first African American performer at New York City's Metropolitan Opera House

____ 9. Actress who married the Prince of Monaco in 1956

____ 10. Famous for writing *Little Women* and *Little Men*

____ 11. Anthropologist who studied primitive cultures. Wrote *Coming of Age in Samoa*

____ 12. Seamstress credited with sewing the first American flag

A. Louisa May Alcott
B. Marian Anderson
C. Stephen Vincent Benet
D. James Buchanan
E. Rachel Carson
F. Roberto Clemente
G. Stephen Foster
H. Robert Fulton
I. Henry J. Heinz
J. Grace Kelly
K. Margaret Mead
L. Betsy Ross

More About Pennsylvania

Use reference books to find an interesting fact about the topics below.

The Lenape people: _____

_____

Quakers: _____

_____

Amish: _____

_____

Hex signs: _____

_____

Mennonites: _____

_____

Pennsylvania Dutch Country: _____

_____

First Continental Congress: _____

_____

Second Continental Congress: _____

_____

Declaration of Independence: _____

_____

Article of Confederation: _____

_____

_____

Valley Forge National Historical Park:

_____

_____

Whiskey Rebellion: _____

_____

Underground Railroad: _____

_____

Elfreth's Alley in Philadelphia: _____

_____

Battle of Gettysburg: _____

_____

Gettysburg Address: _____

_____

Yankee Pennamite Wars: _____

_____

Johnstown flood of 1889: _____

_____

Three Mile Island: _____

_____

Hershey Chocolate Factory: _____

_____

Little League Hall of Fame in Williamsport:

_____

_____

Fort Necessity: _____

_____

The Poconos: _____

_____

Poor Richard's Almanack: _____

_____

_____

Meadowcroft Rockshelter: _____

_____

Let's stop in Hershey to look at the street lights shaped like candy kisses. Do you think we could get some samples at the Hershey Chocolate factory?

182

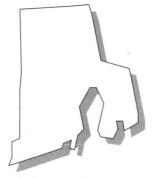

Welcome to Rhode Island

It won't take long to float across the smallest state, but let's not hurry. Lots of history was made in Little Rhody.

Nicknames: Ocean State and Little Rhody

State motto: Hope

State flower: Violet

State tree: Red maple

State bird: Rhode Island Red chicken

State mineral: Bowenite

State stone: Cumberlandite

State shell: Quahog

State song: "Rhode Island"

Capital: Providence

Statehood: Rhode Island was the last of the original 13 colonies to ratify the Constitution on May 29, 1790.

1990 Population: 1,003,464: the 8th smallest in population

Area: 1,214 square miles: Rhode Island is the smallest state.

Neighbors: Connecticut, Massachusetts and the Atlantic Ocean

Did You Know?

• Rhode Island has rivers named the Sakonnet, Seekonk, Pawtucket, Pettaquamscutt, Potowomut, Woonasquatucket, Ponaganset, Chepachet and Moshassuck.

• It doesn't take long to drive across the Ocean State. From east to west, Rhode Island is only 37 miles wide. From north to south, the total distance is only about 48 miles. Many people commute to work farther than that every day.

• The official name of this little state is Rhode Island and Providence Plantations.

• Although it was the first to declare its independence from England, Rhode Island was the last of the 13 colonies to approve the new U.S. Constitution. Many feared they would lose their liberties. Others demanded a bill of rights and the abolishment of slavery. Finally, the state constitutional convention agreed to the Constitution by a 34 to 32 vote.

• The first indoor shopping center in America was the Arcade, built in 1828 in Providence.

• The origin of the Old Stone Mill in Newport is uncertain. Some say it was built by Norsemen in the eleventh century.

Discussion Question: What If?

Although Canada is larger than the U.S. in area, the country has only 10 provinces (states). What if the entire U.S. was divided into only 10 states? How would you divide the U.S.?

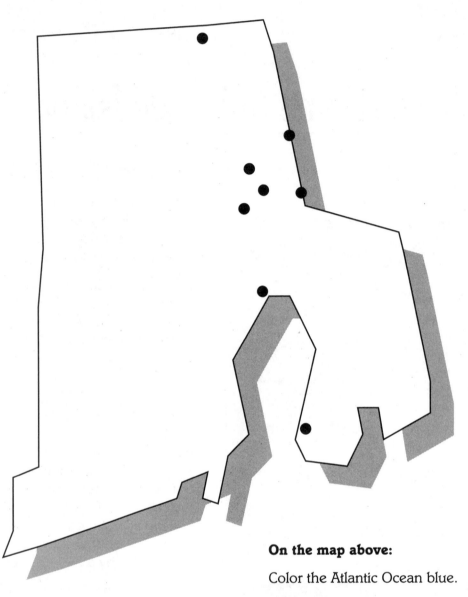

On the map above:

Color the Atlantic Ocean blue.

Color Narragansett Bay green.

Draw a red line to indicate the boundary between Rhode Island and Connecticut.

Label Block Island, a popular recreation area, south of the mainland.

Draw a black line to indicate the boundary between Rhode Island and Massachusetts.

Label these major cities in Rhode Island:

Providence	Warwick
Cranston	Pawtucket
Woonsocket	East Providence
Newport	North Providence

North Pacific Ocean

North Atlantic Ocean

Gulf of Mexico

184

In Search of Religious Freedom

Roger Williams, honored as the founder of Rhode Island, was not the first European to venture into this area. Explorers from Spain, the Netherlands and Italy visited Rhode Island long before Williams founded the first settlement in 1636.

Like many others, Roger Williams left England seeking religious freedom in Massachusetts. He found, however, that although the Puritans wanted religious freedom for themselves, they did not allow the same rights to anyone who disagreed with them.

The governor of Massachusetts ordered Williams to return to England, but he and a few friends fled into the wilderness. With the help of Chief Massasoit, the group survived and eventually settled in a new area they named Providence. Here colonists were allowed political and religious freedom, liberties available in few places at that time.

Known as a safe haven, Quakers, Catholics, French Huguenots (Protestants) and people of many other religious beliefs started their own towns in Rhode Island. Spanish and Portuguese settlers from the Caribbean Islands formed the first Jewish synagogue in Newport in 1763. Rhode Island is also home to the oldest Baptist Church established in Providence in 1775 and the oldest Quaker Meeting House built in 1669 in Newport.

Describe Roger Williams' problems in Massachusetts and his flight to Rhode Island.

Learn more about one of the religious groups that sought religious freedom in Rhode Island.

The Revolutionary War

As the new colonies grew, they began their own industries. They bought and sold goods from other countries. During the early 1700s, England was involved in several costly wars and needed to raise money. They also wished to keep control of the colonies. Parliament passed laws to force the colonists to buy and sell only to England, at prices set by the Mother Country.

One example was a 1732 law that made it illegal to manufacture hats in the colonies of the New World. Other laws restricted selling and manufacturing and forced colonists to sell crops and purchase goods only from England. They were required to pay taxes on many items, like tea, sugar and paper products.

As early as 1764, the people of Rhode Island protested these laws by shooting cannons at a British patrol ship. They burned several British naval ships. The Rhode Island General Assembly suggested that the colonies band together against England.

When the First Continental Congress decided to meet in Philadelphia, the smallest state was the first to elect delegates. A Rhode Islander, Esek Hopkins, became commander in chief of the Continental navy. Rhode Island was the first state to declare independence from England on May 4, 1776.

During the Revolutionary War, British troops took over the city of Newport. Hundreds of houses were burned for firewood. Most of the people fled. French troops and Rhode Island's Black Regiment, made up of former slaves, enabled the colonists to hold off the British until they finally left Newport in 1779.

The following year, 6,000 French soldiers arrived, making Newport their base. With their help, the Continental army was victorious.

Select one of these laws passed by England: The Molasses Act, the Sugar Act, the Stamp Act or the Townshend Acts. How did the law affect the colonists? What was prohibited or taxed by the law?

If you had been a colonist, what would you have done when England passed these laws?

A Little More About Little Rhode Island

Use reference books to answer the assigned questions.

• Five tribes of Native Americans belonging to the Algonquian-speaking group lived in Rhode Island when white settlers first arrived. They included the Niantic, Nipmucks, Narragansetts, Wampanoags and the Pequots.

Describe the culture of one of these early American people.

• Giovanni de Verrazano explored Narragansett Bay in 1524.

What country did he come from?

• Block Island was named for Adriaen Block.

Who was he?

• King Philip's War was fought in 1675.

Who was King Philip? Who fought in this war? Who won?

• Rhode Island is not an island.

How did the state get its name?

• One word appears on the Rhode Island state flag.

What is that word?

• The Brown brothers of Providence, Nicholas, Joseph, John and Moses, were important men in the early days of Rhode Island.

Describe the accomplishments of one of the Brown brothers.

• Rhode Island Reds are the official state bird.

What are Rhode Island Reds?

• The state shell is the quahog.

What is a quahog?

• People can catch both fresh and saltwater fish in Rhode Island.

What are some types of fish found in the waters of this state?

• Jai alai is a popular sport in Rhode Island.

What is jai alai?

• The trees and shrubs at Green Animals Topiary Gardens in Portsmouth are quite unusual.

In what way are they unusual? What does *topiary* mean?

Jai alai looks like fun. Do we have time to watch a game?

Welcome to South Carolina

Let's head to Greenville, South Carolina, for the summer hot air balloon festival. We'll join more than 100 balloons at Freedom Weekend Aloft.

Nickname: Palmetto State
State mottoes: Prepared in Mind and Resources. While I Breathe, I Hope.
State flower: Carolina yellow jessamine
State tree: Palmetto
State bird: Carolina wren
State wild game bird: Wild turkey
State animal: White-tailed deer
State fish: Striped bass
State reptile: Loggerhead sea turtle
State insect: Carolina mantid
State stone: Blue granite
State fruit: Peach
State beverage: Milk
State dance: The shag
State dog: Boykin spaniel
State songs: "Carolina" and "South Carolina on My Mind"
Capital: Columbia
Statehood: South Carolina was one of the 13 original colonies and the eighth state to ratify the Constitution on May 23, 1788.
1990 Population: 3,486,703: the 25th largest in population
Area: 31,113 square miles: the 40th largest state
Neighbors: North Carolina, Georgia and the Atlantic Ocean

Did You Know?

- North and South Carolina were named in honor of King Charles I of England.

- During the Revolutionary War, English soldiers attacked Fort Moultrie at Charleston Harbor. Made of palmetto logs, the fort held even against cannon fire and the South Carolinians won the battle. South Carolina's nickname is the Palmetto State.

- A dance called the Charleston was named for Charleston, South Carolina, but a different dance, the shag became the state's official dance in 1984.

- Wide, white sandy beaches stretch along the northern coast of South Carolina giving this part of the coast the nickname, the Grand Strand. Golfing, deep-sea fishing, boating, swimming and sunbathing are popular tourist attractions here. Myrtle Beach is the unofficial capital of the Grand Strand.

State Animals

South Carolina has a state bird, fish, insect, wild game bird, dog and reptile. Draw a picture and describe one of these state animals.

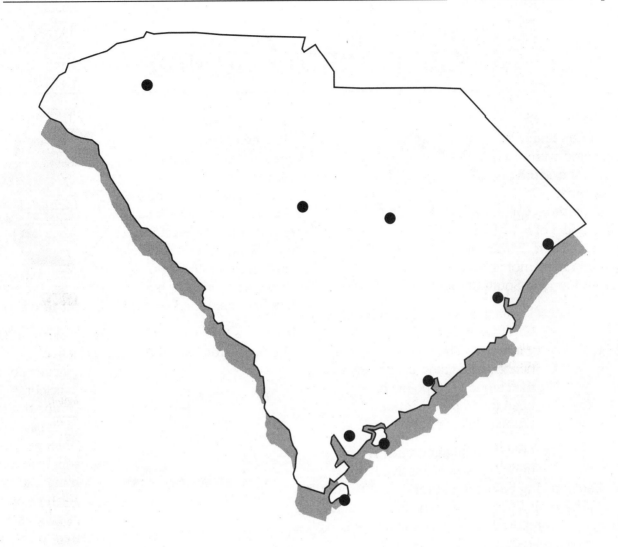

Label the underlined places on the South Carolina state map.

<u>Charleston</u> was the capital of South Carolina from 1670 to 1790. The Dock Street Theater opened in 1736 as America's first playhouse.

In 1790, the capital was moved to <u>Columbia</u>.

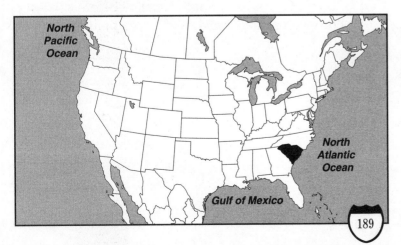

Hopsewee Plantation near <u>Georgetown</u> was the home of Thomas Lynch, Jr., one of the signers of the Declaration of Independence.

Penn School, founded in 1862 in <u>Beaufort</u>, was the South's first school for freed slaves.

<u>Hilton Head Island</u> and <u>Edistro Island</u> are popular resort areas in South Carolina.

<u>Myrtle Beach</u> is another popular vacation spot.

Jesse Jackson was born in <u>Greenville</u> in 1941. He became a preacher and civil rights leader.

<u>Sumter</u> was named for Thomas Sumter, a Revolutionary War leader known as the "Gamecock."

South Carolina is bordered by <u>North Carolina</u>, <u>Georgia</u> and the <u>Atlantic Ocean</u>. On the map above, label their approximate locations.

Early South Carolina

At one time, much of South Carolina was covered with water. At the South Carolina State Museum, visitors can see a life-size model of a 43-foot prehistoric shark. Fossils of camels and mammoths have also been found in South Carolina.

The first people to live in South Carolina arrived at least 11,000 years ago. They were nomadic hunters and gatherers. Many of their stone spearpoints have been found in the South Carolina hillsides.

About 50 different small groups of Native Americans lived in South Carolina long before the European settlers arrived. These people were hunters, farmers and fishermen. They grew corn, beans and squash, crops sometimes called the "Three Sisters" because they were so important. They gathered oysters and clams along the shore.

These early people traveled the rivers and coastal waters in long canoes made from cypress logs. They made clothing and moccasins from animal skins and used Spanish moss as stuffing for mattresses. Clay was used to make jugs and pots. From willow bark they made a medicine similar to aspirin.

In 1521 a Spanish ship anchored in Winyah Bay. The Spaniards invited about 150 Native

Americans aboard for a celebration. Once aboard, the ship set sail, taking their guests as prisoners to Santo Domingo, a Spanish colony in the Caribbean. When they arrived, they were ordered to return the prisoners to their home.

The Cherokees, Cusabos, Coosas, Catawbas, Yamasees, Westros, Congarees and Kiawahs lived in the area that later became South Carolina.

Describe the culture of one of the Native American groups in South Carolina before European settlers arrived.

Settling South Carolina

Early attempts to establish colonies in South Carolina by France and Spain ended in failure because of hunger and disease. King Charles I of England gave a huge amount of land called Carolana (Land of Charles) to eight supporters who were to be the landlords. The land included what later became North and South Carolina. People who moved to Carolana paid rent to the landlords. More than 100 people arrived in 1670 and began building the first settlement called Charles Towne. The landlords permitted religious freedom which brought many French Huguenots, Quakers, Puritans and Baptists to the area.

Besides planting crops for food, the early colonists traded deerskins and furs. They exported grain, timber and beef to England. By 1680, about 1,000 colonists lived in the town we now call Charleston. In 1719 South Carolina became a royal colony ruled by governors appointed by the king.

Rice became an important cash crop because it grew well in the swampy coastlands. Slaves were bought to help with the farming. Large plantations were established by rich families. Slaves were often treated very badly and rebellions occurred.

As more settlers arrived, the Native Americans tried to save their land. Between 1715 and 1717, the Yamasee fought to preserve their way of life and drive the colonists away. They were defeated.

Nicknamed Blackbeard because of his long black beard tied with colored ribbons, Edward Teach, along with Stede Bonnet and other pirates, robbed ships along the coast, often killing passengers and crew. In 1718 the governors of South Carolina and Virginia decided to fight back. Blackbeard was killed in a battle. Stede Bonnet and about 50 other pirates were captured and hung.

Eliza Pinchkey discovered a blue dye made from the indigo plant. The dye was very popular in England, and indigo became the second major cash crop in South Carolina. By the late 1700s, cotton had taken over as the most important crop in South Carolina.

Select one of these topics for a short report:

- How is rice grown?
- How is dye made from indigo plants?
- What was the Stono Rebellion?
- Who were the Sons of Liberty?
- Why did the invention of the cotton gin make cotton a major crop in the South?
- Francis Marion led a group of men against the English during the Revolutionary War. Why was he nicknamed "the Swamp Fox"?
- What role did Denmark Vesey play in the slaves' fight for freedom?

I wonder if anyone dances the Charleston in Charleston, South Carolina?

191

Welcome to South Dakota

South Dakota is quite a bit north of South Carolina. We need to head west, across the Mississippi River, then north to the Coyote State.

Nicknames: Coyote State and Sunshine State

State motto: Under God, the People Rule

State flower: Pasqueflower

State tree: Black Hills spruce

State bird: Ring-necked pheasant

State animal: Coyote

State fish: Walleye

State insect: Honeybee

State mineral: Rose quartz

State gem: Fairburn agate

State grass: Western wheat grass

State song: "Hail, South Dakota"

Capital: Pierre

Statehood: November 2, 1889, the 40th state

1990 Population: 696,004: the 45th largest in population

Area: 77,116 square miles: the 16th largest in area

Neighbors: North Dakota, Minnesota, Iowa, Nebraska, Wyoming and Montana

The Black Hills

Tall tales of Paul Bunyan, the legendary lumberjack are told in several states east of South Dakota. One story says that Paul wanted some ponds for his sawmills, so he dug out the Great Lakes and filled them with water from the Ocean. Not wanting to dump the rubble on the forests of Minnesota, he tossed it into South Dakota. That's how the Black Hills were formed.

What's in a Name?

Badger, Bison and Bull Creek are three places in South Dakota named for animals. How many other places named for plants or animals can you find in South Dakota?

_____

_____

_____

_____

_____

_____

_____

_____

_____

_____

_____

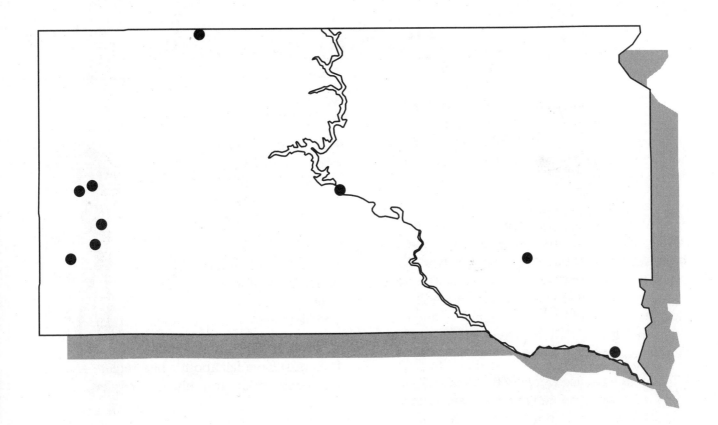

Write the names of the underlined places on the South Dakota state map.

Five states border South Dakota: <u>North Dakota</u>, <u>Minnesota</u>, <u>Iowa</u>, <u>Wyoming</u> and <u>Montana</u>. Label their approximate locations on the map above.

The cemetery in <u>Deadwood</u> is the final resting place of "Wild Bill Hickok" and Calamity Jane.

The Corn Palace in <u>Mitchell</u> displays elaborate murals created from corn and other grains.

A memorial to Crazy Horse is being carved in a granite mountain near <u>Custer</u>.

Dinosaur Park in <u>Rapid City</u> contains life-size sculptures of prehistoric dinosaurs that once lived in South Dakota.

The University of South Dakota in <u>Vermillion</u> houses a large collection of musical instruments from all over the world.

Located at the mouth of the Bad River, <u>Pierre</u> served as the region's headquarters for fur traders and trappers.

The <u>Missouri River</u> cuts South Dakota almost in half.

At <u>Keystone</u>, near Mount Rushmore, visitors pan for gold and take a guided underground tour through Big Thunder Gold Mine.

The city of <u>Sturgis</u> began as a stop for wagon trains on their way to Fort Meade.

Near <u>Lemmon</u>, a small town on the border between North and South Dakota, visitors can view gigantic petrified wood logs up to 10 feet across at the Petrified Wood Park.

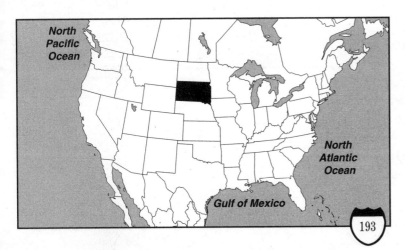

"As Long as the Sun Shall Shine..."

Chief Sitting Bull, born about 1830, spent his life as a warrior and leader of his people, the Hunkpapa Lokota Sioux. The Sioux were a nomadic people who followed the herds of bison across the Great Plains.

Angered at the mistreatment and broken promises to other tribes who had agreed to live on reservations, Sitting Bull declared war on the white settlers in 1865. After many battles, a peace treaty was signed in June 1867. The treaty promised to keep white settlers from the Black Hills "as long as the sun shall shine . . . and the grass shall grow." Within a year, whites had broken the terms of the treaty.

When gold was discovered in the Black Hills in 1874, thousands poured into the area. Sitting Bull refused offers to purchase the land and stood fast against surrendering land or mining rights in the Black Hills. The Sioux believed that the Black Hills region was a holy place — the resting place of the souls of their ancestors.

In December 1875, the government ordered Sitting Bull and his people to leave the Black Hills and live at Standing Rock Reservation. Sitting Bull refused and joined with the Cheyenne and Arapaho. He and his allies defeated General Custer at Little Bighorn in 1876.

Sitting Bull and many others fled to Canada after Little Bighorn but were forced to return in 1881. He was imprisoned for two years before going to Standing Rock Reservation. Buffalo Bill invited Sitting Bull to join his Wild West Show. He agreed to do so but left after one season. He did not like the noise and crowds. Back on the reservation, he worked to improve conditions for his people and build schools for the children. In 1890, Sitting Bull permitted his people to join the antiwhite "ghost dance" movement. When members of an Indian police force were sent to arrest him, a fight broke out and Sitting Bull was fatally wounded.

Discussion Questions

How would you have felt if you had been Chief Sitting Bull? Would you want to be forced to live on a reservation? How would you try to protect the rights of your people?

What if the U.S. government had kept its promises to Chief Sitting Bull and not forced his people to live on reservations?

Write about how Chief Sitting Bull must have felt about white settlers and the U.S. government from his point of view.

_____

_____

_____

_____

_____

_____

_____

_____

_____

_____

_____

_____

_____

_____

Did You Know?

Read these facts about South Dakota. Select one of the activities to complete.

- The pasqueflower was used as medicine by Native Americans. They treated rheumatism with its crushed leaves. Its flowers were used to stop nose bleeds.

Find out about other plants used by Native Americans as medicine.

- *Dakota* is a Sioux word meaning "alliance of friends." Near Mount Rushmore, a monument to a Sioux leader is being carved in a granite mountain.

1. Who designed this monument? When did work begin on it? Who is the subject of the monument? Why is he famous?

- Evidence indicates that people lived in South Dakota 25,000 years ago. About 500 A.D. the people known as Mound Builders settled along the Big Sioux River. By 1250 people who may have been the ancestors of the Arikara constructed fortresses capable of holding up to 5,000 people along the Missouri River. By the 1500s the Arikara inhabited the area. They lived in fortified villages and specialized in agriculture and horse trading.

Learn more about how these early people lived.

- The Sioux, who played an important role in South Dakota history, began arriving in the area in the 1700s.

Write a report about one of the Sioux tribes that lived in South Dakota.

- The Badlands are a barren region in South Dakota filled with strange and beautiful rock formations formed by wind and water over millions of years.

Look at pictures of the Badlands. Imagine trying to find your way through this region. Describe what you see as you ride your horse, looking for a trail through this dry, mysterious area of South Dakota.

- At one time, millions of bison (buffalo) covered the plains of South Dakota.

Write a short poem about how you'd feel standing on a hill looking at a herd of over 10,000 bison.

- The area that is now South Dakota was originally part of the Louisiana Purchase which was bought from France for 15 million dollars.

2. Color the area covered by the Louisiana Purchase on the map below. How much land was included in this purchase? What states were formed from that land?

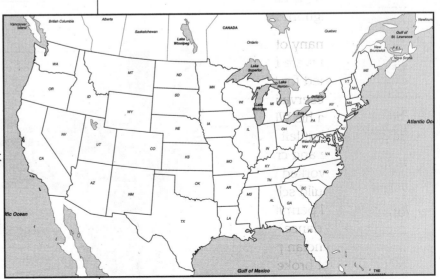

Mount Rushmore

Mount Rushmore is a national monument carved into a mountain in the Black Hills of South Dakota. This granite mountain rises over 6,000 feet above sea level and towers above the neighboring mountains.

The work on Mount Rushmore was designed and done by Gutzon Borglum, an American sculptor and painter. Borglum traveled extensively through the Black Hills area looking for the perfect mountain before deciding on Mount Rushmore.

The original design for Mount Rushmore included sculpting four Presidents from the waist up. Borglum called the project ". . . the greatest thing of its character in the entire world." Difficulties forced Borglum to change and revise his plans several times. In the final design, the four presidential faces on Mount Rushmore are 60 to 70 feet tall.

Borglum began work on Mount Rushmore in 1927 at the age of 60. At his death in March 1941, the project had not been completed. His son, Lincoln Borglum, completed the final work on Mount Rushmore in November 1941.

Who are the four Presidents on Mount Rushmore?

_____

_____

_____

_____

Look at a picture of Mount Rushmore. Note the details carved into the rock. Whose faces would you include if you designed a gigantic sculpture to be carved into a mountain? You could name friends or family members, famous people, past or present or even fictional characters.

Who would you choose?

_____

Why? _____

_____

_____

_____

_____

What would you call your monument?

_____

Why did you select that name?

_____

_____

_____

_____

_____

I wonder when they'll carve my face on a mountain?

On the back of this page, draw your monument or describe how the completed monument would look.

Welcome to Tennessee

From the steep bluffs along the Mississippi River, over hills to the Cumberland Plateau and on to the Great Smoky Mountains, there's lots to see as our hot air balloon floats over Tennessee.

Nicknames: Volunteer State and Big Bend State
State motto: Agriculture and Commerce
State slogan: Tennessee—America at Its Best
State flower: Iris
State wildflower: Passionflower
State tree: Tulip poplar
State bird: Mockingbird
State animal: Raccoon
State insects: Firefly and ladybug
State gem: Tennessee River pearl
State rocks: Limestone and agate
State horse: Tennessee walking horse
State songs: "My Homeland, Tennessee"; "When It's Iris Time in Tennessee"; "My Tennessee"; "The Tennessee Waltz" and "Rocky Top"
Capital: Nashville
Statehood: Tennessee became the 16th state June 1, 1796.
1990 Population: 4,877,185: the 17th largest in population
Area: 42,114 square miles: the 34th largest state
Neighbors: Kentucky, Virginia, Georgia, Alabama, Mississippi, North Carolina, Arkansas and Missouri

Earthquakes in Tennessee?

The largest natural lake in Tennessee, Reelfoot Lake, was formed when an earthquake and its aftershocks rumbled through the state between December 1811 and March 1812. The quakes caused the land to sink in some places. Water from the Mississippi River rushed into one sunken area forming a shallow lake where a forest had once stood.

If an earthquake formed a new lake near your home, what would you name it?

_____

Explain why your name would be a good one for a lake formed by an earthquake.

_____

_____

_____

_____

Discussion Question: What If?

What if the Cherokee and other Native Americans had not been forced to leave Tennessee?

197

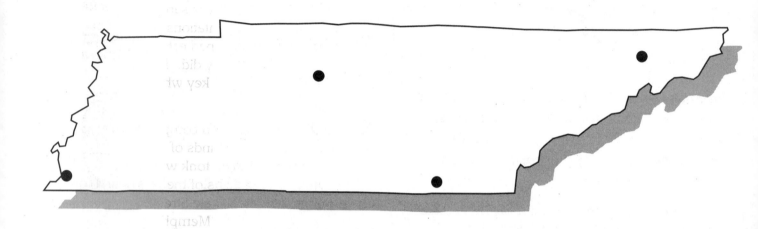

Eight states border Tennessee. Label their approximate locations on the map above.

The Mississippi River forms the squiggly western boundary of Tennessee. Color it blue.

Label the underlined cities on the map above.

Tennessee's largest city, <u>Memphis</u>, was built on the Mississippi River.

<u>Nashville</u>, the second largest city, became the capital in 1826.

On a clear day you can see Georgia, North Carolina, South Carolina and Alabama from the top of Lookout Mountain near <u>Chattanooga</u>.

Each year the National Storytelling Festival takes place in <u>Jonesborough</u>.

Tennessee has some towns with unusual names. How many of them can you find? Add as many as you can to your map: Bells, Halls, Christmasville, Difficult, Friendship, Finger, Only, Wartburg, Wartrace, Gates, Mascot, Paris, Moscow and White House.

North Pacific Ocean

North Atlantic Ocean

Gulf of Mexico

198

More to Discover

Where did much of the music we enjoy today originate? Many styles had their roots in Tennessee. To help students understand the various types of music popular in Tennessee, these activities are suggested.

Tennessee Music

In the eastern mountains of Tennessee, settlers from England and Scotland sang traditional folk ballads. A ballad often tells a story of a person or event. Read the words or play recordings of ballads. Ask students to write a summary of a ballad.

Another type of music that became popular in Tennessee was gospel music. Play some gospel music. Students can write a short poem or story about how this music makes them feel.

The fiddle, banjo, guitar and harmonica were the instruments played most often in Tennessee. Play selections featuring these instruments individually so students can learn how each instrument sounds.

Bluegrass music had its roots in the early string bands common in Tennessee and Kentucky. Bluegrass is characterized by banjo or fiddle music played rapidly, combined with the vocal sounds of early ballads. Play some toe-tapping, foot-stomping bluegrass music for the class simply for enjoyment.

When radio began broadcasting nationally in the 1920s, the music of the Tennessee and Kentucky hills was heard all over the country. The first recordings of "country" music were made in 1927 and the Grand Ole Opry made its debut. Nashville became "Music City, USA."

Hold a barn dance in the gym. Invite students to clap, sing and dance as they listen to the "Nashville sound."

In western Tennessee, slaves sang as they worked on the cotton plantations. Their songs had a strong beat that helped establish a rhythm for the repetitive tasks they did. Many of the melodies were in a minor key which gave the music a sad sound.

In Memphis, W.C. Handy, a composer and performer, combined the sounds of ragtime and honky tonk with the mournful songs of the slaves to write "Beale Street Blues," "Memphis Blues" and St. Louis Blues." As students listen to recordings of blues music, ask them to imagine the roots of that music on the slave plantations of western Tennessee.

In the 1950s, a young man from Mississippi began making records in Memphis. His music combined the styles of country and western with rhythm and blues, and from this combination, a new style of music was formed. We know it as rock and roll. Before long, the unique sound of Elvis Presley was heard all over the world. Although he didn't invent rock and roll, Elvis did more than any other performer to popularize it. His first hit "That's All Right, Mama" led to a recording contract with RCA Victor. Other early hits included "Heartbreak Hotel," "Hound Dog," "Don't Be Cruel," "Love Me Tender" and "All Shook Up." As students listen to some early songs recorded by Elvis, ask them to listen for the influence of country and western and the blues.

Early Inhabitants of Tennessee

Seashells found in Tennessee show that millions of years ago, the area was covered by water. Fossils have also been found of mammoths, mastodons, saber-toothed tigers and other animals now extinct.

The first people to settle in Tennessee arrived about 15,000 years ago. They were known as the Mound Builders because they supported their homes and temples with huge earthen mounds. They buried their dead in smaller, cone-shaped mounds along with pottery, shell spoons and copper breastplates. Clusters of mounds have been discovered near Pinson, Shiloh, Memphis.

The Chucalissa Indian Village and Museum in Memphis is the site of a village founded about 900 A.D. Several village buildings have been reconstructed at this archaeological site by Memphis State University.

By the time Europeans arrived in Tennessee, the Mound Builders had disappeared. By then three main groups of Native Americans lived in Tennessee, the Cherokee, Creek and Chickasaw. They grew corn, hunted deer, wild turkeys and other game. Tennessee was named for Tanasie, an early Cherokee village.

Sequoyah Birthplace Museum in Vonore honors the Cherokee chief who developed a written alphabet of 86 characters for the Cherokee language. Born in the late 1700s, Sequoyah became a silversmith, painter, warrior and scholar. He taught many of his people to read and write. The Cherokee formed their own schools and printed their own books. The huge sequoia trees of California were named for this remarkable man.

Your Own Alphabet

Work with a friend to develop your own alphabet by designing symbols for letters and words. Write messages to your friend in your new alphabet.

What symbols will you use for the letters?

A _____   H _____   O _____   V _____
B _____   I _____   P _____   W _____
C _____   J _____   Q _____   X _____
D _____   K _____   R _____   Y _____
E _____   L _____   S _____   Z _____
F _____   M _____   T _____
G _____   N _____   U _____

What symbols will you use for these words?

friend _____   hello _____   lake _____

happy _____   love _____   mountain _____

school _____   sun _____   far _____

rain _____   yes _____   tomorrow _____

Write this message using your new alphabet:

Hello, friend. I'll see you after school tomorrow. Let's have a picnic by the lake if it doesn't rain.

_____

_____

_____

_____

_____

The Trail of Tears

In 1828, Andrew Jackson was elected the seventh President of the United States. Under his administration, the Indian Removal Act of 1830 was passed. The Cherokee, along with many other Native American tribes were forced from their homelands to the Indian Territory in Oklahoma. They endured terrible hardships along the way. At least 25% of the people died from sickness, starvation and exposure to the cold before they reached Oklahoma. The route of the forced march became known as *nunna-da-ul-tsun-yi*, the Trail of Tears.

Use the scale to determine the total distance of the Trail of Tears.

_____

If a person walked 10 miles a day, how long would it take to get from the Great Smoky Mountains of Tennessee to the Indian Lands in Oklahoma?

_____

Follow the Trail of Tears from Georgia to Oklahoma on the map.

What states did they cross on their forced march?

_____

_____

How would you feel if someone decided you and your family must leave your home and everything in it except what you could carry? Imagine being forced to walk 1,000 miles to a strange, empty land and told you must live there. Write about how this would make you feel.

Learn More About Tennessee

To learn more about Tennessee, check an encyclopedia, atlas and other books about the state.
Find one interesting fact about each of the topics
listed below.

Bluegrass music: _____

_____

Memphis: _____

_____

Grand Ole Opry: _____

_____

Mockingbird: _____

_____

Nashville: _____

_____

Graceland: _____

_____

Chattanooga: _____

_____

Knoxville: _____

_____

Great Smoky Mountains: _____

_____

_____

Cumberland Plateau: _____

_____

_____

Cumberland Gap: _____

_____

_____

Tennessee Valley Authority (TVA): _____

_____

_____

Norris Dam: _____

_____

Clingman's Dome: _____

_____

The Hermitage: _____

_____

Lookout Mountain: _____

_____

The state of Franklin: _____

_____

Davy Crockett: _____

_____

The Parthenon (in Nashville): _____

_____

_____

The Scopes Trial: _____

_____

Tennessee River: _____

_____

Tennessee walking horse: _____

_____

Tennessee River pearls: _____

_____

Coal mining in Tennessee: _____

_____

_____

"Rocky Top, Tennessee"

202

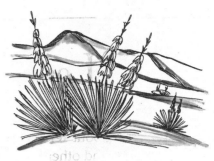

Welcome to Texas

From Tennessee we'll head south and west to Texas. Put on your ten-gallon hat to keep out the sun as we take our time exploring the second largest state in the nation.

Nickname: Lone Star State
State motto: Friendship
State flower: Bluebonnet
State tree: Pecan
State bird: Mockingbird
State fish: Guadalupe bass
State gem: Texas blue topaz
State stone: Petrified palm-wood
State food: Chili
State shell: Lightning whelk
State grass: Sidecoats grama
State song: "Texas, Our Texas"
Capital: Austin
Statehood: Texas became the 28th state on December 29, 1845.
1990 Population: 16,986,510: the 3rd largest in population
Area: 266,807 square miles: the 2nd largest state
Neighbors: Arkansas, Louisiana, Oklahoma, New Mexico, Mexico and the Gulf of Mexico

The Lone Star State Flag

After Texas won its independence from Mexico, it became the Republic of Texas for nine years before joining the United States. It had its own flag and issued its own paper money. Because one star appeared on the flag and money, Texas was called the Lone Star Republic. The Texas state flag is red, white and blue. Red represents bravery, white stands for strength and blue symbolizes loyalty. Color the section around the star blue. The top stripe is white. Color the bottom stripe red.

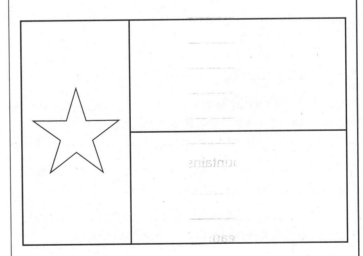

Discussion Question: What If?

What if Texas hadn't won its independence from Mexico?

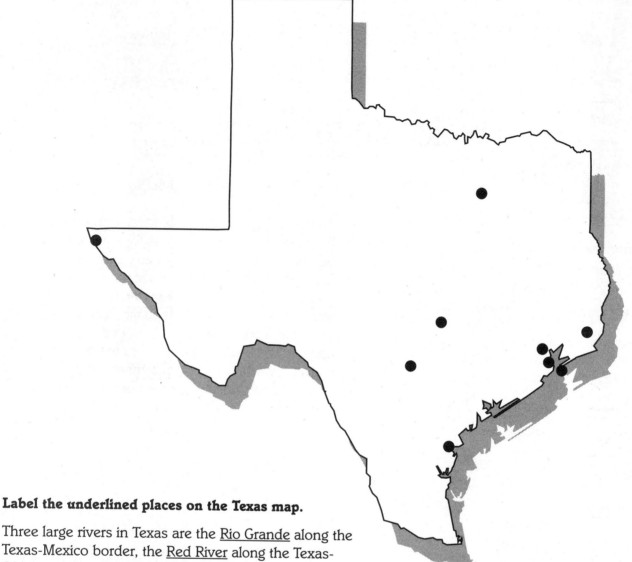

Label the underlined places on the Texas map.

Three large rivers in Texas are the <u>Rio Grande</u> along the Texas-Mexico border, the <u>Red River</u> along the Texas-Oklahoma border and the <u>Pecos River</u> in western Texas.

At Bracken Cave near <u>San Antonio</u> more than 20 million bats may be flying in the cave at once.

Both the Oilers and the Astros play ball at the Astrodome in <u>Houston</u>, the world's first domed stadium.

Texas is bordered by <u>Arkansas</u>, <u>Louisiana</u>, <u>Oklahoma</u>, <u>New Mexico</u>, <u>Mexico</u> and the <u>Gulf of Mexico</u>. Label their approximate locations on the map above.

<u>Corpus Christie</u>, <u>Texas City</u>, <u>Beaumont</u> and <u>Galveston</u> are important ports in Texas.

The Rio Grande River separates <u>El Paso</u>, Texas, from the Mexican city of Juarez.

John Neely Bryan built a home and a store on the Trinity River in 1841. He called the settlement <u>Dallas</u>. Today Dallas is the second largest city in Texas.

<u>Austin</u>, the state capital, was named for Stephen Austin who led the movement for Texas independence.

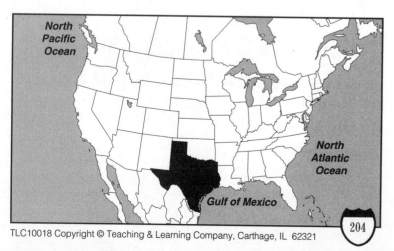

North Pacific Ocean

North Atlantic Ocean

Gulf of Mexico

204

Early Hunters of Mammoths and Mastodons

Millions of years ago, dinosaurs roamed through Texas. Saber-toothed tigers, small horses, camels, mammoths, mastodons and other animals now extinct made their homes in Texas. The first people arrived in Texas about 12,000 years ago. They were hunters who lived in caves. More than 30,000 archaeological sites of ancient burial grounds or rock dwellings have been discovered in Texas.

By the early 1500s, the people of the Caddo Confederacy had formed a group of about 25 smaller tribes who lived in East Texas. They grew corn and other vegetables. Their large, airy homes were built of grass, thatch or branches. The Caddos called each other teshas (friends). This word was changed slightly to the modern word *Texas*.

Along the Gulf Coast, the Karankawas, the Arkokisas and Attacapas lived. Further west in South Texas, the Coahuiltecans lived in the dry desert areas. To the north, the Tonkawas hunted bison.

Other Native Americans in Texas were the Comanches and Jumanos.

In Texas, as in the rest of the nation, battles between the settlers and the Native Americans broke out. In Texas, federal troops and the Texas Rangers were called on. By 1875 most Great Plains Indians like the Apaches, Comanches and Kiowas were forced to move to reservations in Oklahoma.

The early hunters must have been very brave to challenge the huge mammoths and mastodons. Imagine being the leader of a group of about 100 people. Your people need food and want you to lead them in a hunt. How would you plan to kill an animal the size of a mammoth or mastodon? Remember, your people have only stone-tipped wooden spears for weapons.

Below write or draw your plan for the hunt.

Texas Tall Tales

From the time Texas became a state in 1845 until Alaska joined the union in 1959, Texas was the largest state. Texans are proud of their large state and claim that everything in the Lone Star State is bigger and better than anywhere else.

Some things are really large in Texas. Remember, Texas was once home to huge mammoths and mastodons. If you have a "Texas-size" appetite, it means you are very hungry. A "Texas-size" ranch covers much land.

Sometimes Texans use hyperbole. That means they exaggerate. If a Texan claimed that hummingbirds weighed nine pounds in Texas, you would know he was telling a tall tale.

Tall tales are fun to read and write. One of the most famous cowboys in Texas was Pecos Bill who rode a cyclone bareback. This legendary hero is the main character in many tall tales.

Read about this "super cowboy." Write an original story about the adventures of Pecos Bill or another fictional cowboy from Texas.

You could include some of these ideas in your tall tale:

- Texas mosquitos are so big that . . .
- In Texas it rains so hard that . . .
- It gets so hot in Texas that . . .
- It gets so cold in Texas that . . .
- Texas chili is so spicy that . . .
- The mountains in Texas are so tall that . . .
- The fish in the Rio Grande are so large that . . .

- In Texas the rattlesnakes are so fast that . . .
- The thunder in Texas is so loud that . . .
- The wind blows so hard in Texas that . . .

- Texas horses are as smart as . . .
- The cactus in Texas grow as large as . . .
- The cowboys in Texas are as strong as . . .

List some other hyperboles (exaggerations) you could write about Texas.

More About Texas

Select one of the topics below for a short report. Illustrate your report or use pictures from magazines.

- Oil wells have made many Texans very wealthy.

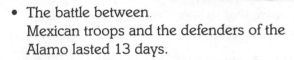

How is oil pumped to the surface? What products are made from oil?

- The battle between Mexican troops and the defenders of the Alamo lasted 13 days.

Write about the battle or about one of the defenders of the Alamo.

- Many early buildings in Texas were made of adobe.

What is adobe? How is it made?

- Many varieties of cactus, sagebrush, mesquite and chaparral grow in the dry western part of Texas. More than 500 varieties of grasses grow in Texas. Pronghorn antelope, armadillos, lizards, alligators and snakes live in Texas.

Find out more about a Texas animal, bird, fish, plant or tree.

- Cattle in Texas are branded to show who owns them. Samuel Maverick, an early Texan, did not brand his herd. His cattle became known as "mavericks." Today, people who do not go along with the usual way of doing things are called mavericks.

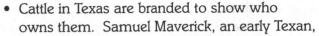

Write a story about someone who is a maverick.

- Cattle drives from Texas to Kansas or Missouri involved a journey of 1,000 miles or more.

What did cowboys do during a cattle drive?

Who was Santa Anna? What role did he play in the Texas fight for independence?

Describe the culture of one of the Native American groups in Texas before white settlers arrived.

What role did the Texas Rangers play in the development of Texas?

How did Fort Worth get the nickname "Cow Town"?

How about stopping for a bowl of world famous Texas hot chili?

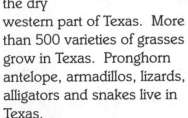

207

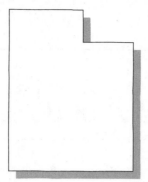

Welcome to Utah

The Beehive State has more national parks than any other state except Alaska. With so many spectacular places to see, it's difficult to know where to begin our tour.

Nickname: Beehive State
State motto: Industry
State flower: Sego lily
State tree: Blue spruce
State bird: Sea gull
State animal: Rocky Mountain elk
State fish: Rainbow trout
State fossil: Allosaurus
State insect: Honeybee
State rock: Coal
State gem: Topaz
State grass: Indian rice grass
State song: "Utah, We Love Thee"
Capital: Salt Lake City
Statehood: Utah became the 45th state on January 4, 1896.
1990 Population: 1,722,850: the 35th largest in population
Area: 84,899 square miles: the 11th largest state
Neighbors: Wyoming, Colorado, New Mexico, Arizona, Nevada and Idaho

Discussion Question: What If?

What if the temperature dropped to -69°F in your state?

Did You Know?

- Utah was named for the Utes who lived there. *Eutaw* means "dwellers in the tops of the mountains."

- Utah averages only 21 people per square mile. Compare that to New Jersey where the average is 995 people per square mile.

- In 1896 Martha Hughes Cannon became the first woman elected as a state senator. The opponent she ran against? Her husband!

- How cold does it get in Utah? On February 1, 1985, a temperature of -69°F was recorded near Logan.

Sites to See

Describe one of these places in Utah. Add pictures or illustrations if possible.

- Arches National Park
- Canyonlands National Park
- Hovenweep National Monument
- Four Corners
- Lake Powell
- Monument Valley
- Natural Bridges National Monument
- Great Salt Lake
- Bryce Canyon National Park
- Zion National Park
- Dinosaur National Monument
- Great Basin
- Golden Spike National Historic Site
- Mormon Tabernacle

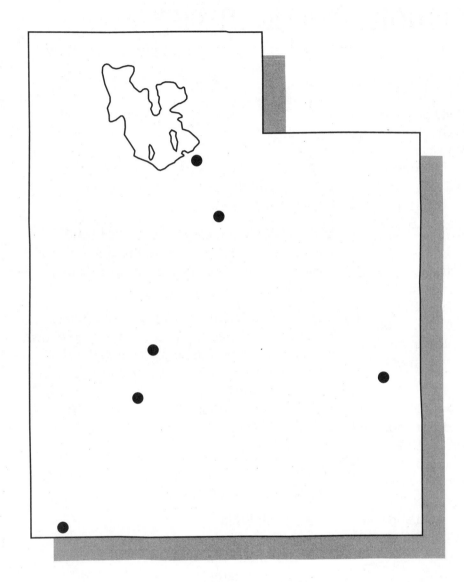

Label the underlined places on the Utah state map.

The Mormons, under the leadership of Brigham Young, founded <u>Salt Lake City</u> in 1847.

<u>Great Salt Lake</u> is seven times saltier than the Ocean.

<u>Provo</u>, another city founded by the Mormons, is the home of Brigham Young University.

<u>Moab</u> is a small town between Arches National Park and Canyonlands National Park.

Brigham Young built a winter home in <u>St. George</u>, a city in southwestern Utah. In 1985, a record high of 117°F was recorded at St. George.

<u>Fillmore</u> was the capital of Utah from 1851 to 1856.

He was known by many as the outlaw, "Butch Cassidy." Born in <u>Beaver</u>, Utah, his real name was George Leroy Parker.

The only place in the U.S. where four states meet is called <u>Four Corners</u>.

Label the approximate locations of the six states that border Utah.

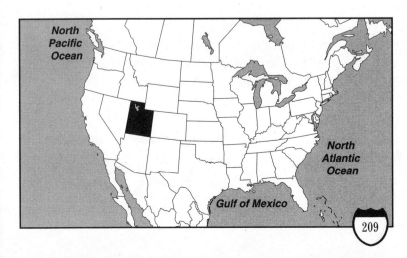

North Pacific Ocean

North Atlantic Ocean

Gulf of Mexico

209

The Mormons Settle in Utah

The story of white settlers in Utah begins in Fayette, New York, where Joseph Smith founded the Church of Jesus Christ of Latter-Day Saints in 1830. Smith reported visions in which he was told he would establish a restored Christian Church. He also received the Book of Mormon which describes the history, wars and religious beliefs of a group of people who migrated from Jerusalem to America between about 600 B.C. and 400 A.D.

The Mormons believed that Jesus Christ appeared in America and that families would be together again in heaven after they died. They believed in polygamy (that men could have more than one wife). Although some people joined Smith, their beliefs were not popular with most people in New York.

The Mormons were forced to move west to Ohio, then to Missouri. They founded Nauvoo, a successful, prosperous town in Illinois in 1839. The number of Mormons continued to grow. When Smith declared he would run for President, many people were angry. They burned the Mormons' farms and crops. Joseph Smith and his brother Hyrum were murdered by a mob in 1844.

Brigham Young became the new leader. He decided to move his people west again to the unexplored Salt Lake Valley. Advance parties went ahead to scout the way, prepare temporary camps and sow crops for those who followed. More than 10,000 Mormons marched west in 1846 to the place that became Salt Lake City. They called their new homeland Deseret, meaning "honeybee."

The Mormons plowed fields, planted crops and dug canals to bring water to the fields. In spite of their efforts, they had little to eat the first year. Many survived by eating sego lily bulbs. The sego lily was later named Utah's state flower. The second year wasn't much better for the set-

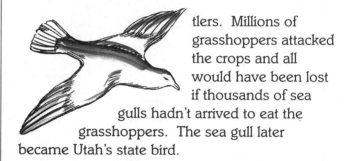

tlers. Millions of grasshoppers attacked the crops and all would have been lost if thousands of sea gulls hadn't arrived to eat the grasshoppers. The sea gull later became Utah's state bird.

In the 1880s Congress passed laws to end polygamy. Mormons ignored the laws. Many were sent to jail. Finally the Mormon Church outlawed polygamy in 1890.

Mormon missionaries to England and other European countries convinced many to join their church. Many converts emigrated to the U.S. and eventually joined the Mormons in Utah. In 1989, the Church of Jesus Christ of Latter-Day Saints reported about 7 million members in 100 different countries.

Select one of these topics or another aspect of the Mormons for a report. Include illustrations or diagrams with your report.

- Joseph Smith
- Brigham Young
- The Book of Mormon
- Mormon Temple
- Mormon Tabernacle
- Mormon Tabernacle Choir
- Beehive House
- The importance of the family
- Genealogical research
- Hardships of the early Mormons
- Opposition to Equal Rights Amendment
- The Mormon's journey from Fayette, New York, to Salt Lake City, Utah

Learn More About Utah

- Utah could well be nicknamed the "Dinosaur State." Scientists discovered the remains of allosaurus, diplodocus, stegosaurus and many other types of dinosaurs in northeastern Utah. Dinosaur tracks were found in southern Utah. Today, high mountains and red-walled canyons cover northeastern Utah at Dinosaur National Monument. More than 140 million years ago this area was flat swampland.

Draw and describe an allosaurus, diplodocus or stegosaurus.

- The earliest people to live in Utah were known as those of the Desert Culture. They were followed by the Fremont Culture and the Anasazi. When European explorers reached Utah, they found the Navajos and Shoshonean-speaking people: Paiutes, Gosiutes, Utes and Shoshones.

Find out more about one of these early peoples who lived in Utah.

- The largest natural lake in Utah is also the largest natural lake west of the Mississippi River. Great Salt Lake covers more than 1,700 square miles. It is seven times as salty as the ocean. Only the Dead Sea contains more salt than the Great Salt Lake.

Why is the Great Salt Lake so salty? Can people swim in the lake? Do any fish or other creatures live in the lake?

How is salt obtained from the lake?

- Seven islands can be found in the Great Salt Lake. Antelope Island is the largest.

What can be found on Antelope Island?

- Between 1800 and 1840, a few hundred fur trappers and traders roamed throughout Utah. Jim Bridger was one of the best known of these "Mountain Men."

What was life like for the Mountain Men?

- Golden Spike National Historic Site at Promontory, Utah, marks the place where the two parts of the nation's first transcontinental railroad joined in 1869.

What does *transcontinental* mean? Why was the completion of a transcontinental railroad important?

- What would you call an animal that was half lion, half tiger? People at the Hogle Zoo in Salt Lake City called the cub, Shasta, a liger when she was born in 1948. This zoo was also home to Princess Alice, a 9,000 pound elephant who died at the age of 78.

Make up an animal of your own by combining two animals. What would you call it? What would it look like? What would it like to eat?

If we land in the Great Salt Lake, do you think our balloon would float?

Welcome to Vermont

Winter is a great time to visit Vermont if you like to ski. There are 1,800 miles of cross-country trails and lots of resorts for downhill skiing.

Nickname: Green Mountain State
State motto: Freedom and Unity
State flower: Red clover
State tree: Sugar maple
State bird: Hermit thrush
State animal: Morgan horse
State fish: Brook trout and walleye pike
State insect: Honeybee
State butterfly: Monarch butterfly
State beverage: Milk
State song: "Hail, Vermont!"
Capital: Montpelier became the capital in 1805.
1990 Population: 562,758: the 3rd smallest in population. Only Wyoming and Alaska have fewer people.
Area: 9,614 square miles: the 8th smallest state
Neighbors: Canada, New Hampshire, Massachusetts and New York
Statehood: When the 13 colonies declared their independence from England, Vermont decided not to join them. The people of Vermont didn't want to be part of any other country or state. They declared their independence on January 15, 1777. The country was called New Connecticut at first. The name was changed to Vermont six months later. In its first constitution, slavery was outlawed in Vermont. Vermont elected its own president, coined its own money and had its own postal service. It became the 14th state on March 4, 1791.

Some of the coins from the country of Vermont are valuable to collectors today.

Design a coin for Vermont. Show what both sides of the coin would look like on the two circles below.

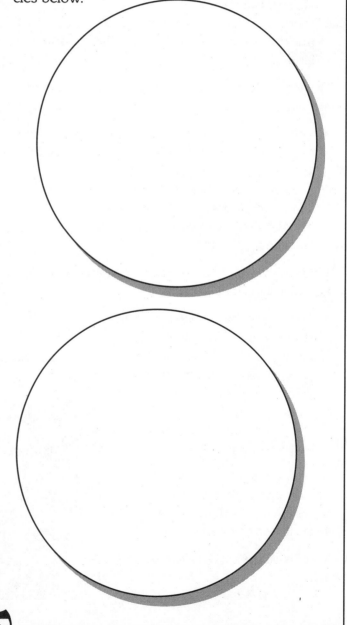

212

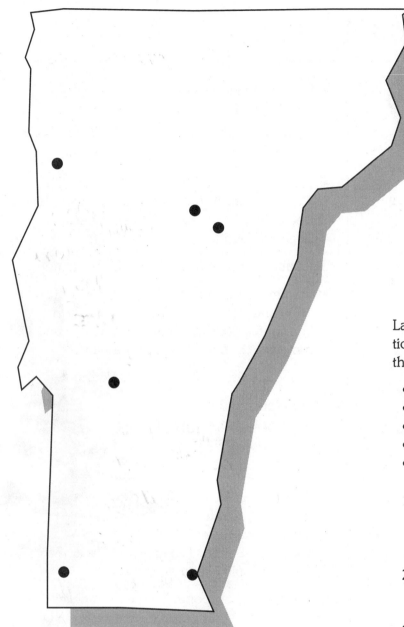

Label these places, or their approximate locations, on the Vermont state map. Then answer the questions below.

- Burlington
- Rutland
- Bennington
- Barre
- Brattleboro

- Montpelier
- Massachusetts
- New Hampshire
- New York
- Canada

1. What direction would you go to get from Bennington to Brattleboro?

   _____

2. Is Montpelier north or south of Rutland?

   _____

3. Which state is west of Vermont?

   _____

4. Which city is closer to New Hampshire: Barre or Brattleboro?

   _____

5. Which city is closer to Canada: Burlington or Montpelier?

   _____

6. Is Bennington closer to New York or Massachusetts?

   _____

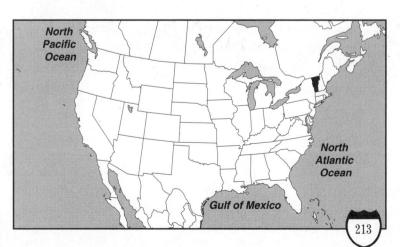

This and That

• Vermont leads the nation in the production of maple syrup, producing about 400,000 gallons a year. It takes 10 gallons of sap to make one gallon of maple syrup.

Describe how maple syrup is made.

• Seventy-five percent of Vermont is covered with forest.

What types of trees grow in Vermont?

• If you like cold weather and winter sports, you'll love Vermont. A temperature of -50°F was recorded in Bloomfield on December 30, 1933.

What is the coldest temperature ever recorded in the state where you live?

_____

• 1816 was called "the year without a summer" in Vermont. Snow fell in June, July and August. Crops failed. Livestock died. The cold spell lasted two years.

Write a short story titled "The Year Without a Summer."

• About 100 inches of snow falls on Vermont's mountains each year.

How many feet would 100 inches of snow equal?

_____

• Wilson Castle, built in 1867, is a 32-room house near Proctor, Vermont.

Draw the floor plan for a 32-room house. Label the rooms (kitchen, dining room, bedroom, etc.).

• Famous people from Vermont include Ethan Allen, Chester A. Arthur, Calvin Coolidge, John Deere, Stephen Douglas, Robert Frost and Brigham Young.

Write about one of these people from Vermont.

• Samuel de Champlain explored Vermont in 1609 and claimed the area for France. Vermont is from the French words *vert* and *mont* which mean "green mountains."

Describe the Green Mountains of Vermont.

• The National Rotten Sneaker Championship is held on the first day of spring in Montpelier. Winners receive savings bonds, foot powder and new sneakers. Sounds like an event Oscar the Grouch would like to attend!

Imagine being a reporter for the *Montpelier Press*. Write a short article for the newspaper about the winning sneakers.

Vermont has over 100 covered bridges, more than any other state. The longest covered bridge still in use can be seen at Windsor. This 450-foot bridge crosses the Connecticut River to Cornish, New Hampshire.

Why were covered bridges covered?

Vermont Firsts

Read about these Vermont firsts. Answer the assigned questions on another sheet of paper.

1. Silos were first used on farms in Vermont.

   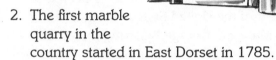

   What are silos used for?

2. The first marble quarry in the country started in East Dorset in 1785.

   What is marble used for?

3. Horses known as Morgans were bred and raised in Vermont in the 1790s to plow the hilly fields of that state.

   Draw and describe a Morgan horse.

4. The first canal built in the United States began operating at Bellows Falls in 1802.

   How long ago was the canal built?

5. Our country's first private military college was established at Norwich in 1819.

   How long ago was the first military college established?

   What was it called?

6. Elisha Otis of Halifax, Vermont, invented the first modern elevator.

   How does the Otis elevator work?

7. Horace Wells of White River Junction was the first person to use laughing gas as an anesthetic for pulling teeth in 1844.

   What type of anesthetic is used by dentists today?

8. The first statewide dairy asso- ciation was formed in

Vermont would be a great place to stop for breakfast. Pancakes and fresh maple syrup! Dee-licious!

Montpelier in 1869.

   How long ago was the Vermont Dairymen's Association formed?

9. Dr. H. Nelson Jackson was the first person to drive across the United States. The trip took him 70 days in 1903 in a car called the Vermont.

   It is 3,217 miles from Portland, Maine, to San Francisco, California. At 55 miles per hour, how many hours would it take to drive that far today?

10. Our country's first Boy Scout troop began in Barre, Vermont, in 1909.

    How many years have the Boy Scouts been around?

11. The first ski tow in the U.S. opened in Woodstock in 1934. The first chairlift was used on Mount Mansfield in 1940.

    Describe how a chairlift at a ski resort works.

12. Ida M. Fuller of Ludlow received the first Social Security check ever issued in 1940. The check was for the amount of $22.54.

    What is your Social Security number?

13. Vermont was the first state to open a tourist agency to bring vacationers to their state.

    Design a poster to encourage people to visit Vermont.

Welcome to Virginia

Relax as we head south and let the breeze carry us back to "Old Virginia," another of the 13 original colonies.

Nicknames: Old Dominion and Mother of Presidents

State motto: Thus Always to Tyrants

State flower and tree: Flowering dogwood

State bird: Cardinal

State animal: American fox-hound

State shell: Oyster shell

State song: "Carry Me Back to Old Virginia"

Capital: Richmond

Statehood: June 25, 1788. Virginia was one of the 13 original states and the 10th to ratify the Constitution.

1990 Population: 6,187,358: the 12th largest in population

Area: 40,767 square miles: the 36th largest in area

Neighbors: Kentucky; West Virginia; Maryland; Washington, D.C.; North Carolina; Tennessee; Chesapeake Bay and the Atlantic Ocean

Famous Virginians

Eight men from Virginia have been elected President of the United States: Thomas Jefferson, James Madison, George Washington, James Monroe, William Harrison, John Tyler, Zachary Taylor and Woodrow Wilson.

Use reference books to help you match the names of these famous Virginians with their achievements.

A. Robert E. Lee   G. Ella Fitzgerald
B. John Paul Jones   H. Patrick Henry
C. Walter Reed   I. Henry L. Marsh III
D. Booker T. Washington   J. L. Douglas Wilder
E. Arthur Ashe   K. Henry Clay
F. Richard E. Byrd   L. Zachary Taylor

1. ____ Discovered how typhoid fever and yellow fever spread

2. ____ Nation's first African American governor

3. ____ Naval commander in Revolutionary War

4. ____ Famous for "Give me liberty . . ." speech

5. ____ Twelfth President, nicknamed "Old Rough and Ready"

6. ____ First person to fly over the North Pole

7. ____ Founded Tuskegee University

8. ____ Famous jazz singer

9. ____ First African American man to win the U.S. men's singles tennis title

10. ____ Famous for saying, "I would rather be right than be President."

11. ____ Leader of the Confederate Army

12. ____ Richmond's first African American mayor

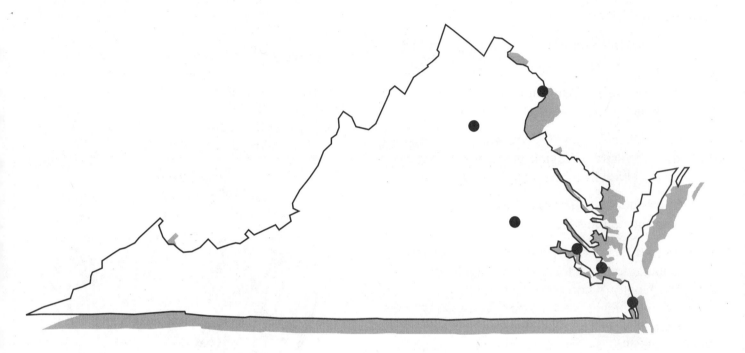

Read these facts about Virginia. Write the names of the underlined places on the Virginia state map above.

The first free school in the United States began in <u>Hampton</u> in 1634.

<u>Williamsburg</u> replaced Jamestown as the capital in 1699. Richmond did not become the capital until 1780.

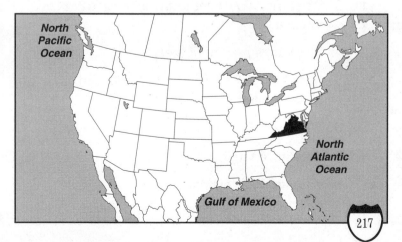

The Virginia Museum of Fine Arts, in <u>Richmond</u>, was the first state-supported art museum in the United States.

Virginia's first public library was established in 1794 in <u>Alexandria</u>.

A small part of Virginia is not connected to the rest of the state. It is called the <u>Eastern Shore</u>.

People enjoy visiting <u>Virginia Beach</u>, a popular vacation spot on the Atlantic Ocean.

In 1989, hundreds of dinosaur footprints were discovered at <u>Culpeper</u>.

Virginia is bordered by <u>Kentucky</u>; <u>West Virginia</u>; <u>Maryland</u>; <u>Washington, D.C.</u>; <u>North Carolina</u>; <u>Tennessee</u>; <u>Chesapeake Bay</u> and the <u>Atlantic Ocean</u>. Label their approximate locations on the map above.

Did You Know?

Read these facts about Virginia. Answer the questions below.

- Virginia was named for Queen Elizabeth I of England, known as the "Virgin Queen."

- The nickname "Old Dominion" was given to Virginia by King Charles II of England.

- The earliest Virginia Colony was much larger than the state of Virginia is today. Eight states were carved from the original land.

- The Little River Turnpike, built in the 1780s, was the nation's first toll road.

- The homes of many former Presidents are popular tourist attractions. George Washington's home on the bank of the Potomac River was in Mount Vernon. Thomas Jefferson designed his 35-room home called Monticello. He supervised its construction which took 40 years to complete.

Montpelier was the home of the nation's fourth President, James Madison. John Tyler, the tenth U.S. President named his home Sherwood Forest.

- Coal is the number one mining product in Virginia. Limestone, sandstone and granite are also mined.

- Virginia can be divided into three regions: the eastern section of the state along the coast is known as the Tidewater. It is also called the Coastal Plain. The Piedmont covers the central portion of the state. *Piedmont* means "foot of the mountain" in French. The Blue Ridge Mountains run in a southwesterly direction across western Virginia. The mountains contain many scenic caverns open to the public including Skyline Caverns, Luray Caverns, Shenandoah Caverns and the Caverns of Natural Bridge.

- The Tomb of the Unknown Soldier in Arlington National Cemetery is a memorial to honor dead American soldiers whose names are unknown.

1. What is the number one mining product in Virginia?

2. Where is the Tomb of the Unknown Soldier?

3. What mountains are found in western Virginia?

4. What does *piedmont* mean?

5. How long did it take Thomas Jefferson to build Monticello?

6. What was the nation's first toll road called?

7. Who gave Virginia its nickname?

8. Who was Virginia named for?

In the Beginning

Prehistoric people settled in Virginia more than 5,000 years ago. They fished and hunted deer, bear and other game. About 2,000 years ago they began planting corn and other crops. The Sequehana and Powhatans built their villages along the coast. The Monacans and Manahoacs lived in the central part of Virginia. The Cherokee lived in the western mountains.

A Cherokee Legend

The Cherokee were amazed when they first met people from Africa and Europe. They told this story to explain why people have different colored skin:

When it was time to make people, the creator built an oven. Then he formed three figures out of dough, but he did not know how long to bake them. He took the first one out too soon. It was not done enough. The descendants of this "underdone" figure are white people. The creator waited a bit longer and took out the second figure. It was light brown and became the ancestor of the Cherokee and other Native Americans. The creator was so pleased he forgot to watch the oven, and the third figure baked too long. It turned very dark in color. The figure became the ancestor of all black people.

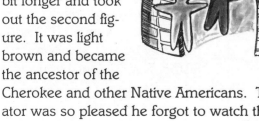

Pocahontas

Captain John Smith helped establish the original colony at Jamestown in 1607. While out hunting, he and two others were captured by the Powhatans in 1608. John Smith was saved from death by the chief's daughter, Pocahontas. She later married John Rolfe, a successful planter. Their marriage began an eight-year period of peace between the settlers and the Powhatans.

Write a conversation that might have taken place between Pocahontas and her father when she convinced him to spare captain John Smith's life.

A Tour of Historic Virginia

Because Virginia was the site of the first European town in the New World, the state played an important role in the early history of our country.

Match these historic events with the sites on the map. Write the letter of the event by the correct place.

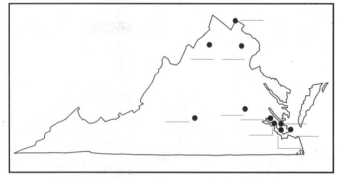

A. England's first permanent settlement was founded at <u>Jamestown</u> in 1607.

B. One of the final battles of the Revolutionary War occurred at <u>Yorktown</u> where George Washington's army defeated British troops under General Cornwallis.

C. At <u>Harper's Ferry</u>, John Brown led a group of abolitionists on a raid of an arsenal in 1859. They wished to arm runaway slaves and establish a free state in the mountains.

D. Virginia seceded from the Union on April 17, 1861. A month later <u>Richmond</u> became the Confederate capital.

E. The first major battle of the Civil War was fought near <u>Bull Run Creek</u>.

F. The <u>Shenandoah Valley</u>, called the "Granary of the Confederacy," was the site of many battles as the North fought to control the Confederates' food supply.

G. More than half of the battles of the Civil War were fought in Virginia. The battle between the two ironclad ships, the *Monitor* and the *Merrimac* was fought at <u>Hampton Roads</u> in 1862.

H. The Civil War ended when General Robert E. Lee surrendered to General Ulysses S. Grant at <u>Appomattox</u>.

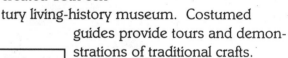
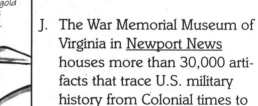

I. Visitors enjoy touring Colonial <u>Williamsburg</u>, an elaborately re-created 18th century living-history museum. Costumed guides provide tours and demonstrations of traditional crafts.

I hear there's gold in the sand at Virginia Beach.

J. The War Memorial Museum of Virginia in <u>Newport News</u> houses more than 30,000 artifacts that trace U.S. military history from Colonial times to the present.

Welcome to Washington

As we travel to the Evergreen State in the Pacific Northwest, watch for beautiful Mount Olympus, named for the mythical home of the Greek gods.

Nickname: Evergreen State
State motto: By and By
State flower: Coast rhododendron
State tree: Western hemlock
State bird: Willow goldfinch
State fish: Steelhead trout
State gem: Petrified wood
State colors: Green and gold
State dance: Square dance
State song: "Washington, My Home"
Capital: Olympia
Statehood: Washington became the 42nd state on November 11, 1889.
1990 Population: 4,866,692: the 18th largest in population
Area: 68,139 square miles: the 20th largest state
Neighbors: Idaho, Oregon, British Columbia and the Pacific Ocean

Did You Know?

- Washington was named for the first President, George Washington.

- National forests and parklands cover more than one-third of Washington.

- Mount St. Helens, which erupted in 1980, is now protected as a national monument.

- A rare variety of quartz called Ellensburg Blue is found only in central Washington.

No Laughing Matter

Native American children in Washington and along the Pacific Northwest coast had many handmade toys. Boys played with miniature canoes, bows and arrows. Girls played with carved wooden dolls with hair of bark or fur. They also enjoyed games like ones we play today—games like tag, hide and seek and king of the hill.

Both children and adults enjoyed the "laughing game." They divided into two teams. The team members stared at each other with sad faces. Whoever smiled or laughed first was the loser.

Divide up into teams of three or four and play the laughing game.

Label the underlined places on the Washington state map.

Washington is bordered by the province of <u>British Columbia</u> on the north, <u>Idaho</u> on the east and the <u>Pacific Ocean</u> on the west. Label their approximate locations on the map above.

The <u>Columbia River</u> forms part of the southern border between Washington and <u>Oregon</u>.

Ships travel through the <u>Strait of Juan de Fuca</u> to enter Puget Sound.

The <u>San Juan Islands</u>, a group of 172 small islands, are located in <u>Puget Sound</u>.

On a clear day, Mount Rainier, the highest mountain in Washington, can be seen from <u>Seattle</u>, more than 60 miles away.

The city of <u>Tacoma</u> started in 1852 at the site of a water-driven sawmill.

<u>Olympia</u>, the capital of Washington, began as a shipping port for logging companies.

The residents of <u>Yakima</u> were disappointed when the Northern Pacific Railroad laid tracks four miles away, leaving them without a railroad depot. Residents jacked up their houses, put them on wheels and rolled them closer to the tracks.

Other major cities in Washington are <u>Spokane</u>, <u>Bellingham</u>, <u>Vancouver</u>, <u>Bremerton</u> and <u>Kennewick</u>.

At the Sign of the Totem Pole

Before white settlers arrived, a group of Makah people lived in a village in Washington near the Pacific Ocean. The people wrapped themselves in animal skins for warmth and slept on raised platforms on woven mats of reeds and bark. They stored clothing, tools, hunting and fishing gear in baskets and wooden boxes. One house in the village contained a carved totem pole that looked like the back fin of a killer whale. The totem pole was painted black and decorated with hundreds of otter teeth.

How do we know so many details of this Makah village? A mud slide destroyed part of the village 500 years ago, covering everything in its path—people, houses, dogs, tools and totem poles. Much of the village was frozen in time. In 1970, a heavy storm washed away some of the mud. Scientists discovered thousands of items preserved under the mud.

The Makah were one of several Native American groups called the Totem Pole Indians who lived along the Pacific Northwest coast from Washington to Alaska.

Not all Native Americans carved totem poles. A totem pole was like a sign that told about the people in a home or village. A house totem pole told a family's story and identified their clan. Important people and events would be carved into the pole.

Some totem poles were 80 feet tall and included several carved figures perched on top of each other. The figures could be of people, animals, fish, birds or mythological creatures. Many were brightly painted and intricately carved.

Carved poles were also used to mark graves, as welcome signs for visitors or to mark special places. The largest ones were carved from whole trees by trained craftsmen and took a year or more to complete.

Design a personal totem pole that represents your life or your family. Draw it on another sheet of paper. In the space below, explain why you used each figure, decoration, shape and color.

_____
_____
_____
_____
_____
_____
_____
_____
_____
_____
_____
_____
_____
_____
_____

Learn More About Washington

Use reference books to find an interesting fact about each of the topics listed below.

Olympic National Park: _____
_____

Mount Rainier National Park: _____
_____

North Cascades National Park: _____
_____
_____

Grand Coulee Dam: _____
_____

Expo '74: _____
_____

Space Needle: _____
_____

Mount Rainier: _____
_____

Mount St. Helens: _____
_____

Mount Olympus: _____
_____

Hudson's Bay Company: _____
_____

Cape Disappointment: _____
_____

Puget Sound: _____
_____

Cascade Mountains: _____
_____

Olympic Peninsula: _____
_____

Red Delicious and Golden Delicious: _____
_____

Chinook and sockeye salmon: _____
_____

Boeing Company: _____
_____

Tacoma Narrows Bridge: _____
_____

Fort Spokane: _____
_____

Fort Vancouver: _____
_____

Hell's Canyon: _____
_____

The Seattle monorail: _____
_____

Peace Arch State Park: _____
_____

"Fifty-Four-Forty or Fight" _____
_____
_____

There's Mount St. Helens. She seems to be steaming a little bit. I hope she doesn't blow her top.

224

Welcome to West Virginia

Let's stop for a while at Monogahela National Forest. It covers 840 acres in the Mountain State and includes Blackwater Falls, Blackwater Canyon and many limestone caverns.

Nicknames: Mountain State and Panhandle State
State motto: Mountaineers Are Always Free
State flower: Rhododendron
State tree: Sugar maple
State bird: Cardinal
State fish: Brook trout
State animal: Black bear
State colors: Blue and gold
State song: "The West Virginia Hills"
Capital: Charleston
Statehood: West Virginia became the 35th state to join the Union on June 20, 1863.

1990 Population:
  1,793,477: the 34th largest in population
Area: 24,231 square miles: the 41st largest state
Neighbors: Ohio, Pennsylvania, Maryland, Virginia and Kentucky

Did You Know?

- West Virginia has been called the Switzerland of America. The Alleghenies and the Blue Ridge Mountains, plus the rugged Appalachian Plateau give West Virginia its nickname, the Mountain State.

- West Virginia was part of Virginia until 1861. By a large majority, the voters of western Virginia favored becoming a separate state. Wheeling became the new capital. Political leaders considered several names for the new state including Kanawha, Allegheny and Augusta. On June 20, 1863, Congress approved West Virginia as the 35th state. During the Civil War, Virginia joined the Confederate States while West Virginia remained with the Union, even though many in the Eastern Panhandle fought in the Confederate Army.

- After the Civil War, Virginia asked West Virginia to reunite and form one state again. When West Virginians refused, Virginia presented the state with a bill for millions of dollars to pay off the state debt incurred before the two states separated. It took the courts 45 years to settle the case. Eventually West Virginia paid $12.4 million to Virginia.

- The famous feud between the Hatfields and the McCoys began during the Civil War. The Hatfields from West Virginia sided with the South. The McCoys, across the border in Kentucky, enlisted in the Union Army. When a pig ran away from one family's farm, the other family claimed it. Fueled by their political differences, this incident was enough to start a family feud which lasted for several generations.

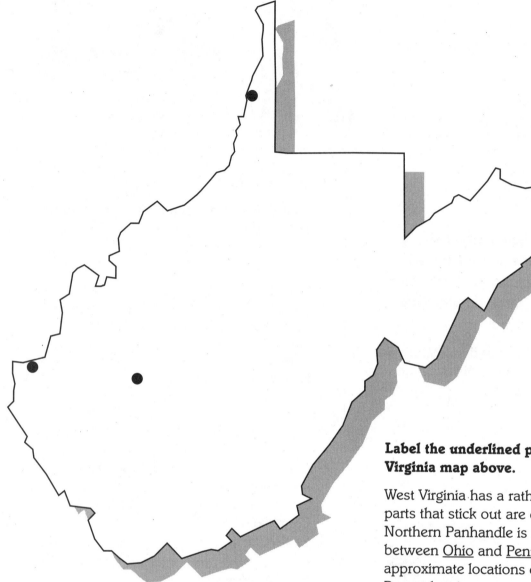

Label the underlined places on the West Virginia map above.

West Virginia has a rather odd shape. The two parts that stick out are called panhandles. The Northern Panhandle is a narrow strip of land between <u>Ohio</u> and <u>Pennsylvania</u>. Label the approximate locations of Ohio and Pennsylvania.

The Eastern Panhandle is bordered by <u>Virginia</u> and <u>Maryland</u>. Label their approximate locations.

<u>Kentucky</u> borders West Virginia on the southwest. Label its approximate location.

Most of West Virginia has a moderate climate with warm, humid summers and mild winters. The average high temperature in July is 87°F in <u>Charleston</u>. One hundred inches of snow can fall in the central and northeastern mountains.

<u>Huntington</u> is located on the Ohio River.

In the early days, Fort Fincastle protected the village of <u>Wheeling</u> in the Northern Panhandle.

North Pacific Ocean

North Atlantic Ocean

Gulf of Mexico

226

West Virginia Pioneers

The first people to live in West Virginia were the nomadic hunters who arrived about 15,000 B.C. Archaeologists have found tools and arrowheads of these people who hunted mammoths, mastodons, camels and other animals now extinct.

Over thousands of years, different groups of people lived in West Virginia, including those known as the Mound Builders. At the largest mound in West Virginia, called Grave Creek Mound, scientists found the skeleton of a person seven and a half feet tall.

No one knows what happened to the Mound Builders or why their civilization died out about 500 A.D. By the time Europeans began exploring the land, the mounds were overgrown with trees and shrubs.

Although many tribes hunted in the area, few groups made their permanent homes in the rugged land of West Virginia. Early explorers and settlers discovered some small Shawnee, Mingo and Tuscarora villages.

People began exploring and mapping West Virginia in the 1670s, but few pioneers moved to the area until after 1725. Even then, the population grew slowly. Most early settlers lived in the Eastern Panhandle region called western Virginia.

Slowly, the pioneers moved west. Conflicts occurred with tribes who resented white settlers living in their traditional hunting grounds. In 1763 King George III of England banned further settlements west of the Alleghenies, hoping to end the conflicts between colonists and Native Americans. People from the Netherlands, Germany, Scotland and Ireland ignored the order. So did the English colonists.

The abundant forests of West Virginia provided the early pioneers with wood to build homes. Building a log cabin required much hard work and most homes were small—about the size of a two-car garage. A central fireplace provided a place to cook and heat for the home. They hunted deer, bear and wild turkeys and planted corn, potatoes and squash.

Discussion Questions

- Many animals once found in West Virginia and other states are now extinct. How do you think they became extinct?

- What do you think might have happened to the Mound Builders?

- Why do you think people ignored King George's law not to settle west of the Allegheny Mountains?

- Why do you think the early colonists believed West Virginia was the "far west"?

- What do you think it would have been like for a large family to live in a log cabin?

- What do you think children did for fun? What kinds of chores do you think they had to do to help their parents?

Industry Grows in West Virginia

Salt was the first major industry in West Virginia. Commercial salt mines opened in Bulltown, Clarksburg and in the Great Kanawha Valley in the early 1800s. Not only was salt important as a seasoning, it was needed to preserve meat.

Another early industry began at a large iron making plant which opened in 1794. At its peak, the plant produced two tons of iron a day.

The railroads helped the industrial growth of West Virginia. In 1873, Huntington was linked by railroad to Norfolk, Virginia, and coal could be sent to new markets on the Atlantic coast. Needing coal to fuel the steam-driven engines, the railroad became an important customer for West Virginia coal.

Coal, first discovered in 1742, eventually became the major industry in West Virginia, providing jobs for thousands. Cotton may have been king in many neighboring states, but coal was king in West Virginia. In 1870, 600,000 tons of coal came from the state's mines.

For miners and their families, coal provided jobs, but wages were low and the work was difficult. Besides long hours of heavy work, the mines were dark and unsafe. Cave-ins, explosions and other types of accidents occurred. Miners often worked knee-deep in water. Company towns grew up around the mines. Workers rented homes from the mine owners and bought their goods in a company-owned store, at prices set by mine owners.

Union strikes for better pay, shorter hours and safer working conditions were often bitter battles between workers and owners. Dependence on coal mining led to the state's problems with unemployment and poverty. When coal prices fell, thousands lost their jobs.

New industries like lumbering, glassmaking, production of chemicals, sand and gravel, tourism, salt mining and the discovery of petroleum and natural gas have made West Virginia less dependent on King Coal.

Select one of the topics below for a report.

- Write a story about what you think it would be like to work in a coal mine in the early days.

- How is salt mined? What else is salt used for besides a seasoning?

- How is coal mined? Compare conditions in West Virginia's coal mines today to conditions 100 years ago.

- Select one of the industries in West Virginia. How has that industry helped the people of West Virginia?

So many mountains! No wonder they call this the Mountain State!

Welcome to Wisconsin

Only a few more states left to visit. Some might say we've left the best until last as we go "forward" to Wisconsin. Each year in early June, thousands travel to Wisconsin to watch the Great Wisconsin Dells Hot Air Balloon Rally.

Nicknames: Badger State and America's Dairyland

State motto: Forward

State flower: Wood violet

State tree: Sugar maple

State bird: Robin

State animal: Badger

State fish: Muskellunge (muskie)

State insect: Honeybee

State mineral: Galena

State rock: Red granite

State song: "On Wisconsin!"

Capital: Madison

Statehood: Wisconsin became the 30th state on May 29, 1848.

1990 Population: 4,891,769: the 16th largest in population

Area: 56,150 square miles: the 26th largest in area

Neighbors: Michigan, Illinois, Iowa and Minnesota

Famous Wisconsinites: Edna Ferber, Robert LaFollette, Georgia O'Keeffe, Spencer Tracy, Orsen Wells, Frank Lloyd Wright, Laura Ingalls Wilder, John Muir, Maureen Daly, Woody Herman and the Ringling Brothers. Harry Houdini, the famous magician and escape artist, was raised in Appleton.

Land of Lakes

Wisconsin has nearly 15,000 lakes, rivers, streams and creeks—so many that Wisconsin ran out of names for them. There are 51 named Beaver Creek and 74 named Long Lake. Lake Winnebago, the largest inland lake in Wisconsin, covers 215 square miles. The word *Wisconsin* comes from the Chippewa word meaning "the gathering of waters."

Why does Wisconsin have so many lakes? Have you ever heard of Paul Bunyan, the giant lumberjack? Paul's big Blue Ox, Babe, used to get very thirsty, so Paul scooped out all those lakes with his shovel.

Although tall tales are fun to read, the thousands of lakes in Wisconsin were not exactly scooped out by Paul Bunyan's huge shovel. They were formed by glaciers which moved south from Canada like a giant bulldozer. Much of Wisconsin was covered by the glaciers during the last Ice Age. The enormous walls of ice flattened mountains and formed valleys. When the ice melted and the glaciers retreated, thousands of lakes, streams and creeks remained.

Write your own "tall tale" about why there are so many lakes in Wisconsin.

229

Locate Lake Winnebago on the map above. Color it blue.

Write the names of these major Wisconsin cities in the correct places on the map: Madison, Milwaukee, Racine, Green Bay, Kenosha, Appleton and Sheboygan.

Draw a red line along the border between Wisconsin and Illinois.

Draw a blue line along the border between Wisconsin and Minnesota.

1. What famous river forms much of the border between Wisconsin and Minnesota?

   _____

2. What two Great Lakes border Wisconsin?
   Lake _____ and Lake _____

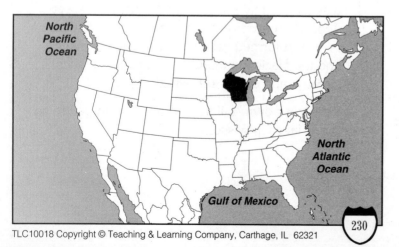

Early Inhabitants of Wisconsin

Big game hunters and their families arrived in Wisconsin 13,000 to 14,000 years ago. As the huge glaciers retreated, nomads followed the herds of mastodons, giant beavers, deer, caribou and elk which headed north. Some of these people continued to move north. Others settled in the area.

Further migrations to Wisconsin continued for the next 10,000 years. By the time white settlers began arriving in Wisconsin, they found villages of Winnebago, Fox, Illinois, Kickapoo, Menominee, Miami, Ojibwa, Ottawa, Potawatomi, Sauk and Sioux.

Look at a map of Wisconsin. List cities, lakes and rivers named for Native American tribes.

_____

_____

_____

_____

_____

_____

Meet the Red Earth People

They called themselves the **Mesquaki**, "the red earth people." We know them as the Fox. They lived on a hilltop on the south shore of Lake Butte des Morts from 1680 until they were driven out by the French.

For 50 years the Fox controlled the fur trade along what is now known as the Fox River. The French, however, also wished to control the fur trade and launched military expeditions against the Fox village in 1716, 1728 and 1739.

Scientists have uncovered the remains of a 10- to 15-acre village of several thousand inhabitants. They have identified residential areas, refuse areas, areas for processing animal carcasses, gardens and cornfields. The village itself was surrounded by a wooden palisade (high fence). Many of the Fox probably lived outside the palisade and sought safety in the village in times of war.

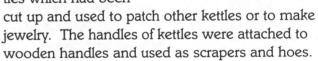

Scientists have discovered broken pottery and stone tools; French muskets; musket balls; glass beads; animal, deer and fish bones. They discovered parts of brass kettles which had been cut up and used to patch other kettles or to make jewelry. The handles of kettles were attached to wooden handles and used as scrapers and hoes.

This site is unique in several ways. It's the only known place where the Fox once lived. The first major battle in Wisconsin between Europeans and Native Americans took place here.

Why is it important to preserve the Fox village site and other places where early Native Americans once lived? What can we learn from studying these places? Write your answers on another sheet of paper.

Ginseng, an Unusual Wisconsin Crop

Ginseng, a root called the "elixir of life," is used in China, as a remedy for many diseases, to relieve stress and fatigue, to alleviate joint stiffness and improve athletic performance. "Cold" ginseng (grown in a cold climate like Wisconsin) is good for cooling the body. Ginseng is also used in soups and as a seasoning for various dishes.

Ginseng was first discovered by white settlers near Montreal in 1716. In Colonial times, wild ginseng could be found in southern Canada,

across the northern U.S. and even as far south as Kentucky and West Virginia. Native Americans knew the plant by many names and used the root for medicinal purposes. To the Cherokee, ginseng was known as "Little Man" because its shape resembles the human form. The Chippewa, Creek, Pawnee, Iroquois and Sioux also used ginseng as a medicine.

Between 1820 and 1903 nearly 17 million pounds of wild American ginseng were exported to China. Today, 95% of the ginseng grown in the U.S. is raised in Wisconsin. Ninety percent of Wisconsin's ginseng is raised in Marathon County. Thanks to growers in Marathon County, the U.S. is currently the third largest exporter of ginseng in the world.

Raising ginseng is time consuming, expensive and labor-intensive. Ginseng must be protected from a variety of diseases and pests. Once land is used to grow ginseng, it cannot be used for that purpose again. The crop takes from four to six years before it can be harvested. Ginseng roots are gathered in fall, cleaned and hung to

dry in a heated shed. One hundred pounds of fresh roots yield about 25 pounds of dried roots. A good acre yields about 2,000 pounds of ginseng.

Growers from China come to Marathon County to inspect the crop. They may sort the ginseng according to size or by the shape of the roots. They may chew it to determine the flavor. The ideal color is a root golden on the outside and white inside. Once the roots are bought, they are packed and shipped to China for resale.

Corn, pumpkins, apples, sunflowers, potatoes, beans, beets, peas, hay, oats, cabbage and cranberries are also grown in Wisconsin.

Learn more about how ginseng or other Wisconsin crops are grown, where they're shipped and what they're used for.

Learn More About Wisconsin

Select one of the topics below for a short report. Illustrate your report or use pictures from magazines.

• Describe the culture of one of the Native American groups in Wisconsin before white settlers arrived.

• Who fought in the Fox Indian War? Why? Who won?

• Learn more about a person from Wisconsin or about someone like Jean Nicolet, Louis Joliet, Chief Oshkosh or Father Marquette who played an important role in Wisconsin's history.

• Why is Ripon known as the Birthplace of the Republican Party?

• How did the Treaty of Paris affect Wisconsin?

• Why is Wisconsin nick-named the Badger State? Hint: Not because of the badgers that live there.

• Why is Wisconsin known as America's Dairyland?

• Trace the origin of the names of three places in Wisconsin.

• Why was lead mining important to the development of Wisconsin?

• What are some of Wisconsin's natural resources? Why are they important?

• Black bear, white-tailed deer, mink, badgers, ducks and geese live in Wisconsin. Find out more about a Wisconsin animal, bird, fish, plant or tree.

• Make a collage. Cut out pictures and words from magazines and maps to make a Wisconsin collage. Include pictures of people, places, barns, animals and crops, or the names of cities and places in Wisconsin.

I wonder if the brown cows give chocolate milk?

233

Welcome to Wyoming

From the Grand Tetons to the Grand Canyon of Yellowstone, Wyoming has grand mountains and deserts, woods and plains.

Nicknames: Equality State and Cowboy State
State motto: Equal Rights
State flower: Indian paintbrush
State tree: Plains cottonwood
State bird: Meadowlark
State mammal: Bison
State gem: Jade
State song: "Wyoming"
Capital: Cheyenne
Statehood: Wyoming became the 44th state on July 10, 1890.
1990 Population: 453,588: the 50th in population. Wyoming averages only five people per square mile.
Area: 97,809 square miles: Wyoming is the 9th largest state.
Neighbors: Montana, Idaho, Utah, Colorado, South Dakota and Nebraska

The Equality State

In December 1869, long before Wyoming became a state, a woman's suffrage bill was passed granting women the right to vote and hold public office. Two months later, Esther Hobart Morris became the nation's first female judge when she was appointed as justice of the peace in South Pass City. Her statue stands before the main entrance to the state capitol building in Cheyenne.

Women first served on juries in Wyoming in 1870, but that practice was discontinued a year later and women were rarely called for jury duty until 1950.

In 1870, Eliza Swain, a 70-year-old grandmother, became the first woman to cast a ballot in a general election. Other women from Wyoming made history as the first to be elected to public office and as first woman state senator.

Discussion Questions: What If?

What if women had never been allowed to vote or hold public office in the United States?

What if all women in the United States had been allowed to vote and hold office as early as 1776?

What if a woman became President?

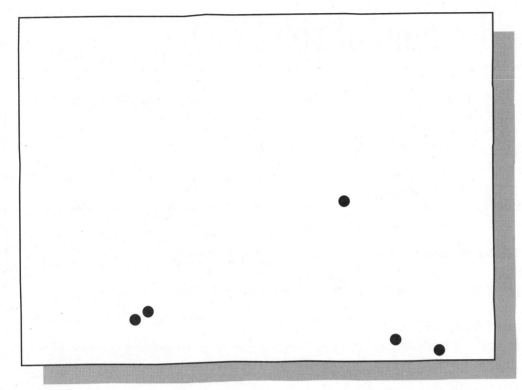

Scale

0 15 30   60

Miles

Label the underlined places on the Wyoming state map above.

Cheyenne was the first Union Pacific railroad station in Wyoming.

For a scenic drive through the mountain passes of Curt Gowdy State Park, take Happy Jack Road (State Highway 210) from Cheyenne to Laramie, another city that started as a railroad station.

Oil drilling began near Casper in 1888. Its first oil refinery opened in 1895.

Rock Springs started as a stop on the Overland stagecoach route in 1862.

The city of Green River is known as the Trona Capital of the World. What is trona? What is it used for?

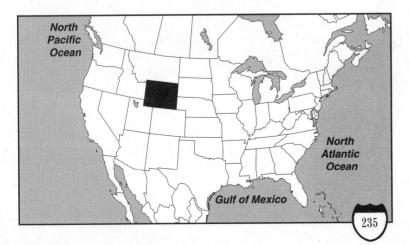

Wyoming is a rectangular state with straight lines along all four borders.

1. How far is it across Wyoming from east to west? _____ miles

2. How far is it across Wyoming from north to south? _____ miles

3. Which state is north of Wyoming?

   _____

4. Which three states are along the western border of Wyoming?

   _____

   _____

   _____

5. Which two states form Wyoming's southern border?

   _____

   _____

6. Two states border Wyoming on the east. What are they?

   _____

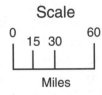

The Legend of the Cowboy

Many cowboys worked on the cattle and sheep ranches in Wyoming. Some worked on the railroad or followed huge herds of cattle on cattle drives. Some fought the Sioux, Cheyenne, Arapaho and other tribes who were trying to protect their homelands. The cattle ranchers fought with the sheep ranchers. Bandits and robbers fought with everyone.

In stories and movies, we see cowboys as romantic heroes who led adventurous lives. "Buffalo Bill" Cody helped give cowboys an exciting, romantic image. His traveling show, "Buffalo Bill's Wild West and Congress of Rough Riders of the World" thrilled audiences in the United States and Europe.

Can you imagine what the life of a cowboy might have really been like? Keep in mind that cowboys spent many long hours in a hard saddle. They had no air conditioning during the hot summers nor any protection from the blazing sun. They worked outside in blizzards and thunderstorms, with only the heat from a campfire to warm them at the end of a long day. They didn't have indoor plumbing, running water or microwaves. In winter, they couldn't go to the grocery store to buy fresh fruit and vegetables. They ate a lot of beans and tough dried meat called jerky. They rarely took baths. Many couldn't read or write.

Write a story about a day in the life of a real cowboy.

_____

_____

_____

_____

_____

_____

_____

_____

_____

_____

_____

_____

_____

_____

_____

_____

_____

_____

Land of Spectacular Natural Wonders

Where can you find magnificent snowcapped mountains, huge lakes, glaciers, deep canyons and gorges, rushing rivers and waterfalls, eerie rock formations, dry deserts, treeless plains, geysers, volcanoes and hot springs? Wyoming has them all.

Select one of the topics below for a report. Include pictures and illustrations.

- Describe the Red Desert and the plants and animals that live there.

- What is the Continental Divide?

- Compare the Grand Canyon of Yellowstone to the Grand Canyon in Arizona.

- What is the Great Divide Basin?

- Describe Wind River Canyon.

- Yellowstone's Lower Falls drop almost twice as far as Niagara Falls. Describe these spectacular falls.

- What does Devil's Tower look like? How did it get its name? How was it formed?

- What is Jackson's Hole?

- What types of fossils have been found at Fossil Butte?

- Describe the Red Canyon and the plants and animals that live there.

- What was found in Mummy Cave?

- What makes Old Faithful erupt?

Hot Air Ballooning in Wyoming

Hot air ballooning is a popular sport in Wyoming. Riverton holds an annual summer Hot Air Balloon Rally. The Desert Balloon Extravaganza takes place each year in Rock Springs.

Discussion Question

Why do you think traveling by hot air balloon would be popular in Wyoming?

Grand Teton National Park

The area surrounding the Teton Mountains in western Wyoming became a national park in 1929. The park includes the beautiful, rugged Teton Mountains which are part of the Rockies. The lakes at the base of the mountains are also part of the 500-square-mile park.

Grand Teton National Park has something found in few other places in the U.S.—12 small glaciers. The highest peak is Grand Teton, 13,700 feet above sea level. Visitors enjoy camping, canoeing, swimming, hiking, fishing, horseback riding and studying nature.

Unscramble these groups of letters to discover some animals that live in Grand Teton National Park.

1. nobis _____

2. stabbir _____

3. lek _____

4. rerlssuiq _____

5. someo _____

6. rabes _____

7. reed _____

8. gleesa _____

9. reevab _____

10. xof _____

11. grroophnsn _____

12. grabdes _____

Wyoming, a Wildlife Haven

Not only is the scenery spectacular in Wyoming, the trees, plants, birds and animals that live there are also quite amazing.

Learn more about the wildlife in Wyoming. Select one of the plants or animals listed below. Draw a picture of it and write 10 facts about it.

- moose
- grizzly bears
- lynx
- bison
- coyotes
- pronghorns
- falcons
- osprey
- pelicans
- rails
- muskie
- lichens
- ponderosa pines
- Engelmann spruce
- greasewood
- buffalo grass
- Indian paintbrush
- saxifrage
- kinnikinnick
- elk
- catfish
- mountain goats
- mountain lions
- mule deer
- trumpeter swans
- whistler swans
- bald eagles
- golden eagles
- grayling
- prairie rattlesnake
- Douglas firs
- sagebrush
- yuccas
- arnicas
- aspens
- flax
- columbine
- mahoganies
- Rocky Mountain bighorn sheep

Discussion Question: What If?

What if the government had never set aside any areas as national parks?

Yellowstone National Park

People would enjoy visiting Yellowstone simply to see the beautiful rock formations, deep canyons, roaring waterfalls, steep mountains and abundant wildlife. These sights are great, but they are not why the park is so special. The many thermal wonders make Yellowstone truly unique. *Thermal* means "caused by heat."

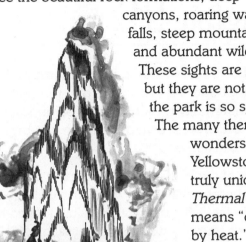

When John Colter and other early explorers told of seeing steam coming from the Earth, of brightly colored pools of boiling water and mud, of hot springs and geysers that spouted fountains of hot water, people thought they were making up stories.

Long ago, **volcanoes** erupted in Yellowstone. Deep in the Earth is a layer of molten rock called **magma**. When a volcano erupts, magma (lava) is pushed to the surface. When **lava** cools, it hardens into rock. Huge cone-shaped mountains may form from the lava. Flowing lava formed many of the landscape features in Yellowstone.

The volcanoes are no longer active, but the earth below the surface remains very hot. When water trapped below ground is heated, it expands and turns to steam. As water expands, pressure causes the water to find a way out. Water that bubbles up to the surface becomes a **hot spring**. Bacteria and algae that live in hot springs may cause the water to look brown, yellow, orange or green.

When steam rises through puddles of mud, **mud pots** are formed. The mud bubbles, burps and blurps like pudding boiling in a pot on the stove. Another thermal oddity in Yellowstone are **fumaroles** which shoot out hot gases and steam from holes in the Earth.

The best known thermal feature of Yellowstone is Old Faithful, a **geyser** that "blows its top" every 40 to 100 minutes. *Geyser* comes from an Icelandic word meaning "gusher." A geyser is a fountain of hot water that shoots into the air. Each time Old Faithful erupts, water shoots up 100 to 184 feet and lasts about four minutes.

The rushing waters of Yellowstone River cut a deep gorge called the Grand Canyon of Yellowstone. The canyon is 24 miles long and 1,200 feet deep in places.

In 1872 Yellowstone become the world's first national park. It gets its name from rhyolite, a yellow rock found there. The park covers 3,472 square miles, mostly in Wyoming.

Which thermal feature of Yellowstone would you most like to see? Why?

Find out more about volcanoes, hot springs, mud pots, fumaroles or geysers.

Write a short poem or story about Old Faithful.

Myths are stories used to explain something in nature. Make up a myth to explain why Old Faithful erupts.

Look! Old Faithful is about to erupt!

239

Welcome to Washington, D.C.

Although it's not part of any state, Washington, D.C., is the center of our nation's government.

Nicknames: Nation's Capital and Capital City
District motto: Justice for All
District flower: American Beauty rose
District tree: Scarlet oak
District bird: Wood thrush
Major industries: Government and tourism
1990 Population: 606,900
Area: 69 square miles
Neighbors: Maryland and Virginia across the Potomac River

Did You Know?

The *D.C.* in *Washington, D.C.,* stands for District of Columbia, named in honor of Christopher Columbus.

George Washington selected the site in 1791. The land was donated by the state of Maryland. Washington, D.C., became the U.S. capital in 1800.

In most cities, when you visit a mall, you plan to do some shopping. In Washington, D.C., the Mall is a large public park near the Capitol.

When the center of government moved from Pennsylvania to Washington, D.C., in 1800, there were 126 clerks on the government payroll. Today, about 400,000 people in the Washington area work for the Federal government.

Washington, D.C.s earliest inhabitant may have been an 80-foot brachiosaurus or a triceratops. One hundred fifty million years ago, dinosaurs lived in the cypress swamp that is now our nation's capital.

Building of the Washington Monument began in 1848, but money ran out when the obelisk was only 160 feet tall. Mark Twain said it looked like "a factory chimney with the top broken off." The 555-foot tall structure wasn't finished until 1885. When a steam elevator was installed, women and children weren't allowed to ride in it because it was considered too risky. They had to climb the 898 stairs if they wished to reach the top.

Select one of these famous places for a report. Include pictures or illustrations with your report.

• Washington Monument
• Capitol Building
• White House
• Lincoln Memorial
• Jefferson Memorial
• Treasury Building
• Supreme Court Building
• Vietnam Veterans Memorial
• Library of Congress
• Smithsonian Institution
• National Archives
• National Gallery of Art
• Kennedy Center for the Performing Arts

Discussion Question: What If?

What if our government still had only 126 people working for it?

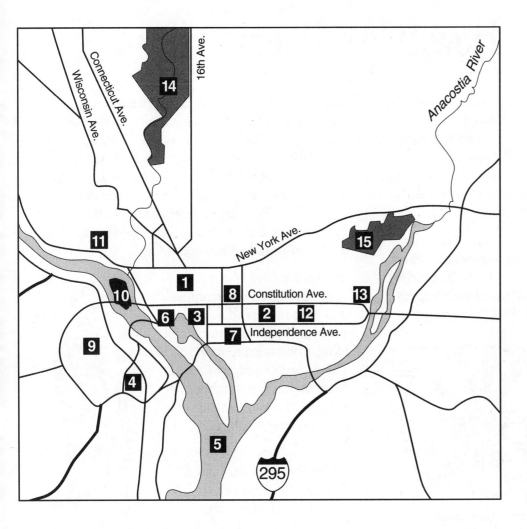

Look at the street map of Washington, D.C. Write the number next to the name of each Washington, D.C., landmark.

_____ Lincoln Memorial

_____ Supreme Court Building

_____ Capitol Building

_____ White House

_____ Washington Monument

_____ National Gallery of Art

_____ Smithsonian Institution

_____ Theodore Roosevelt Island

_____ Union Station

_____ The Pentagon

_____ Arlington National Cemetery

_____ National Arboretum

_____ Potomac River

_____ Georgetown University

_____ National Zoological Park

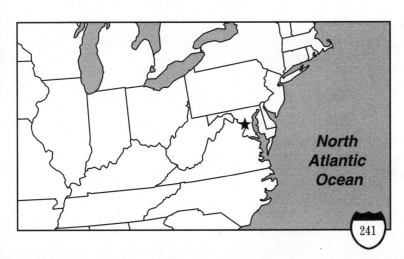

How It All Began

By 1790, the newly formed United States already had eight temporary capitals. George Washington knew the country needed a permanent center of government. The site of the capital was chosen for its central location. If a central location were chosen today, the capital would probably be in Kansas or Nebraska.

President Washington selected Pierre Charles L'Enfant, a French soldier, engineer and architect, to draw up the plans for the new city. He laid out the city in the shape of a wheel with streets as spokes of the wheel and the Capitol in the center. His plans were grand, with magnificent wide avenues. If a house, a store or even a tree stood in the way of a planned street,  L'Enfant wanted it torn down. Many people felt he was too rigid with his plans, and the city would cost far too much to build. He was finally fired. When he left, he took his detailed plans for the city with him. The task of completing the city fell to his assistant, Andrew Ellicott.

The first two major government buildings planned were the home of the President and a meeting place for Congress. Although several other official buildings joined the White House and Capitol during the early years, the city looked more like a country village than a great center of government. Only a few hundred wooden houses stood along the streets. The unpaved roads were dusty avenues in dry weather and lanes of mud in rainy weather. Cows and pigs wandered through the streets. Corn grew on Pennsylvania Avenue. The city did not grow very fast. For the first 10 years, only one police officer was needed for the whole city.

During the War of 1812, British troops invaded the capital. They piled up everything that would burn and set the Capitol and White House on fire. The Capitol burned to the ground. A heavy rainstorm put out the flames in the White House, but the building was gutted. The next day more buildings, offices and homes were set on fire. By the time the British soldiers left, Washington was a burned-out, smokey mess.

During the Civil War, soldiers again occupied Washington, this time to defend it. Union soldiers camped in the White House ballroom and on the Mall. The basement of the Capitol became the army bakery. A slaughterhouse was set up near the Washington Monument.

When the Civil War ended, thousands of former slaves moved to Washington. There weren't enough houses or water. Ditches served as open sewers and disease swept the city. President Lincoln's son, Willie, died of typhoid fever.

In 1871 the President appointed a governor to the city. Finally, sewers and sidewalks were installed. Street lamps were lit and roads paved. Washington, D.C., began looking like the great capital envisioned by George Washington nearly 100 years earlier.

Write a short story about what it might have been like to live in Washington, D.C., during the first 100 years.

Home of the Presidents

How was a decision made for the design for the President's home? A contest was held. James Hoban, an Irishman, won the contest with a plan that resembled a grand Irish manor house. The first foundation block was laid on October 12, 1792, on the 300th anniversary of the day Columbus landed in the New World.

When John and Abigail Adams moved in, the building wasn't completely finished. The place was drafty. The roof leaked and the walls weren't plastered. There was no place to hang laundry, so the First Lady had it hung in the East Room to dry.

George Washington was the only President never to live in the White House. Many Presidents and First Ladies have made changes to the original home. It wasn't called the White House until after it was painted and restored after being burned by the British during the War of 1812. Andrew Jackson had running water piped in. Millard Fillmore bought the first cookstove. James Polk had gaslights installed, and Benjamin Harrison brought in electricity. William Taft had a huge bathtub installed, and President Franklin D. Roosevelt put in a swimming pool.

So many changes were made over the years that the White House was in danger of collapsing by 1948. President Harry S. Truman called for a complete reconstruction of the building, a project that took four years to complete.

Today the White House has 132 rooms. Besides the first family's private quarters, the Oval Office and staff rooms, the White House has kitchens and supply rooms; a dentist's office and medical clinic; rooms for a barber and a florist; a movie theater; carpentry, paint and upholstery shops and an electrical center.

Imagine being a friend of someone who lived in the White House and going there to spend the day. What would you like to do and see if you could explore the home of the President?

The Capitol

Jenkin's Hill was chosen as the site for the nation's capitol building. Dr. William Thornton won $500 in a contest for the best plan. His design featured two identical wings, one for the House of Representatives and one for the Senate, joined by a round, domed center room called a rotunda.

George Washington laid the cornerstone for the capitol with a silver trowel on September 18, 1793. Lack of workers, money and materials caused many delays. Seven years later when Congress was scheduled to move in, only the north wing was ready. The Senate, House of Representatives, Circuit Court, Supreme Court and Library of Congress all squeezed into the one completed area. In summer it was so hot, people called it "The Oven."

After fire destroyed the building in 1814, the Capitol was eventually rebuilt to the original plans. As more states joined the Union, more room was needed for the additional members of Congress. The building was enlarged in 1851. The Senate and House of Representatives each had their own wing of the Capitol. The central rotunda area became a marketplace. Street vendors sold their wares and rubbish littered the floors. In 1864 Congress decided to clean up the rotunda and get rid of the vendors.

The sculpture "Freedom" on top of the Capitol dome was put in place in 1830. In 1959 the Capitol was enlarged again. President Dwight D. Eisenhower

laid the new cornerstone with the same silver trowel George Washington had used for the original building. Today the Capitol contains 540 rooms.

Select one of these topics for a report:

- What is the difference between the Senate and the House of Representatives?

- How large is the Capitol in square feet? What are some of the rooms used for?

- Describe Statuary Hall.

- Describe "Freedom," the statue on top of the rotunda.

- Why are people who come to the Capitol hoping to influence a vote called "lobbyists"?

- What are pages? What do they do at the Capitol?

- Why is Statuary Hall called Whispering Hall?

Answer Key

Arkansas

What Can You Find in *Little Rock*? page 14

cell	lick	rote
cello	like	tell
cite	litter	tic
colt	little	tick
core	lock	tie
cot	locker	tier
cotter	lore	till
ice	lot	tilt
ill	ore	tire
ire	otter	tock
irk	relock	toe
kill	rice	toll
killer	Rick	tore
kite	rill	tote
krill	roe	trice
let	role	trick
lice	roll	trill
		troll

California

Bits and Pieces, page 18

The first Mickey Mouse cartoon was *Steamboat Willy*.

Name the Sport, page 20

1.	San Diego Padres	baseball
2.	San Diego Chargers	football
3.	Los Angeles Dodgers	baseball
4.	Los Angeles Rams	football
5.	Los Angeles Raiders	football
6.	Los Angeles Kings	hockey
7.	Los Angeles Lakers	basketball
8.	Los Angeles Clippers	basketball
9.	San Francisco 49ers	football
10.	San Francisco Giants	baseball
11.	California Angels	baseball
12.	San Jose Sharks	hockey
13.	Oakland A's	baseball
14.	Golden State Warriors	basketball
15.	Sacramento Kings	basketball

Who's Who? page 20

1. John Steinbeck
2. Jack London
3. Sally Ride
4. Shirley Temple
5. General Patton
6. Richard Nixon
7. Ronald Reagan
8. Ansel Adams
9. Mark Spitz
10. Joe DiMaggio

Colorado

Map Activity, page 25

Milwaukee, WI	1,038 miles
New York, NY	1,794 miles
Miami, FL	2,197 miles
Seattle, WA	1,341 miles
Boston, MA	1,998 miles
Dallas, TX	784 miles

Note: Information is from the 1994 Rand McNally Road Atlas. Students may get slightly different numbers depending on the source they use.

Florida

What Can You Find in *Tallahassee*? page 37

alas	heal	sell
ale	heat	set
all	heel	shalt
allah	lash	shale
ash	lass	sheet
ate	last	shell

TLC10018 Copyright © Teaching & Learning Company, Carthage, IL 62321

ease	late	slash
easel	leash	sleet
east	least	stale
eat	less	stall
hale	let	steal
hall	sale	tale
halt	salt	tall
has	sash	tassel
hassle	sat	tea
haste	sate	teal
hat	seal	tease
hate	seat	tell

Life in the Waters of Florida, page 39

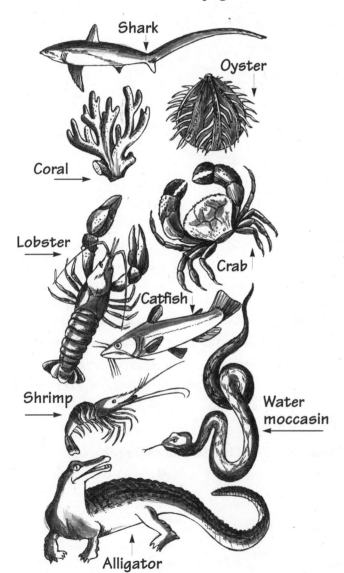

Shark

Oyster

Coral

Lobster

Crab

Catfish

Shrimp

Water moccasin

Alligator

Georgia

Find Out More About Georgia, page 47

1. King George II of England
2. James Ogelthorpe
3. cotton gin
4. boll weevil
5. peanuts, peaches
6. Juliette Low
7. Augusta
8. Jackie Robinson
9. Martin Luther King, Jr.
10. Savannah
11. manatees
12. Jefferson Davis, Robert E. Lee, Stonewall Jackson
13. Dahlonega

Hawaii

The Islands of Hawaii, page 51

1. Hawaii—Big Island
2. Maui—Valley Island
3. Lāna'i—Pineapple Island
4. Moloka'i—Friendly Isle
5. O'ahu—Gathering Place
6. Ni'ihau—Forbidden Island
7. Kaua'i—Garden Isle

Idaho

Map Activity, page 54

1. British Columbia
2. Montana and Wyoming
3. Nevada and Utah
4. Washington and Oregon

Illinois

Big Eight, page 58

3 Chicago, Illinois
8 Dallas, Texas
7 Detroit, Michigan
4 Houston, Texas
2 Los Angeles, California
1 New York City, New York
5 Philadelphia, Pennsylvania
6 San Diego, California

Map Activity, page 59

1. The "Tall State" is 385 miles long from north to south.
2. Springfield to Chicago is 202 miles.

The Windy City, page 61

1. The Sears Tower is 110 stories—1,454 feet tall.

All About Illinois, page 62

1. Bears—football, 2. Black Hawks—hockey,
3. Bulls—basketball, 4. & 5. Cubs and White Sox—baseball
6. Ronald Reagan was born in Tampico, Illinois. Abraham Lincoln was born in Kentucky, and Ulysses S. Grant moved to Illinois from Ohio.
7. Because glaciers once covered most of the state, Illinois is very flat.

Indiana

Indy 15, page 65

1. B.	6. A.	11. B.
2. A.	7. A.	12. A.
3. B.	8. B.	13. A.
4. B.	9. A.	14. B.
5. A.	10. A.	15. A.

The Indianapolis 500, page 66

These cities are within 500 miles of Indianapolis: Birmingham, Charleston, Chicago, Cincinnati, Cleveland, Des Moines, Detroit, Louisville, Memphis, Milwaukee, Pittsburgh and St. Louis.

Kansas

Good Question! page 75

1. Dorothy
2. Laura Ingalls Wilder
3. Unsuccessful presidential candidates
4. International Forest of Friendship
5. Carry Nation
6. Emmet Kelly
7. Gwendolyn Brooks
8. Walter P. Chrysler
9. Amelia Earhart
10. Fort Hays

Kentucky

In the Early Days of Kentucky, page 81

The turtle had one friend start the race and two other friends waiting along the course. As the rabbit came to the first ridge, one turtle crossed ahead of him, then hid in the woods. At the next hill, another turtle waited and again crossed the ridge ahead of the rabbit. The turtle who won the race waited at the end of the course for the rabbit to show up. When he saw the rabbit coming, he came out of hiding to cross the finish line first.

Who's Who in Kentucky? page 83

1. D., 2. C., 3. A., 4. B.

Louisiana

How Many Is XIV? page 84

1. 10		5. 12
2. 5		6. 40
3. 16		7. 67
4. 4		8. 32

Maine

Who's Who? page 93

1. C., 2. A., 3. F., 4. B., 5. D., 6. E.

TLC10018 Copyright © Teaching & Learning Company, Carthage, IL 62321

Massachusetts

Who's Who from Massachusetts? page 102

1. Francis Bellamy
2. Susan B. Anthony
3. Elias Howe
4. Samuel Adams
5. John Adams
6. John Quincy Adams
7. Abigail Adams
8. Paul Revere
9. John Hancock
10. Julia Ward Howe
11. Eli Whitney
12. Ben Franklin
13. Samuel Morse
14. Clara Barton
15. Lucy Stone
16. Nathaniel Hawthorne
17. Dr. Seuss
18. Calvin Coolidge
19. Arthur Fiedler
20. John F. Kennedy
21. George Bush

Michigan

Motor City, Michigan, page 106

Explorer (Ford)
Bobcat
Cadillac
Ranger (Ford)
Pontiac
Ford
Fairlane (Ford)
Oldsmobile
Buick
Dodge

Minnesota

Who's Who and What's What? page113

1. K.	8. P.
2. B.	9. D.
3. E.	10. J.
4. G.	11. F.
5. Q.	12. M.
6. C.	13. N.
7. L.	14. A.

Mississippi

Exploring Mississippi, page 116

1. Louisiana
2. Choctaw and Chickasaw
3. Spain
4. gold
5. Mississippi, Canada
6. Andrew Jackson, Oklahoma

Mississippi Musicians, page 117

1. A., 2. C., 3. B., 4. C., 5. A., 6. C., 7. A., 8. C., 9. B., 10. C.

Note: Students may come up with different answers than the ones given. For example, Elvis began as a blues and gospel singer before becoming famous for rock and roll. Bobbie Gentry mostly sang ballads, etc.

Montana

More About Montana, page 126

1. Helena was originally named Last Chance.
2. Yellowstone National Park is partly in Montana, Idaho and Wyoming.
3. Pompey's Pillar was named for the son of Sacagawea.
4. Chief Joseph was the Nez Perce leader.

New Hampshire

From A to Z, page 139

1. BEAVERS
2. BLACK BEARS
3. BLUE JAYS
4. BOBCATS
5. CHIPMUNKS
6. DUCKS
7. EASTERN COYOTES
8. ELK
9. FINCHES
10. FOXES
11. GROUSE
12. LIZARDS
13. LYNX
14. MINK
15. MOOSE
16. MUSKRATS
17. OPOSSUMS
18. OSPREYS
19. OTTERS
20. GEESE
21. PHEASANTS
22. PORCUPINES
23. RABBITS
24. RACCOONS
25. SHREWS
26. SQUIRRELS

About New Hampshire, page 140

1. The Old Man of the Mountain
2. White
3. "beautiful water in a high place"
4. *Ranger*
5. Since 1920 the first presidential primary has been held in New Hampshire. These elections determine the final candidates for President.
6. Mount Washington
7. Indian Stream Republic
8. A breed of chickens developed in New Hampshire in the early 1900s

New Jersey

All About New Jersey, page 143

1. Trash Museum
2. Campbell Museum
3. Fort Lee
4. *The Great Train Robbery*
5. Samuel B. Morse
6. Judy Blume
7. James Fenimore Cooper
8. Stephen Crane
9. Hawaii, Rhode Island, Delaware, Connecticut
10. Trenton
11. Henry Hudson
12. Giovanni da Verrazano
13. New York, Pennsylvania, Delaware
14. Woodruff Indian Museum
15. Garden State
16. wigwam

New York

About New York, page 151

1. Philadelphia
2. California
3. baseball
4. football
5. hockey
6. basketball
7. 64 feet
8. New Netherlands

Map Activity, page 152

1. Quebec, Ontario
2. Erie, Ontario

Who's Who from New York? page 155

1. Washington Irving
2. Herman Melville
3. (Lyman) Frank Baum
4. Maurice Sendak
5. Eleanor Roosevelt
6. Jonas Salk
7. Anna Moses
8. Henry Louis "Lou" Gehrig
9. baseball
10. Kareem Abdul-Jabbar
11. Millard Fillmore

The Rest of New York, page 156

1. apples
2. cherries
3. pears
4. beans
5. lettuce
6. cabbages
7. corn
8. potatoes
9. Fort Orange
10. Lake Placid

TLC10018 Copyright © Teaching & Learning Company, Carthage, IL 62321

12. George Gershwin
13. Fiorello Henry LaGuardia
14. Norman Rockwell
15. Theodore Roosevelt
16. Franklin D. Roosevelt

North Dakota

Map Activity, page 163

1. Bismarck   49,256
2. Fargo   74,111
3. Grand Forks   49,425
4. Minot   34,544

Ohio

Slow Reading, page 166

1. 1968
2. $1825

Name These Famous Ohioans, page 169

1. John Glenn
2. Neil Armstrong on July 20, 1969
3. Robert McCloskey
4. Thomas A. Edison
5. Ulysses S. Grant
6. Rutherford B. Hayes
7. James A. Garfield
8. Benjamin Harrison
9. William McKinley
10. William H. Taft
11. Warren G. Harding
12. Orville and Wilbur Wright
13. *Uncle Tom's Cabin*
14. Zane Grey
15. Annie Oakley
16. Ransom Olds
17. Steven Spielberg

Sports Spotlight, page 169

1. Reds, Indians
2. Browns, Bengals

3. Cavaliers
4. Canton, Ohio
5. Jesse Owens

Oklahoma

Something to Crow About, page 173

1. blue jays
2. swallows
3. sparrows
4. herons
5. cardinals
6. robins
7. quail
8. crows
9. doves
10. orioles
11. egrets
12. roadrunners

Pennsylvania

What Can You Find in *Pennsylvania?* page 178

ail	line	sane
aisle	linen	sap
Alan	Linsey	save
ale	lip	say
aline	lisp	seal
alive	live	sin
alpine	lye	sip
Alvin	Lynn	slain
Ann	nail	slap
Anna	nap	slave
Anne	nape	slay
Annie	nave	slip
ape	nay	sly
apse	nil	snip
Asia	Nile	snipe
Asian	nine	spa
Aspen	ninny	Spain
Ava	nip	span
avail	pail	spay
avian	pain	spin
aye	pal	spine
easily	pale	spy
easy	pan	sylvan
Eva	pane	Sylvia

evil	pansy	vail
inn	pave	vain
isle	pay	vale
Ivan	peal	van
lain	pen	vane
Lana	penny	vase
lane	pie	via
lap	pile	vial
lava	pin	vie
lave	pine	vile
lay	plane	vine
lean	play	Yale
lei	sail	yap
Lenny	sale	yelp
Levi	Salina	yen
Levy	saline	yes
lie	saliva	yip
lien	salve	

Who's Who? page 181

1. D.	7. H.
2. E.	8. B.
3. F.	9. J.
4. I.	10. A.
5. C.	11. K.
6. G.	12. L.

South Dakota

Did You Know? page 195

1. A monument to the Sioux leader, Crazy Horse, was started in 1948 by Korczak Ziolkowski.
2. About 800,000 square miles of land was included in the Louisiana Purchase. This area included the present states of Louisiana, Arkansas, Missouri, Iowa, Nebraska, South Dakota and most of Oklahoma, Minnesota, North Dakota, Kansas, Montana and Wyoming, plus part of Colorado.

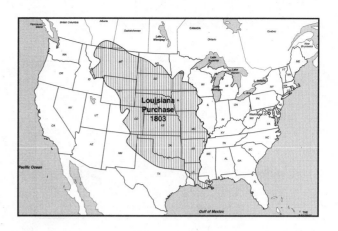

Vermont

Map Activity, page 213

1. east
2. north
3. New York
4. Brattleboro
5. Burlington
6. New York

Virginia

Famous Virginians, page 216

1. C.	7. D.
2. J.	8. G.
3. B.	9. E.
4. H.	10. K.
5. L.	11. A.
6. F.	12. I.

Did You Know? page 218

1. coal
2. Arlington National Cemetery
3. Blue Ridge Mountains
4. "foot of the mountain"
5. 40 years
6. Little River Turnpike
7. King Charles II
8. Queen Elizabeth I

A Tour of Historic Virginia, page 220

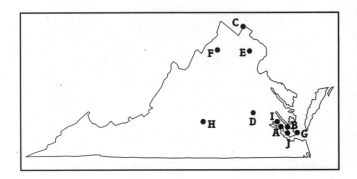

Wisconsin

Map Activity, page 230

1. Mississippi
2. Michigan, Superior

Wyoming

Map Activity, page 235

1. 362 miles
2. 275 miles
3. Montana
4. Idaho, Montana and Utah
5. Colorado and Utah
6. South Dakota and Nebraska

Grand Teton National Park, page 238

1. bison	7. deer
2. rabbits	8. eagles
3. elk	9. beaver
4. squirrels	10. fox
5. moose	11. pronghorns
6. bears	12. badgers

Washington, D.C.

Map Activity, page 241

6   Lincoln Memorial
12   Supreme Court Building
2   Capitol Building
1   White House
3   Washington Monument
8   National Gallery of Art
7   Smithsonian Institution
10   Theodore Roosevelt Island
13   Union Station
4   The Pentagon
9   Arlington National Cemetery
15   National Aboretum
5   Potomac River
11   Georgetown University
14   National Zoological Park